Relearning to Tea

Relearning to Teach challenges the seemingly complex teaching profession and the various initiatives, strategies and ideas that are regularly suggested. It explores how teaching methods are used without a clear understanding of why, which leads to ineffective teaching that is *believed* to work – but ultimately doesn't. Cutting through the clutter of conventional teacher guidance, David Fawcett tackles myths head on, sharing the latest research and explaining how this will look translated to a classroom environment.

The book breaks down the complexities of teaching into manageable chunks and offers practical advice on how to take charge of your own CPD to become a more reflective and successful practitioner. Focusing on what's most relevant and helpful to build effective teaching practice and self-improvement it raises key questions such as:

- Is lesson planning just a box ticking exercise?
- Why do students remember in lessons, but forget in tests?
- Is asking more questions beneficial?
- Is feedback actually worth it?

Relearning to Teach is a must read for all teachers looking to pinpoint the *why* of teaching methods and to gain an understanding of the reasons why various pedagogies are used within the classroom.

David Fawcett has been a teacher for over ten years in English secondary schools. He is also a speaker, trainer and organiser of multiple teaching conferences in the UK. His goal is to make teachers more aware of what might work in the classroom by bridging the gap between educational research and everyday practice.

Relearning to Teach

Understanding the Principles of Great Teaching

David Fawcett

Routledge
Taylor & Francis Group

LONDON AND NEW YORK

First published 2020
by Routledge
2 Park Square, Milton Park, Abingdon, Oxon OX14 4RN

and by Routledge
52 Vanderbilt Avenue, New York, NY 10017

Routledge is an imprint of the Taylor & Francis Group, an informa business

British Library Cataloguing-in-Publication Data
A catalogue record for this book is available from the British Library

Library of Congress Cataloging-in-Publication Data
A catalog record has been requested for this book

ISBN: 978-1-138-21385-2 hbk
ISBN: 978-1-138-21386-9 pbk
ISBN: 978-1-315-44744-5 ebk

Typeset in Bembo
by Swales & Willis, Exeter, Devon, UK

Contents

Foreword

I first met David Fawcett five years ago at Pedagoo London, one of the first so-called education unconferences, where I was the keynote speaker. It was my first such gig and I desperately wanted to say something meaningful for the audience who had turned up, on a Saturday, in great numbers. For weeks ahead of the event, I pondered what I would say to a group of ordinary teachers who had decided to take the reins of their own professional learning, through networks established on Twitter and informed by the insights of the first wave of teacher bloggers, in a way that was virtually unheard of at the time.

Being an English teacher, I had long been used to deploying metaphors as analogies for making sense of our world, and I was keen to do so on this occasion. So it was that I first came upon the story of the Trojan Mouse. The story occurs in the realm of the inelegantly named "penetration testers" who work with organisations to deliberately hack their servers and infect their software with non-deadly viruses. One such organisation had held the view that its defences were unbreachable, not unlike the great ancient city of Troy, and had challenged their "penetration tester" to prove them wrong.

Following multiple attempts at a head-on attack, the hackers decided to try another approach. Working their way through social media sites, they identified employees of the company who might prove to be ineffective as gatekeepers and sent each of them a complimentary USB computer mouse in the post. These mice had been disassembled, rewired to include the harmless-but-trackable virus, before being reassembled, repackaged and dispatched. And then the "penetration testers" waited. Before long, one of the employees took their mouse to work, plugged it into the system and the hack was completed: the walls of Troy fell and the Trojan Mouse took the credit.

In my presentation, I compared the delegates to the Trojan Mouse. Like it, they were bringing different ideas about what teaching could and should look like, sound like and feel like into their schools right under the noses of the traditional gatekeepers to professional learning, their leadership teams, many of whom appeared to be asleep on the job. Too much bad practice had accumulated for many of these Trojan Mice to tolerate any longer and quietly they set about "infecting" their internal networks with "viruses" brought in from the outside. It was a reminder of the agency of individual teachers and their ability to change, from within, the vital business of our schools.

I concluded the presentation with an invitation for the colleagues there on that day, the Trojan Mice, to become "guerrilla teachers", adopting tactical approaches to liberating themselves, their classrooms and their colleagues from the top-down control of their school leaders acting under a rather dubious reading of the Ofsted agenda, and even more suspect understanding of what research was saying about teaching and learning. David understood exactly what I was trying to say and it was only a few months later that he, along with Jennifer Ludgate, created their own unconference, which aptly mirrored my call-to-arms, not least of all in its title, the Teaching and Learning Takeover. This conference (we appear to have dropped the un- from the title, which I still feel is something of a shame) is still going strong and is my must-attend event of the educonference year.

What this book shows to me is that David is still the archetypal Trojan Mouse. In it, he continues to grapple with concepts that are vital for teachers and does so within his own classroom. In it, he shows a refusal to be pigeon-holed, drawing in research evidence from across the so-called traditionalist/progressive divide and applying it within his own classroom. He demonstrates a complete lack of complacency, questioning his own past practice whilst never being fooled into thinking that he has reached the end-point of his enquiries. In short, in this book he takes an utterly pragmatic, rather than dogmatic, approach and this is what makes what he has to say worth the time it takes to read it. It is clearly a book written by a Trojan Mouse, intended to be read by Trojan Mice who need to know that they are not alone.

Five years have passed since I first met David and, with it, a lot of water has passed under the bridge. What appears not to have altered in the slightest is his determination to be better and, to paraphrase Dylan Wiliam, he does so not because he is not good enough, but because he knows that he can be even better. That humble confidence is what exudes through the chapters in this book in order to help others be better. And that confident humility is the very quintessence of what I would want in a teacher working with the children in my school or, for that matter, working with my own children. To be both Trojan and Mouse is no easy feat but David, and this book, do so and do it well.

Keven Bartle
Headteacher
Canons High School

Preface
Am I a good teacher? (Or just a used car salesman?)

If you cast your mind back, can you remember your first day as a teacher? Can you remember the first term, the first year or even the first few years of your career? The nervousness as you take on such an enormous responsibility. The moment you teach *that* class for the first time. The enjoyment you get from a student who really grasps what you've taught them.

Four years of learning how to become a teacher left me with the desire to make a difference to people's lives that had been the main reason for coming into the profession. I remember those first few years as some of the hardest but most valuable moments in school. This is the time where you get to grips with systems and procedures. Organising your lessons and managing planning becomes more efficient. Tackling behaviour becomes more effective as you put systems and structures in place. Those first few years were when I learnt the day-to-day logistics of being a teacher. I can still remember meeting my first tutor group and having to quickly learn how to guide and support so many different characters. I still remember department meetings and trying to soak up all the information given to me. I remember my first real outings with extra-curricular clubs and the pride of managing a team on my own.

Reflecting back on the good old days is fun. However, you will also remember, vividly, times in when you could have done things better. The lesson that didn't go so well. The students whose behaviour escalated because of how you managed a situation. The assessment results lower than you ever expected. At the time those moments can be soul destroying. "How is it that I am working so hard yet students just don't seem to be performing well?"

In the early stage of my career I felt very lucky. I got a job at my first attempt in an absolutely fantastic school. I settled in very quickly and formed a strong bond with my colleagues in the department. I was promoted to a teaching and learning role within the first three years. In a wider remit, I was given opportunities to lead, implement and develop teaching across the whole school as part of an energetic team. I would run INSET sessions and teaching programmes and launch whole-school initiatives. I quickly got my name out among staff and became somebody who expressed their opinion on matters of teaching and learning.

I remember to this day the interview that secured me that key promotion, in particular the presentation I delivered on my philosophy and vision for the role. Candidates were seated together in the library. One by one we gave our presentation to the interview panel and other candidates. Armed with whizzy PowerPoint slides, I began explaining how I would drive the role forward. I referred to my principles, the logistics and laid out my five year plan. I would use students as exemplars and draw upon metaphors from life, the workplace and industry to capture the imagination of the audience. It was an opportunity to demonstrate my thinking around teaching and learning and lay out the foundations of my practice. At the end of a nervous five minutes, the head of RE and member of the interview panel caught me off guard. I was waiting for gruelling questions and a critique of my ideas. Instead, she simply turned to me and said, "Bloody hell David, you'd make a great used car salesman."

I didn't realise it then but that statement had some truth over my first six years as a teacher. The responsibility of my role, my work within the department and my support of teachers had led me to believe that I was a "good" teacher. Someone who knew what they were doing in lessons. Someone you could go to for ideas. What it also did was blind me to what was actually going on.

At the end of that six years with some extremely average results I began asking myself that very question from earlier: "How is it that I am working so hard yet students just don't seem to be performing well?" I spent hours planning ever more eye catching lessons, incorporating the latest ideas I could find and creating unique resources. I covertly sought advice and endeavoured to introduce these glamourous ideas into lessons. I had my GCSE bottom set class up out of their seats to make things as interactive as possible. I created multi-level task sheets to give students choice. I created PowerPoints with more slides than there were minutes in the lesson. Time spent this way meant I wasn't able to properly check books or look at the data and see what was actually going on.

At the end of this period I sat myself down. When an internal interview for an AST post was unsuccessful I realised that things weren't as rosy as I had believed. The interview day was tough, rounded off by two students getting into a scuffle in my interview lesson. I had misunderstood completely what being a teacher at that level actually entailed. I realised that what the head of RE had said a few years earlier was probably true: I was a used car salesman masquerading as a teacher. The vehicles (lessons) I was delivering to customers (students) on a daily basis maintained turnover but provided no real benefit or service in the long term. I could talk the talk, the lessons might look glamourous, but underneath the hood there was nothing more than a scrambled together mix of bits and pieces. I knew what an engine looked like, but didn't understand how it worked.

Four years of university and six years of teaching had taught me the skill of organising myself as a teacher. Through my own fault I had been seductively wooed by a plethora of ideas that had no real benefit. I had completely missed learning the craft of teaching. I had overlooked the basics – the foundations of what good teachers actually do in their classes. And what was worse, I had shared these hollow ideas with others.

I made the decision to start afresh, to begin a huge reflection process and think more deeply about the following:

- What am I currently doing now?

- Is it working? If not, why isn't it working?

- Is teaching this way making me feel happy at the moment of delivery (in the lesson), AND, at the time when I measure the impact (assessments and tests)?

- What are the fundamentals of teaching? What do we do every lesson, every day that has the biggest impact on learning?

- What is a more efficient way of working that won't impact my work-life balance?

- What is the evidence out there that particular approaches actually work?

- How can literature, articles and research papers challenge my approach and way of thinking?

- Can I realistically get better as a teacher?

- How?

- By when?

- What would I need to start with first?

- And what would a 1 per cent improvement in this look like?

This is not an exhaustive list and could change from person to person. Take a few moments to answer these questions yourself. What areas would you like to work on and improve? Do you assign yourself meaningful time to develop these areas? I know from experience that time is usually the limiting factor. With the ever-increasing demands that teachers face, it feels like our own professional development is repeatedly sacrificed for what we claim are "more important tasks". Those reports that need to be done are more urgent than reading up on feedback methods. The data inputting of classes that comes before looking at better ways to challenge students in lessons. Catching up with emails prioritised over seeking how to engage more students with better questioning. If we're not careful, these tasks, important as they are, can dominate our time and push the soul of our job, teaching and learning, out of the picture.

This can't be the case. Improving teaching is one of the most important things that schools can do and something that we as teachers have to be constantly mindful of. In fact, as Viviane Robinson found in her 2009 Curee research summary, "[p]romoting and participating in teacher learning and development" has the most significant impact on student outcomes. The Sutton Trust's 2011 interim statement confirms this, highlighting the huge differences in student outcomes between very effective teachers and poorly performing teachers. Helping teachers become better teachers is a big deal.

At the 2012 SSAT National Conference, Dylan Wiliam told delegates that to become elite in whichever field you are in takes a decade of deliberate practice. This practice is "an effortful activity that can be sustained only for a limited time each day"; such practice is "neither motivating nor enjoyable – [but] it is instrumental in achieving further improvement in performance". Getting better is therefore a tough task, one that needs constant attention and focus. Wiliam went on to say that "currently all teachers slow, and most actually stop, improving after two or three years in the classroom". Six years into my career and I was a prime example of wasting time on the road to becoming the expert teacher we apparently all have the potential to be.

At year six in my career it was time for a complete rethink. Time to relearn how to teach. Time to think pragmatically and break teaching down into its core fundamentals. Identify the day-to-day elements such as planning, questioning and feedback. The logistical side, from data to curriculum design. The student domain, such as revising and exam technique. I began surrounding myself with as much teaching and learning literature as possible. I looked not at the how but at the *why* of teaching. What was it that made explanation great? Why don't students remember what I've taught them? What does challenge for all look like?

This book isn't an absolute. It won't make you the finished article – not by a million miles. It doesn't promise you perfect methods of teaching because teaching is complex and what works for one person may not work for another. But understanding the *why* of teaching and learning will certainly clarify your thoughts and help you make informed decisions about what you do for students. There are no quick fixes, no silver bullets or miracle cures. These only paper over the cracks, which will inevitably break open later down the line. The key is to understand a principle and start small. Choose the right class to trial an idea with and then evaluate its impact. If it works, begin growing it, adapting it to the rest of your teaching and then beyond.

Don't throw out everything. There are things that you do every day that are brilliant and have real impact on helping students learn. Identify the good elements of your teaching, the good habits, the keepers. Be confident in the foundations you have already laid and build upon them. Find time to look at those good habits and see where you can make that 1 per cent improvement. Even the best things we do can be that bit better.

Go rogue – be brave. Don't go against school policy, be responsible for your development. Try things outside the school's SEF that you think will make a difference. Research elements of pedagogy that may not be on your department's wider agenda. Always ask *why*!

Be open-minded about ideas but sceptical enough to cut through to the core of the approach. You will probably have to unlearn some of the deeply engrained habits that you have formed over the years. It may feel tough but there will be positives.

There may be things that go against your beliefs. But what if those beliefs are ineffective or even fundamentally flawed? What if there is a better way? Some of the ideas you come across can be counter-intuitive. Don't just dismiss these. They offer insights into the complex world of teaching and learning.

If you take nothing else from this book, take the idea that if you have the passion and the drive to get better, the commitment to set time aside and the focus to deliberately practise your craft, you really can make a difference. What follows is what I found out about the key areas of teaching. You'll find common problems, key messages from research and the fundamental principles for each area. As Dylan Wiliam said at the SSAT 2012 conference:

"Every teacher needs to improve, not because they are not good enough, but because they can be even better".

Six years in a career is a long time to realise that you can be that bit better. Accept the challenge, empower yourself and begin that journey to greatness.

I hope you enjoy.

David

References

Robinson, V. M. J., Hohepa, M., & Lloyd, C. (2009) *School leadership and student outcomes: Identifying what works and why, Best Evidence Synthesis*. Wellington: Ministry of Education.

Sutton Trust, The. (2011) *Improving the Impact of Teachers on Pupil Achievement in the UK – Interim Findings*. London: Sutton Trust.

Acknowledgements

There was once someone on Twitter who said that my acknowledgements list would be huge – and indeed it is. And it is because I have learnt so much from so many people. The generosity of some to read over chapters, provide links to articles, lending me books, supplying a story or simply bouncing ideas around has been nothing short of phenomenal. It is so humbling to be in a profession where people will actively help each other to be better at what they do. And I guess that's because what we do is so important as it affects the futures of so many students. Without the generous time that people have given up, this book would not have been finished.

To the one who privately messaged me on Twitter, without understanding what this book was trying to do, and nearly made me pack it all in – I've done it.

For opening and closing this book – thanks to Kev Bartle and Chris Moyse. Both of you have inspired me to be a better teacher.

For those that contributed stories and have learned similar things that I have along the road, I thank you all. To Stephen Lockyer, S. Pavar, Nancy Gedge, Peter Blenkinsop, Lee Donaghy, James Theobold, Harry Fletcher-Wood, Helen Rogerson, Cristina Milos, Stuart Lock, Shaun Allison, Louise Hutton, Phil Stock, James Hughes, Jo Facer, Calum Lacey, Josh Chandler, Damian Benney, Wendy Daley, Mark Enser, Marianne Fox, Dawn Cox, Dan Brooks, Mark Miller, Andy Tharby, Michael Tidd, Kristian Still, Pete Pease, Lindsay Philips, Drew Thomson, Chris Moyse, Hin-Tai Ting, Doug Lemov, Kat Howard, Katie Yezzi, Susan Strachan, David Didau and John Tomsett.

For those who pointed me in the right direction of research; Mark Healy, Phil Stock, Cristina Milos, Harry Fletcher-Wood and Veronica Yann.

For those that lent me books; Claire Doherty, David Doherty, Heather Leatt, James Hughes, Graeme Bowden and Graeme Eyre.

For those who bounced ideas around via email, tweets or Skype: Doug Lemov, Kenny Pieper, Katie Yezzi, Dawn Cox, Caroline Spalding, Helene Galdin-O'Shea, Chris Curtis, David Didau, Nancy Gedge, Debbie Light, Dylan Wiliam, John Biggs, Geoff Petty, Veronica Yann, Cristina Milos, Yana Weinstein and Pooja K. Agarwal.

For the colleagues who put up with me as I got really geeky about teaching and learning; Shaun Riches, Neil Chance, Fran Bennett, Marianne Fox, John Fenlon, Pete

Pease, Petrina McCulley, Ria Allan, Aly Egerton, Ashleigh Thomson, and my amazing department. To my brilliant PGCE and SCITT students James Hughes, Matt Wagstaff and Jamie Williams who I bombarded much of this information to – apologies. I hope it helped.

And to the one man who started this all off (yes, it's his fault!), Chris Fuller. One year of working with him opened up the world to social media, research and wanting to better myself.

And finally, to my family. To Emma who clearly felt the strain of writing this book but supported me so well. To my Dad who helped with the family to get it out there. And to my two amazing daughters, Niamh and Effie, who inspired me to write this and distracted me enough when I found the whole process tough. These guys mean the world to me.

Introduction

In his 2003 paper, "Teachers Make a Difference", John Hattie writes about what affects student achievement. He identifies six major variables: student, home, school, principal, peers and teacher. Before we discuss his findings, take a moment to look at that list again. What order would you put them in? Which one has the most influence on student achievement and which the least?

Interestingly, Hattie found that students accounted for around 50 per cent of the variance. What students bring to the table is a huge predictor of achievement. A high-ability student will probably achieve well. Four of the other five factors – home, school, principal and peers – only accounted for about 5–10 per cent each, but teachers account for about 30 per cent of the variance. "*It is what teachers know, do, and care about which is very powerful in this learning equation*" (p. 2). He goes on:

> I therefore suggest that we should focus on the greatest source of variances that can make the difference – the teacher. We need to ensure that this greatest influence is optimised to have powerful and sensationally positive effects on the learner. Teacher can and usually do have positive effects, but they must have exceptional effects. We need to direct attention at higher quality teaching, and higher expectations that students can meet appropriate challenges.
>
> (p. 3)

In over ten years of teaching I have yet to meet a teacher who doesn't put the development of others – their students – first. We want to do all we can to help set them up for the rest of their lives.

Hattie argues, though, that we must have *exceptional effects*. But, as Dylan Wiliam (2012) states, this could take ten years of deliberate practice. Many teachers have the best intentions to improve but things get in the way. Ask yourself this: *how often does your personal CPD takes a back seat?* Do admin tasks mean that CPD drops down your list of priorities? Do you sometimes find quick fixes because time just doesn't allow you to come up for air? I've seen first-hand how colleagues scramble things together before performance management reviews just to pass them. That's not fully engaging in your own CPD, that's just avoiding getting moaned at.

For many, improvement simply means trying out new ideas that have been passed on from colleagues, the internet, social media or books. Chatting to other teachers and sharing methods is one of the most common ways that our repertoire builds. We magpie, borrow and implement. It is time efficient and freshens up what we do in lessons. If it works for them, it must work for us. Surely there's no harm in that? Well, maybe there is. Maybe we should be wary of quick fixes that we don't fully understand. In Graham Nuthall's excellent book, *The Hidden Lives of Learners*, he writes:

> There is, however, a potential problem with ideas and models about how to teach. In most cases, there is a description of what to do and how to do it, but no description of why it might work. There is no explanation of the underlying principles on which the method or resources have been constructed. The result is that teachers are constantly being encouraged to try out new ideas or methods without understanding how they might be affecting student learning.
>
> (p. 14)

If we're not careful, we could head down the route of having a toolkit full of shallow teaching methods that we won't know how to adapt when things go wrong, because we don't really know why they worked in the first place. We also have to be extremely aware that what works in the classroom of one teacher won't necessarily work in the classroom of another. Understanding the principles and the fundamental components that make great teaching is a much more profitable route to take.

What I hope this book will do is help you scrutinise the art of teaching. It has split teaching into the core components which we are exposed to on a daily basis. Using these fundamentals it poses questions I have heard numerous times over the years; questions such as "Why do they seem to remember in lessons, but then forget it in the test?" and "For all the time and effort, is feedback actually worth it?" It then aims to unpick the principles behind these fundamentals that make them work, allowing us to adapt them to our own classrooms and unique set of circumstances.

The book could be a front to back read, and then become a "dip in" book when you want to develop a specific area. It hopes to spur you on to prioritise your own development. It aims to show you that what goes on in classrooms can be amazing and that we can all be that little bit better. Habits are difficult to break. We can sometimes become set in our ways. We can also be enticed by the fads, the silver bullets, and fail to see what actually works. I've worked with many amazing teachers who have taught me first-hand how to be better at my job. This book is about reaffirming what you do and giving you the confidence to share what you do more widely. If we take Hattie's advice and want to have "exceptional effects", maybe it's time we give a little more time to developing what we do, understanding why teaching methods work, and ultimately get that little bit better.

David Fawcett

References

Hattie, J. (2003) *Teachers make a difference: What is the research evidence?* Paper presented at the Building Teacher Quality: What does the research tell us ACER Research Conference, Melbourne, Australia. Available at: http://research.acer.edu.au/research_conference_2003/4/

Nuthall, G. (2007) *The Hidden Lives of Learners.* Wellington, NZ: NZCER Press.

SSAT (2012) *SSAT National Conference 2012 Keynote 2.* Available at: www.youtube.com/watch?v=r1LL9NX1hUw&list=PLyoKDRCO9tQygjjCGmKChL-13G2dUX8pf

Isn't lesson planning just a box ticking exercise?[1]

Planning the perfect lesson – is there such a thing?

Lesson planning was part of my professional training more than 20 years ago and I, as a young teacher, followed the script for a while without ever questioning the general scheme. It seemed to work and why wouldn't it? It had both a logical flow and a simple, clear structure: set your objectives, design the activities, and then check for understanding. As one's experience grows, however, you come to the realization that things should be simple but not simpler than they are, and that attending to nuance and complexity is the basis of excellence. The students were, indeed, learning: they were involved in all activities during the lesson, they had very good scores on tests, both national and international, and their feedback was always positive. Yet, over the course of a school year, small gaps would emerge, and connections between their previous learning and new content seemed to form with more difficulty than I expected. What was I doing wrong? I was planning according to the strategies I had learned and I stuck to the well-known cycle (objectives-activities-feedback) consistently.

Initially, I tried to address the issue by working on details: Should I time this and that activity differently? Should I use a different resource? Should I vary the type of feedback students give? and so on. Although some of these choices had an impact on student performance, it was temporary and it did not bring the desired change in the bigger picture. Then I began to look at the structure of planning as a whole and reversed two of the three components: what if designing assessment prior to activities makes it clearer for me to anticipate student learning? This small decision resulted in an important shift that forced me to look closer at aspects that previously I did not quite connect. Before I would plan for increased difficulty but I would rarely consider complexity of a concept that is, connecting it with more curricular elements. Also, now I could clearly plan for potential misconceptions because as soon as you ask yourself, "How will the student learn this?", you begin to anticipate difficulties a learner experiences in the process. I also started to look at knowledge, concepts, and skills more holistically and, in the attempt to make them more coherent and integrate them in a whole, I started to plan for longer periods of time. Long-term planning was another change that resulted in greater learning gains because it made me think hard of how these elements enable students to connect, transfer, and consolidate their learning.

(Cristina Milos, Teacher, Rome)

Years of teaching has led me to notice an obsession with planning a "perfect" lesson. Through discussions in staff rooms, meetings or social media, there are many teachers who long to find out the mix that is right. We share, we borrow, we adapt and deliver. We aim to combine various ideas together to make a lesson of pure learning gold and leaves students in awe of the greatness that they have just experienced. There are many opinions on lesson planning as well. "Have you tried using the x framework?" "Make sure your lessons consist of . . . You'll never fail". "Always start your lessons with a . . .". If you seek it, you will find it.

Part of this problem may span from lesson observations. Although not required any more by Ofsted, the necessity for a large number of schools to grade lessons has led to a culture of dependency. How many times over the years have you seen teachers panic more with an observation coming up than they do with the other lessons in that week? How many times after giving detailed feedback do you find the only thing that the teacher wants to know is what grade they got – not how well the planning of the lesson led to improved levels of learning? And why is this the case? Maybe because we feel that this observation is a measure of our performance as a teacher?

Lesson planning may also be hindered by the fact we honestly seek to find a "best method". We hear of educational panaceas that will "improve learning by X per cent" and "ensure all of your lessons are outstanding". We genuinely want to do well and the bombardment and confusion about what actually works makes it difficult to see what would be best for us. Then there are school priorities, whether it's differentiation, literacy, numeracy, SMSC, feedback or more. With good intentions, we then look for ways to get them in our lesson. The culture of being magpies and adopting ideas without fully understanding them leads to them being implemented not as they were intended, and results aren't what we expect.

The thing is that if we are not careful, lesson planning can become a box ticking exercise. For years, my lesson planning took numerous twists and turns. In essence, the core stayed the same but the rest fluctuated term by term. Having a starter ready for the students to work on, sharing knowledge, answering some exam questions and wrapping it up with a plenary became the norm. Add to this the 30-slide PowerPoint, the numerous worksheets, the card sorts, filling in blanks, getting facts from around the room and all of the other pyrotechnics and things became shallow and unnecessarily complex. Students would either be restless or so active that they weren't really learning anything. They were simply the passengers on a huge ramble where I failed to consider whether they were actually being challenged to learn anything. Lessons had no meaningful recall, no real methods to embed and engrain knowledge. Instead they simply looked good. But maybe I need to be honest and realise that I was the main part of the problem. My first problem was referring to lessons as single entities. This brings me to my first principle.

---

1 A lesson is the wrong unit in time

As a trainee teacher and NQT, the obsession was thrust upon me that I needed to look at planning perfect, isolated lessons. I remember late nights filling out lesson plans provided by my university, that separated a lesson into various sections (and sub sections). I would look at a topic and break it up into fragmented components and spend 60 minutes trying to get my students to learn it. I knew what I needed to get through, and with timings of each activity scripted down the side column, I even knew when I needed to move on. Once I had taught this lesson, I could tick it off and plan the next topic. Everything was neatly organised into these lessons and I could pop them into my folder to exemplify that I was becoming a lesson planning expert. Or was I?

Ask yourself these questions:

- What is wrong with planning isolated lessons?
- Do we focus too much on planning perfect lessons?
- What is a perfect lesson?
- If I've taught them this topic on this particular day, does it mean that they've actually learnt it?
- Is a single lesson long enough to teach them a complex or difficult concept sufficiently?
- What happens if students still don't understand what you've taught them at the end of the lesson?
- Why might some people (including me) be so focused on planning individual lessons?

At first glance, you might say this problem is isolated purely to trainee teachers. Obviously, as a novice teacher we need guidance on how to structure lessons: A plan allows us to practice putting a lesson together, and gives us some guidance on what to do. But maybe this narrow view formed a habit where I focused on learning as single lessons? I can't say it happens in all teacher training providers, but this focus on isolated lessons is common as Kat Howard, an English teacher from Leicestershire, also experienced.

> The course itself is geared towards planning for the perfect "learning moment," when this is not a realistic demonstration of how the learning process works. By additionally placing such emphasis upon grading lessons as a key component of the completion of a training session, it detracts from the value of learning over time, which leaves the candidate completely unprepared for the day-to-day requirements placed upon them within schools.

And it's an experience that others, such as English teacher Susan Strachan, have also encountered.

As an ITT my training focused on how to plan a good lesson (singular), not how to plan a scheme of learning or how to plan a longer series of lessons. So, armed with this meagre knowledge I would happily spend 3–4 hours planning the "perfect" lesson, or so I thought. How naive of me to think that spending triple or more time on one lesson was productive or sustainable and, although I know that planning does get quicker and easier with time, choosing to plan single lessons in isolation meant that this was never going to happen.

So scrap planning lessons? Is that what you're saying?

Knowing what we do on a day to day and lesson by lesson basis is important. What I am suggesting is a more holistic view. As Head of Maths, Bodil Isaksen (2015), writes: "A lesson is the wrong unit of time": We need to think of it in the context of the whole unit or scheme of work. The fluidity of the lesson should be dependent on what you taught before, and based on what your formative assessment told you, what you need to teach today. As David Didau, an English teacher and author once told me, "Planning individual lessons encourages narrow thinking and thus promotes short term performance over learning. It's better to plan sequences". I totally agree with this sentiment. Yet, at times, usually during times when we are being observed, we still become focused on planning that illusive outstanding lesson (whatever that is?). Planning should be viewed as long term process.

When chatting to numerous teachers about how people plan lessons, one of the overwhelming themes that came back was the fact that more experienced teachers seem to seeing planning as a longer unit of time. They're not planning six or seven isolated lessons in one go, but are instead thinking of a larger long-term goal where they want the class to end up, and planning how to get there. Take this for example.

Working with PGCE students for the past few years, some of them feel liberated when they watch some of my department teach and see that when the 60 minutes up and the lesson isn't finished, we leave it there knowing we'll pick it up from here next lesson. In some of the schools they've visited, that lesson needed to have been completed – not left to carry over. But why? Why cram everything in when you could ultimately end up with students who have covered the content, but learnt nothing?

Seeing lessons as a larger period of time allows us many more benefits that we might have initially not considered. By focusing on isolated lessons, we may have the thought that what needs to be taught today, has to be taught today. We break a subject into small chunks, which in turn causes us to block them. Today's lesson is about discrimination towards women in sport. Tomorrow's is about the role of the media. Next week's is about role models. Looking at this, both you and I can see there is an obvious link between all three lessons. There has been (historically) a lack of women role models in sport, a lack of coverage by the media highlighting women role models, probably as a result from historic stereotyping and discrimination towards women in sport at all levels. All of these are seriously interlinked. However, planning lessons one topic at a time may miss the bigger context and connections on offer.

If you have ever come across the work of Robert Bjork (1992), you will know that what we see happening in lessons to what is actually learnt is completely different. In a well-designed perfect lesson, we may leave feeling that every student has understood the content and learnt it. We've taught it, we asked them questions, they've completed work and all the students seemed to have grasped it. However, have they really learnt it? What we might have seen is performance rather than learning. They are not the same thing. If we decide to plan in blocks, we may be given the false impression that students are really picking things up. However, to really learn things, students need to revisit these topics numerous times over a curriculum. Each time we space them out, force them to retrieve them or interleave them with other topics, we are helping them to remember it better next time. That is learning. Planning in isolation doesn't help this process or way of thinking.

Planning in isolation can also cause us to feel pressured to finish up and move on. With curriculum time so precious, there is the temptation to start the next lesson with a new topic. The comeback is that if we allow misunderstanding to build up, we have a lot of learning gaps to cover at a later date when time is even more precious. Is it not better to nip things in the bud before they develop into serious misconceptions? Being flexible and seeing beyond isolated lessons will help that.

And finally, even though it has been widely debunked (Bartle, 2013; Coe, 2015), there are still those who seek to see perfect progress in a perfect lesson. Observers analyse whether lessons show that students have rapidly picked things up and learnt them. We can therefore feel obliged to show this progress in isolated lessons. However, you and I know, based on what I mentioned in the last paragraphs, that learning happens over time. We need to think beyond isolated moments and look at learning over weeks and months, units and schemes, terms or years. Think bigger, break boundaries and be brave.

But I still need to plan my lessons for tomorrow

I am now going to appear to contradict myself but there is a reason why. It is vital we plan learning over a longer period of time. When I first started teaching, I didn't and my students suffered for it. And I don't think I can stress enough how we should look at a series of lessons rather than individual ones. However, there is the fact that for your lesson on Thursday period three when you are teaching Year 10 how the inverted U theory affects performance of an athlete with different levels of arousal, you need to start that lesson in a particular way and move through a series of sections until your lesson finishes. And that is the critical point. We still have to teach these lessons and as teachers we still need to have a format or structure. It may not be as prescribed as it was when they were novices, but they still have a way they plan individual lessons. They have a series of sections organised in a particular order for a particular reason. I did but it didn't work. Others do and are masters in this true art. Planning is difficult and probably I suspect one of the areas that people may start with when relearning their craft. With all this in mind, where could you begin?

But which frameworks, structures or taxonomies should I use? (And what do they all mean?)

Geoff Petty, one of Britain's leading experts on teaching methods, once told me that there isn't a huge abundance of research specifically on lesson planning. Of those where there is, he issued caution by saying:

> However, you can't separate the planning and structure from the delivery when it comes to research really. Also, lessons contain so many elements it's impossible to know which bit is doing the work and which bit is holding the learning back. So researchers tend not to look at the lesson planning as a whole, but instead concentrate on its elements. So they try to sort out "what works best" by picking off small strategies one by one, rather than looking at the enormity of lesson planning.

When trying to find specific research on different planning formats, frameworks and structures, it's quite difficult to find anything conclusive. There are numerous different planning frameworks out there, but how can you tell if it's worth investing time in? Which way of planning lessons would bring about the best results for students? I have tried countless methods over the years and each worked with varying successes. What this made me realise is that maybe it's not the framework or the piece of paper you fill in that makes the difference. Maybe there's some commonality between all of the methods? Maybe there are underlying principles in them all that contribute to making learning successful? Rather than ripping each one apart and dismissing them, maybe there are lessons in their design we can learn from. Instead of just seeing what the planning format looks like, maybe I could understand how they were designed and why they might lead to increased student achievement. And that's what I hope to do in the next section. I've been that person who has tried the million different methods. Some worked, some didn't, but here is what I learnt about each of them.

Accelerated learning cycle

One of the first ways of planning I was introduced to came from Alistair Smith (1998) and has been developed with Cramlington Learning Village. Whilst investigating the idea of Learning to Learn, this particular format for a lesson grabbed my attention. Because of my lack of experience as a new teacher, I hadn't ever considered a lesson in itself being a cycle. I had only seen a lesson as a one-way street. The notion of looping the learning allowed many opportunities to formatively assess what students were learning, and re-teach. If you've never seen the format before, it follows this process (see Figure 1.1).

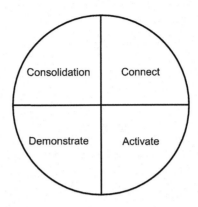

Figure 1.1 Accelerated Learning Cycle

Connect

Grab the attention of the learner, to the learning, in that lesson. It's about showing the bigger picture so students can contextualise what it is that they will be encountering. In this stage, we explain why what they will be learning is useful.

It's important therefore to share the objectives and success criteria – make it clear what we are aiming for by the end of the process, and how we get there. One crucial element for me, we need to connect with what has previously been learnt, or what students already know.

Activate

Learners find the information and begin to make sense of it. We need to use a variety of mediums to do this. They will need to describe, reflect and speculate. They will need to solve problems and make meaning of the content.

Demonstrate

Learners show that they have understood the content or topic. Teachers need to provide opportunities for learners to demonstrate, share and receive feedback on their progress. Misconceptions may be addressed in an effort to move forward.

Consolidation

Students have the chance to consolidate learning through meaningful review. They reflect on what they've learnt, and where they need to go next. Activities can be pair, small group or whole class activities. We also look ahead and preview the next lesson and begin to lay the foundations.

What can you learn from this? For me, it shows that lessons are part of a bigger picture and should be a cycle. Things aren't linear, it prompts me to keep referring back to other lessons, topics and concepts.

It tells me how important it is to put today's topic into the bigger picture. I need to bring in other topics where relevant and show how it all fits together.

It also points out that I need to connect to prior learning. In the next chapter I talk about the importance of background knowledge, schema and how students might already know about the lesson you're about to teach. Finding this out and building upon it is pretty important.

Finally, it builds upon the foundation that students need to make meaning, and really show they understand the content they are learning. They need to receive feedback on this so that they can move learning forward, into future lessons.

The cycle has pitfalls, but this section is about learning messages. And some of the key things that it does do well are things we should do in our own planning.

TEEP

TEEP originated back in 2002 with work by the SSAT, some underpinning work by Professor Daniel Muijs and David Reynolds, and an action research project by the Gatsby Charitable foundation. Developed as a Teacher Effectiveness Enhancement Programme (TEEP), it consists of a number of fundamental principles including; collaborative learning, Assessment for Learning, thinking for learning, accelerated learning and the TEEP learning cycle. It has some very close ties with the Accelerated Learning Cycle, and was also part of a project run at Cramlington Learning Village.

TEEP is quite complex, but at the heart of it, things like Assessment for Learning (AfL), the idea of thinking for learning, and the cycle itself are the most prominent for me.

Assessment for learning

TEEP uses AfL as an important tool in its process. It recognises that any assessment taken in lessons should improve learning – whether that is in the form of formative (during) or summative (at the end). It needs teachers to plan times to give quality feedback and make changes to their teaching as it happens . . . all very sensible.

Thinking for learning

I am uncomfortable about some of the methods that TEEP recommends, such as De Bono's thinking hats and Anderson's taxonomy, but it does make the important point that students must be made to think about the information they are being taught so learning becomes long lasting. It insists that we stay away from superficial learning but should go into real depth. Apart from the way in which they want to do it, this again seems sensible. We do indeed need to differentiate between long-term learning, and the performance we see in a lesson.

The TEEP learning cycle

This is very similar to the Accelerated Learning Cycle. It involves:

- Preparing the environment – Resources, room layout, etc.
- Agree learning outcomes – Sharing them with students so they know what is coming up.
- Introduce new information – As it says on the tin.
- Construct meaning – Practice developing their knowledge and understanding of the topic.
- Apply to demonstrate – Completing tasks or activities that force students to demonstrate what they have learnt. Applying learning in new challenging situations.
- Review – Developing metacognitive awareness and reflect on what has been learned. Challenge students to make their learning explicit.

TEEP feels unnecessarily clunky and complicated. However, looking for messages from different planning styles:

For me, it made me realise that AfL needs to happen, and it needs to be done properly so that we can see where students are going, and whether I need to change my teaching to address misconceptions and difficulties.

It highlights the importance of reviewing lessons to see if they support superficial learning or promote students to think hard about the topic. If we want to have a chance of things being committed to the long-term memory, thinking hard helps.

Project based learning (PBL)

Students work on a project over an extended period of time – from a week up to a semester – that engages them in solving a real-world problem or answering a complex question. They demonstrate their knowledge and skills by developing a public product or presentation for a real audience.

As a result, students develop deep content knowledge as well as critical thinking, creativity, and communication skills in the context of doing an authentic, meaningful project. Project Based Learning unleashes a contagious, creative energy among students and teachers.

(Buck Institute for Education Website)

PBL was something I came across after reading Ron Berger's *An Ethic of Excellence* (2003). According to the BIE, it has a number of design elements to it:

1. Key knowledge, understanding, and success skills – The project needs to be focused on learning goals (standards-based content and skills such as problem solving, communication etc).

2. A challenging problem or question – Which frames the project. Students have to solve this challenge.

3. Sustained inquiry – Students must engage in rigorous, extended process of asking questions, finding resources, and applying information.

4. Authenticity – It needs a real world context, tasks and tools.

5. Student voice and choice – Students make decisions about how they work and what they create.

6. Reflection – Students and teachers reflect on learning, the effectiveness of their work and how to overcome obstacles.

7. Critique and revision – Students give, receive, and use feedback to improve their work.

8. Public product – Work is displayed publicly to people beyond the classroom.

There are words of warning when it comes to doing a project. Done well, some schools such as High Tech High, produce some absolutely amazing pieces of work that do not look like school students have created them. The work is so beautiful, so detailed, and so professional looking, you might question whether it was a child who produced it. However, researchers such as Kirschner et al. (2006) warn that minimally guided instruction, such as open projects like PBL, are actually not an effective way of learning.

Bearing in mind it might not be the best way to teach, there are some elements of PBL which are really worth knowing.

First, the relentless pursuit of excellence is absolutely fundamental. Yes, working within a PBL framework can take time, but ask yourself if the work that your students produce on a regular basis is beautiful? I know for sure that mine isn't. But why can't we make exceptional the norm, not settling for mediocracy?

Second, the way PBL uses feedback to help students redraft work is amazing. Students may redraft numerous times until a piece of work is of a standard good enough to be showcased. And it has become the norm. But how many times do our students redraft work until it is brilliant? We can expect better.

Finally, how often does the work that students produce just go on your desk, and then back to the students? It's a conversation, on paper, between you and the student – is there any surprise they don't take as much pride as those who use PBL? In PBL, work is showcased publicly so students ensure it is of a standard worthy enough to have people view it.

Bloom's taxonomy

Bloom's, for many, is one of the first methods that they may have come across in terms of planning or structuring lessons. Designed under the leadership of Dr Benjamin Bloom in 1956, the taxonomy isn't actually a planning tool, but has been used by some as one. Its aim was to classify educational learning of objectives into levels of complexity and specificity. It can be used to plan objectives, assessments and activities. The most familiar part of the taxonomy is the cognitive domain (see Figure 1.2).

Remembering

This involves remembering facts, terms, concepts and answers. It doesn't necessarily mean students understand the terms, just what things are.

Understanding

Demonstrating an understanding of facts and ideas. Normally involves organising, comparing, describing and interpreting.

Applying

This involves using the knowledge that the students have acquired – maybe to solve problems. It could include identifying connections between concepts, relationships between facts, and ultimately applying them to situations.

Analysing

This involves analysing the information and breaking it down. It needs students to look at how bits relate to each other, making inferences or finding evidence to support ideas.

Evaluate

Using information to highlight positives and negatives, pros and cons, advantages and disadvantages. To evaluate, the student needs to compare it against a criteria.

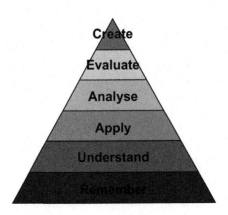

Figure 1.2 Bloom's Taxonomy

Create

Putting ideas together to form a whole. It's about building a structure or pattern. Can students create a solution using what they know?

I used Bloom's to consider challenge in my lessons – am I moving up the taxonomy and stretching students? It made me think about what students need to know, understand, and be able to apply. After this, can they analyse and evaluate information, before creating a solution to demonstrate they have grasped the concept.

The issue for me though is twofold. Firstly, people jump up the taxonomy too quickly, sacrificing students' understanding.

Secondly, it talks about stages, rather than what makes up the topic we're teaching. If I want to do that, I'd use the final planning tool – SOLO taxonomy.

SOLO *taxonomy*

SOLO Taxonomy is a framework that started out as a joint project between Kevin Collis and John Biggs. Kevin was interested in Piaget's stages of development as exemplified in school subjects, following the work of Edwin Peel. John was interested in study behaviour and linked up with Ference Marton's work on phenomenography. SOLO was a child of Piaget and Marton, tuned up to their own context. It eventually formed the framework for designing intended outcomes and rubrics as in the 2011 edition of Teaching for Quality Learning at University. The taxonomy itself (which stands for the Structure of the Observed Learning Outcome), "is a means of classifying learning outcomes in terms of their complexity, enabling us to assess students' work in terms of its quality not of how many bits of this and of that they have got right" (as explained by John Biggs via email).

The taxonomy is set out in a hierarchical format with a number of stages. Each stage describes the increasing level of complexity gained as students learn a new topic. With the help of John Biggs, here is a description of the various stages (see Figure 1.3):

Pre-structural – Pre-structural responses simply miss the point or use tautology to cover lack of knowledge or understanding. These responses can be quite sophisticated, such as the kind of elaborate tautology that politicians use to avoid answering questions, but, academically, they show little evidence of relevant learning.

At this stage the student demonstrates that they have little or no understanding of the topic. You begin questioning students in your plenary and knowing you should really stop whilst ahead of the game, you throw out one more question. A student sat right at the front offers a blank expression or complete mish-mash answer. It's this stage, the pre-structural, which highlights a real lack of understanding.

Uni-structural – The student has grasped a single isolated element of the subject. The beauty of SOLO purely for planning means that we can use this level in many ways. As a measure of observed learning, it points to the fact that a student has only grasped one particular concept, fact or piece of information from a particular moment of learning. If we were asking a student to recall a topic, they may only be able to come up with one particular

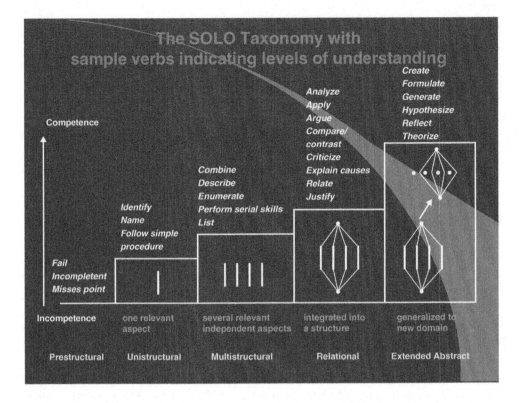

Figure 1.3 SOLO Taxonomy

element of it without much detail or depth. They "deal with terminology, getting on track but little more". Uni-structural points to the students grasping only singular elements of a topic with limited ability to add detail and information.

From a planning perspective, thinking about the uni-structural element can be very helpful. When looking at your next topic, what is the key fundamental piece of information that students must know? This isn't lowering expectations; it's merely breaking down the topic and prioritising that piece of knowledge that once learnt can help understanding of the rest of the topic.

Multi-structural – Here the student is able to describe concepts, list facts or define multiple pieces of information. As Biggs says, "Here, the students see the trees but not the wood. Seeing trees is a necessary preliminary to adequate understanding, but it should not be interpreted as comprehending the wood". There is no link between pieces of information and the student cannot explain how they relate. It shows that there is an understanding of this topic in isolation, but the wider picture is not yet understood.

From a planning perspective it's good to use this to help pull out specific aspects of the topic you are teaching. It's the foundation which leads to subsequent learning but connections between them are yet to be established. In your next topic, what are the key things that must be learnt? What are the definitions or key points of each?

Relational – When we get to the relational stage, we begin to develop our understanding about the relationships between pieces of information. As Biggs goes on, here

> The trees have become the wood, a qualitative change in learning and understanding has occurred. It is no longer a matter of listing facts and details. This is the first level at which "understanding" in an academically relevant sense may appropriately be used.

Now when we ask students to explain a topic, they can compare, analyse and relate ideas. Here we begin to see a greater insight into the students understanding of the topic.

From a planning perspective, we can use this to identify what connections we need to teach students. How will you help them see the relationships between information and provide a greater insight into the topic as a whole?

Extended Abstract – Whereas the Relational level stays with the given, Extended Abstract goes beyond the given. The theory or content being talked about is expanded to incorporate new domains. It links in other topics that overlap, as and allows you to look at the topic in an abstract way.

From a planning perspective, this is where I connect learning and show a bigger picture. What other topics could you bring into your lesson? What questions could you pose that really change the concept you are teaching?

The key point from SOLO is that it helps map out the components of a topic. It helps me clearly see what I need to teach, what the relationships are and how things fit into a bigger picture. Some people hate SOLO because of its complex terminology – I get that. I purely use it as a planning tool.

Aren't taxonomies just a distraction and overly complicated?

Don't get me wrong, taxonomies face criticism and SOLO and Bloom's are no different. In fact, both have come under a lot of scrutiny in some quarters for either being overly complicated or because they rank their stages as a hierarchy.

What are the concerns?

For SOLO it seems to be questions like: How much do students need to be part of the SOLO taxonomy process? Do they have to know the names of the various stages? I've used SOLO taxonomy for a number of years and I would probably say, no, they don't. There is an argument that such awareness would allow student to be part of the learning process. But I have also used SOLO where the process isn't explicitly for students, for my own planning purposes instead. It's now become a thing behind the scenes and using it this way, the outcomes have been the same or even better. As I plan lessons, I look at SOLO as a framework and use it in two ways in which the students are not explicitly part of the process.

1. To deconstruct a topic so I know exactly what I need to teach and how to put it all back together again – I worked with a colleague Ian Williamson a back in 2015. At that time, I was asked to sit with him and explain how SOLO worked. Obviously, as

a very experienced teacher who had seen fads and gimmicks come and go, he was hesitant about SOLO. I asked him to pick a topic from the GCSE specification so that we could break it down and plan it. We focused on the key principle what elements students had to know and terminology they had to acquire. We discussed how sections interlinked and applied them to examples before looking at how previous topics tied in. At the end of it I simply looked at the notes and jotted the symbols next to the things we wrote. Yes, I guided the conversation with SOLO in mind, but without mentioning it at all, we had mapped out a topic using SOLO as a framework. And that isn't the first time that's happened. SOLO, purely in my own opinion, is really helpful at working out what we need to teach. When a topic is made up of a number of complicated concepts, SOLO helps to unpick them. When some topics have so many intricate components and complex relationships, we need to be very aware of them so we teach them well enough. As a planning tool, it can help clarify what we're teaching and remind us of the relationships involved.

2. To give some direction – When I'm teaching a less familiar topic, there are moments when I have a planning blank where I can't think of what exactly I want students to do with the information I am teaching. The verbs associated with SOLO can be a good prompt here. Do I want them to evaluate, relate, apply, list or theorise? At this point in a lesson would it be better to get them to list or define, classify or predict? That little nudge can be helpful and lead the lesson into various levels of challenge which might not have been apparent.

The second issue that has come up, and is very similar to Bloom's, is the insistence that we need to treat it as a hierarchy and get to the top as fast as we can. As Yazz would say, the only way is up. But for some this becomes a measure of how challenging their lesson is and getting there as quickly as possible is the only goal. If my lesson is at the upper end of the taxonomy, I must be an excellent teacher. Unfortunately, getting to the higher end of SOLO might be more challenging for your class, but is this because it's relevant and pitched correctly, or because we've skipped quickly past the important knowledge, facts and definitions, which leaves the challenging tasks difficult to learn? I'll explain more in the questioning chapter, but the (perceived) lower levels of the taxonomy (and Bloom's) are as important, if not more important, than the (perceived) higher levels.

And this then poses my last question. With SOLO as a hierarchy, do we just need to head up? Would there be a problem with starting the lesson with an Extended Abstract type question to act as a hook? Here is what we're going to try and solve, now let's set about learning how. If we move up to a relational level, does this mean we can't drop back down to multi-structural one? Some may see that as the lesson going backwards. But what if most of the class don't get it, would you simply plough on because the hierarchy tells you to? As John Biggs once told me:

Yes SOLO is a hierarchy but whether you can go up and down depends on how you are using it. I recommend its use now as a means of designing outcomes at an appropriate level. Thus, if all you want is for students to have an acquaintance with a range of topics then multi-structural is enough. If your aim is for students to apply a concept to solve a problem then relational; if to solve an unseen problem then extended abstract is appropriate. Then you design rubrics for the concept or topic using SOLO from U to EA to see if the desired level has been reached.

The same can be said for Bloom's as well. There are still those who misinterpret it and view the lower end of the taxonomy as a stage not as important or as desired as some of the higher levels. The lower ends might seem shallow and unchallenging, but without them the upper levels wouldn't work.

Finally, we've talked about how SOLO terminology could be overly complicated for students. Although the same isn't apparent for Bloom's, it is hard to explain progression between levels. With SOLO it's pretty obvious. I know something, I know other things, I see how they link together and so on. I've yet to hear a student (if used explicitly with them) say "I've fully applied this now Sir, can I move on to analyse it?" The language isn't very fluent. Moving from one stage to another for a student can be complicated. But if you don't share it and use it purely as a teacher planning tool, you won't have this problem.

So which do I use then?

Planning is the architectural structure of great learning. Get it right and lessons can lead to great gains in understanding and application. Get it wrong and it can be the downfall of your efforts. I have heard teachers passionately promote a particular way of teaching how a taxonomy, a pro-forma or a methodology can transform what is happening in the classroom. I have to admit, I have been lured in by these Pied Pipers. Drawn in by the allure of student outcomes and increased learning. The noise of how "my way of planning creates expert level learners who will retain everything you teach, achieve academic excellence and be able to juggle a dog, cat and mouse at the same time". Such promises are short lived. Instead of trying to find a way to plan a lesson or a method for structure, understanding why you should plan in a particular way would be more beneficial. And that is the point of the previous section. Too many times we tell others, innocently, to "do it this way". However, look at the structure, see what it aims to do and understand why it does. Knowing this means you probably don't need a structure.

Ok, so the lesson format is sorted, but you mentioned about planning bigger. How?

Too many times over the years, I looked at lesson planning the wrong way round. I always got my plan or my (now-) blank bit of paper and thought, what do I need to do first? I planned from start to end in isolated lessons. I used to constantly think about how A linked to B and then to C without a really clear process or direction. It would limit my thinking to filling a lesson with activities rather than focusing on the learning that I wanted to take place. It made me fall into the trap of planning fragmented day-to-day lessons on discrete topics instead of creating coherent plans backwards from a long-term end goal. How am I going to start this lesson? What task will I get them to do? What activity should follow after that? When talking to teachers and relearning how to plan lessons, I found that I had actually gone about it the wrong way. I should have instead taken on board my second principle.

---

2 Always plan backwards

In *Visible Learning for Teachers*, Hattie stresses that lessons should be about learning and

> Learning starts with "backward design" – rather than starting from the textbooks of favoured lessons and time-honoured activities. Learning starts with the teacher (and preferably also the student) knowing the desired results (expressed as success criteria related to learning intentions) and then working backwards to where the student starts the lesson(s).
>
> (2012, p. 104)

As a reason for doing this, Hattie went on further:

> Knowing our intentions and what success of a lesson should look like before we start to plan is the essence of such backward thinking. Such knowing allows us to improvise and change during the process of teaching, while reluctant to change the notion of success.
>
> (p. 119)

As a teacher with years of experience, we have a model of what excellence may be. If our content knowledge is good, we know the multiple layers of the topics we teach, including what the highest level is. Backward planning offers a number of benefits. Notably, and probably most importantly, it forces us to begin with the end product in mind. It makes us think of what our outcome should be and gives us a better mental model of what students should be achieving. It allows us to set expectations high because we know we will have to plot the path to reach it. When you know what the endpoint is, whether this is the level of knowledge or quality of work, we can quickly get back on the right path if a lesson takes an unexpected turn. Without this end goal in mind, a lesson can be unnecessarily messy.

As a trainee teacher or NQT, backward planning was well beyond me. Time in schools or at university only taught me to do the following:

- Pick a topic
- Make a list of two or three superficial outcomes (which I didn't really use at all)

- Think about a starter
- What activity would I do next?
- Is there another activity, maybe slightly harder, that I could add in?
- Do an exam question
- Maybe have a plenary
- Done
- Have I added in literacy, numeracy, SMSC, differentiation and any other number of bolt-ons?

Alongside this would obviously be my questions, my explanations and the 30 different card sort or colouring in activities. If you look at it, all I would be doing is picking a topic and just ticking parts of it off.

As I look back, I realise how far I've come but can see how many mistakes I used to make. I sacrificed depth of learning in order to make lessons fun. Planning from start to finish moves things on one step at a time. But unless I have an end goal in mind, how do I know if I've got there? How do I know if I've pushed the students as far as I could? You're in danger of missing a trick of getting students to be amazing.

You're a bit dramatic, David

Maybe. Maybe just thinking about my planning more carefully all those years back would have produced the same outcomes, whether it was through normal planning or backwards planning. However, I don't think it would. I really believe that planning in reverse is the key. What would I recommend now?

Setting standards, outcomes and goals high – like, really high!

One of the first things we should do when mapping out a lesson or series of lessons is focus on what the outcome should be. In Chapter 5, I talk about the benefits of aiming high and something called the Pygmalion effect – how students can astonish us if we push them right to the edge of their comfort zone.

By backward planning, we can spend valuable time thinking about where we want our students to end up. Is it to create an exceptional piece of writing? Is it to understand a concept in great depth? Starting at the end allows us to focus on quality, which, as Hattie said earlier, does not change even if the direction of the lesson does.

Pick an upcoming topic you will be teaching and then ask yourself the following questions:

- What is it that you ultimately want students to achieve?
- What does this outcome look like?
- What would excellence look like?
- What makes work of this standard?

- What knowledge do students need to get them here?
- What skills do they need in order to achieve that?
- What is needed to get to excellence in this topic?
- Working backwards, what are the steps to get here?
- What is needed to get to the stage before excellence, and then the stage before that, and before that . . .

So, what was your topic? What is the highest end point you want your students to achieve?

Work backwards and map out, in order, the sequence of learning that must take place before you get there. It may take more than one lesson to get there – that's not an issue at all.

Planning backwards requires us to know our curriculum, specifications and exams inside and out, and be able to push students to the highest level. Be brave, push boundaries and challenge students to reach an outcome which may have surpassed initial thoughts.

You're going to throw something in now with a warning aren't you?

Of course! I've warned you already about taxonomies. However, SOLO taxonomy, for me, was the thing which really helped me plan backwards. I know it has its critics because of its terminology, and how some have used it incorrectly, but using it solely for planning has been the clarity I needed.

Whenever I plan a topic now, the first thing I do is think of what the highest possible thing could be at that moment for my students. This end point needs to be challenging, but at the same time needs to allow me the opportunity to teach the students what they know. In SOLO taxonomy terms, this aspirational level is called the Extended Abstract level.

Using Media in sport as an example, at the end of this topic, I want students to understand the role that media has in the sports industry, and whether it is a good or bad thing for performance and participation rates? As media expands, will it help or hinder sport?

Students have to evaluate, reflect, generalise, hypothesise and imagine. All of the things that the Extended Abstract stage requires. It will force students to think hard about the topic and form opinions, judgements and predictions about the impact of media. It's quite complex, it will draw in other topics such as sponsorship, gender and elements of psychology in sport (whether athletes can help media pressure). Knowing this is the end point, I can now work backwards.

Brining us to the relational level, I know I will need students to be able to compare the various media outlets and the impact they have. I need students to classify reasons for media to have a positive or negative affect. I need students to begin to explain the causes that media has on sport, such as how watching role models will inspire young athletes to take up sport, or copy techniques to improve their performance. I need to show them how everything links.

At the stage before, called the multi-structural, students would need to know everything they can about media. Without this stage, the earlier ones can't work. This is the one I need to spend most of my time on so my students have such a grasp on the content knowledge, they can manipulate it to make considered conclusions later on. Knowledge is power.

This then leads me to the beginning. We call this the uni-structural stage. For me, I always think about what is the one thing that every student must know in this topic. I need students to know and understand what is meant by "media". It sounds simple, but that's part of the problem with planning. People try to make planning so complex, when in fact we should try to keep it as simple as possible. Without knowing what on earth I mean about media, students won't be able to hook the subsequent information to anything in their memory. This is the beginning of my schema. Going to town at the start, means that we can build this schema and have a better chance of committing things to memory over time. If I mention media in six months' time, hopefully, because of the importance of this starting stage, students will be able to unlock a wealth of information from their prior knowledge. Maybe.

One of the points I'm trying to highlight is that using this process, I am not thinking about how I will teach the topic, I'm thinking about what I will teach. What students need to know. What students need to understand. It's a big difference and one that people sometimes forget. I urge you not to. If like me, you never use it for anything else, SOLO is a great way to map out a topic from back to front. Worth a try, I hope.

Backward planning helps plan lessons with an assessment in mind

Oh the number of times I put an assessment in at the end of a lesson for good measure. I would get towards the end of my planning and think how I needed an exam question or two to get students to think about the content. On the face of this there is no harm at all in doing that. Exams contain exam questions, testing is a good way to develop memory, and getting some sort of assessment lets me get a taste of what students do or don't know.

The issue though is this always made assessment a summative task in mind. It made the shoe-horning of an exam question an afterthought. I didn't really think too much about the type of question, only that the question was from that particular topic. Anything would do.

The benefit of planning backwards means that I know what I want to achieve, so I can therefore design a way to assess this has been met straight away. If I want to see if students can explain how the muscular system and skeletal system interact to create movement, I will make sure I have something in there towards the end to do just that. Rather than blindly throwing in a task for good measure, I now know the specific way I will gather evidence that students are beginning to grasp this concept. This changes everything.

Take the media example from the previous section. Once I know what components make up my topic, I need to start thinking about how I can assess them along the way. Once again, I will start backwards.

I think about a form of extended answer that students write. Whether this is a stock exam question from the exam board, or one I create myself. I work out what students need to know in order to answer this. I even try answering this myself. Doing so allows me to check its validity, its level of challenge, as well as giving me a model to share with students later on. If my plan won't help students answer this, I go back to it and amend it.

Planning assessment doesn't just have to be at the summative end of the spectrum. I would also need to map in times along the way when I need to asses formatively. This could be after a difficult concept has been taught. It could be at the stage when I go from teaching knowledge, to the time I ask them to manipulate and use this knowledge. Sticking with SOLO taxonomy, it's usually when I move from the multi-structural (developing solid content knowledge) to the relational (pieces this knowledge together). I do it here to check misconceptions from isolated facts and information, before asking students to pull them all together. Get that wrong and students could confuse concepts or associate incorrect elements.

So, what could you do at that point? Well-planned out questions to start with. Mini-whiteboards, if used well, are good. But my favourite has to be using hinge questions. I talk more about them in Chapter 3, but they are a way to get an answer from every student about a difficult topic before deciding whether to move on or not.

Planning backwards helps you tell a story

I'll mention it more later in Chapter 2, but Daniel T. Willingham (2009, p. 66) refers to stories as being psychologically privileged. He talks about how the memory treats stories differently than other types of materials. As I go on to explain in Chapter 6, how many times can you remember a good anecdote or tale, yet forget the simplest of facts. Stories are effective in helping content become memorable and interesting.

Willingham explains a number of reasons for this, but from a backward planning element, one reason stands out more for me.

In *Why Don't Students Like School?* (2009, p. 69), Willingham explains that stories require low to medium difficulty inferences. As a result, you must think about the meaning of a story throughout. Thinking about meaning is excellent for memory, as it is usually the meaning that we want our brains to remember. Willingham also explains that stories provide structure. So, knowing about one part of a story normally requires us to remember what happened before that part (to explain why this thing is happening) and where this fits within the bigger context of the story. Again, these multiple routes to information help with memory.

And that's where we can use it. If I use my SOLO media plan from earlier in this principle, I could have a story to attach it to. I could have a story of how the media, in the case of David Beckham after World Cup 98, attacked him so viciously. This highlights the negative aspect. However, I could twist the tale and talk about how he was made a hero after his free kick against Greece in 2001 secured England's qualification to the World Cup 2002. I could use it to talk about the various media types, showing examples of some of the bias, hype and sensationalism. How his influence as a role model inspired youngsters. How numerous children tried to copy his technique of that amazing free kick. One story can tie so much into it. And when we talk about it months down the line, that story, being psychologically privileged, will help draw out the content from memory.

So, is there a bigger story that you could work backwards with and tie in content? Could you use that story to map the topic out with? Start at the end, work back, and use it to help information become more accessible in students' memories.

Planning backwards helps you to be aware of cognitive overload

I'll go into a lot more depth in Chapter 3 but in the short term, cognitive overload occurs when a teacher gives students too much information, or creates too many distractions, and they can't process the information effectively. As a quick introduction, imagine we had a difficult concept to explain. How many times have you, like me, stared to explain it, only for students to look blank faced a minute in?

Knowing what the bigger concept is allows you to break it down into smaller, more manageable chunks. It allows you the ability to work out what prior knowledge is needed to build new knowledge, so that you can teach it more effectively. It allows you to identify examples that may need to be sequenced in order to get to the lesson outcome, so that things aren't confusing.

Doing these things allows you to have cognitive load in mind. And knowing that it's important, I'll go into much more depth in Chapter 3.

And finally, it switches the focus from activities to learning

And this is a very important point. As pointed out by Nancy Gedge, a consultant teacher at the Driver Youth Trust, planning backwards is important, "otherwise we become fixated on the funky activities we want to use and forget about why we choose particular ones". Rarely does planning backwards make you think of what activity or task students will do. Instead it allows you to do my third principle.

---

3 Plan learning first – then think about activities

Teachers like shiny things. I remember the days when I crammed hexagons, diamond nines, card sorts, differentiated learning cards, challenge cards and more into lessons. The problem of working in this way was highlighted to me by Katie Ashford, a Deputy Head-teacher in London: "Just remember the golden rule: If a resource takes longer to make than to deliver, don't do it!" This quickly became my new mantra.

If we are not conscious of the process, planning a lesson can quickly become an amalgamation of activities, mish-mashed together and squeezed into the hour slot. Working this way makes us pay attention to the "what" of a lesson, rather than the "why" and poses four problems.

1. The lesson becomes more about doing rather than understanding – When I first started teaching theory lessons, after picking the topic I needed to cover, I would ask myself "What could I get my students to do today?" I would look at cool ways to get students engaged in my lessons: PowerPoint, "Thunk" activities, mind mapping, quizzes, card sort, group work, a hot seat activity. I hadn't begun the planning process with an end outcome in mind: There was no thought behind exactly what I wanted students to learn. Instead the lesson was more about doing things, an explosion of activity with fragments of learning.

2. Things can become overly complicated – "Sorry Sir, what is it we're supposed to be doing?" Activities, when designed well, can complement learning. In fact, they can work in harmony. However, if an activity is extremely complicated, students working memory will be paying more attention to the activity itself, rather than what it's trying to teach them. This ties in closely with my next point.

3. They remember what they did, not what they were supposed to learn – Daniel T. Willingham (2009) states that "memory is the residue of thought". When students are thinking hard about a concept, really focusing their attention on it, there is a good chance that it will stick over time. However, if a student can only remember the time they stuck labels on their partner to identify the different bones, without remembering what the names of those bones were, we have to ask ourselves "have we forced our students to attend to the wrong things?"

4. We mistake busy for learning – There has been many a time where either myself or a colleague has come into the staffroom and said "I did a really good activity today. All of the kids were really engaged". We are all keen to hear more and the activity is explained. It sounds good, it seemed to have the kids engaged and the teacher saw them all busily working away. A word of caution: Professor Rob Coe (2015) warns this might be a poor proxy for learning. Sometimes being busy and engaged doesn't necessarily mean that learning has taken place. On the other hand, a quiet classroom may not seem to have much learning going on in comparison but here there might be lots. A well-designed activity which links directly to what is being learnt can come in many different forms: If you want to know if any learning took place, see what they remembered two weeks down the line.

What I am trying to say is keep it smart. Activities seem to be the vital ingredient in getting students engaged. But as Richard Cheetham MBE, a Senior Fellow at the University of Winchester once told me, students will learn better when intrinsically motivated. Lesson after lesson of elaborate activities may not result in learning. Instead it may burn us out or may make us feel like circus performers. Our focus should be on what we want students to learn. What are the facts? What are the concepts? What are the relationships between topics? Lesson activities can therefore take a back seat until we've planned this out first.

But ultimately, there will come the time when you need to design the activity to compliment the learning. It would therefore be important to ask yourself the following questions from David Didau (2013), an English teacher and author from Somerset:

1. Is it going to encourage students to think about the content of lesson, or will it be a distraction?

2. Is there an easier way to get them to think about what's important?

So, it seems that what I am saying is keep it simple, not boring. You'll benefit from it in the long run. And that leads me to my next principle.

---

4 Keep it simple

We have an idea of a long-term plan. We plan backwards and understand how to get to this end point. We look at what needs to be learnt first and later plan activities. Next, we need to be brave and keep lessons simple. And there's a number of reasons why.

What are your Rondos?

Part of Barcelona FC's legendary success under coach Pep Guardiola was due to his training method, the "Rondo". The simple drill involves a "piggy in the middle" situation, with team mates keeping the ball away from defenders. Every day, for around 20 minutes, players would practice pressing, finding space and retaining possession in a Rondo. Each day the Rondo would vary slightly, but every day the Rondo would be used. The result was a team that could out pass, out press and out play opponents. This deliberate practice was the cornerstone of training and is part of the success that Barcelona achieved.

When I spoke to Doug Lemov, an author and English teacher in America back in 2016, we chatted about the process of planning as teachers. In this discussion, Doug spoke about a number of things to keep planning simple. The first question he said we should ask teachers is "What are your Rondos?"

In a time where we are looking for the next glitzy activity, Doug suggested we should ignore the cult of novelty where we change things on a daily basis to keep interest. Instead we should keep things much simpler. By overcomplicating the planning process, we spend too long trying to invent new things. We instil a cost every time by having to teach students a new strategy each day, which in turn takes time – time that might have better been used to focus on learning. Doug suggested doing what Guardiola does and choose your best systems and re-run them every lesson. If a particular way you start lessons work very well, do them again. If how you get students to read from texts is effective, do it again. If the way you model examples or structure with your class provides clarity, do it again. For me, "Do now" tasks, retrieval practice quizzes, writing scaffolds and modelling excellent work all fall under my Rondos. Look at the way you plan lessons. If things you do have a positive effect on learning, ensure they become your rondos and do them repeatedly.

Plan collaboratively

> Planning can be done in many ways, but the most powerful is when teachers work together to develop plans, develop common understandings of what is worth teaching, collaborate on understanding their beliefs of challenge and progress, and work together to evaluate the impact of their planning on student outcomes.
>
> (Hattie, 2012, p. 41)

One of the best ways to avoid overcomplicating a lesson is through collaboratively planning with colleagues. They can help you see sticking points. Help you see where things may need more time. They can help you assess whether particular points in the lesson might confuse students. They can also help you work out whether things are too complicated. The art of planning takes years. In the early days we become hooked on delivering "glamourous lessons" packed full of content. As we get more experience, it seems we refine the way we teach and understand that less is more. Experience takes time though and we can develop bad habits before we spot them and begin to rectify it. Imagine what a teacher of ten years could offer an NQT +1? Planning collaboratively does take precious time, but making it a consistent routine could certainly help make lessons simpler.

But how simple is simple?

As we mentioned earlier with activities, engagement doesn't always mean that you need whizzy lessons. In fact, as we explore in the next chapter, they can actually hinder learning. Lesson planning can in fact be refined down to one simple focal point, which can be adapted to suit the learners as required. As Mary Myatt, an education adviser and writer told me:

> The key to planning is simplicity. When we have a rich resource such as a demanding text, an artefact or other stimulus, we can use this to explain, model and ask questions. It is important to plan for the top and to unpack the ideas through talk. There is often no need for worksheets as these often put limits on learning. Much better to use knowledge organisers containing the key concepts, vocabulary and essential information, which learners are expected to know, over time, inside out. There is likely to be more impact in keeping things simple, not overcrowding with resources and instead, letting the material speak for itself.

From experience, I was never brave enough to use one source for an entire lesson. How on earth could that fill 60 minutes? This may be at one end of the spectrum, but compared to lessons full of activities, simple ones may benefit learning. And one reason for this is our working memory and cognitive overload. I am now going to be overly simplistic as I go into a bit more detail in the next chapter about this process.

When we are thinking about things, we process it in our working memory. The working memory is the place where we hold information ready for processing. We use our working memory all of the time. Even now as you read this page, you are using your working memory to hold the words, ready for our brain to process meaning. The issue is that our working memory has a limited capacity. Back in 1956, George Miller, a cognitive psychologist from Princeton University, proposed that working memory can only hold seven plus or minus two pieces of information at any one time. This has been argued over the years, with current psychologists insisting that number may in fact be lower. If we overcomplicate our lessons, we run the risk of overloading working memory and causing confusion and reduced learning.

Tied into this is what cognitive psychologist Daniel T. Willingham (2009, p. 80) calls "attention grabbers". If we are not careful, our whizzy lessons can grab student's attention in the wrong way, meaning they think more about activities or glamorous parts of our lessons rather than the learning itself. Graham Nuthall (2007, p. 104), in his book, discusses how students' recollection of information can be affected by the type of activity we design. He states "sometimes memory for the task itself is longer lasting than the content the task was designed to teach". This is something we need to be mindful of.

Going back to my skeletal system lesson, after students have stuck bone labels onto their partner, they may end up coming away remembering they stuck things to their partner, rather what the labels were explaining or representing. If I demonstrated the elephant toothpaste experiment in science (worth looking it up online), students may remember how I got some chemicals to explode foam over the classroom ceiling, rather than understanding exothermic reactions, catalysts and covalent bonding. Again, simple doesn't mean cut these out or be boring. But it does mean we need to be mindful of our student's limitations and what is it that we exactly want students to remember? The thing we're trying to get them to learn or the complicated whizzy activity? And as Mary continues to explain:

> And yes I have seen both: overcomplicated often means that completing the tasks become more important than checking for understanding, where the piece of paper becomes more important than the pupils. Simpler lessons flourish as long as the resource is rich – much more time needs to be given to this I think, rather than quick activities downloaded from the internet.

Complicated can also mean that there is more opportunity for things to go wrong. It can mean that there are more chances for things to go off tangent, get confused or mess up. Simple avoids that. Complicated also means that lessons can feel constrained. Knowing you have seven things to get through, have you got the flexibility explore a worthwhile line of questioning, conscious that you only have 30 minutes left to get through the remaining elements of a lesson.

My advice, as with many experienced teachers, is that (probably) less is more. Pick a rich source, an excellent question, a great text or rich resource. One which really compliments the aim of the learning and allows true depth of understanding. Work out what students need to know and then plan activities around this. How will you use this resource to highlight gather knowledge? What questions could you pose? What will allow you to gain an insight into what they know? How could they develop their writing using this resource? In what ways can you make the source really interesting?

How could you use this resource to draw in other knowledge and make links? And finally, linking to my next principle, how will you get students to think?

---

5 Memory is the residue of thought

In his book *Why Don't Students Like School?*, Daniel T. Willingham bases his third chapter on the principle, "Memory is the residue of thought": Whatever students are asked to think about, they will remember.

When we plan lessons, we can sometimes be focused on what students will do, rather than what students will be thinking about. We should be thinking of what it is we want them to learn, and working back to see how we get there. At each stage we can then scrutinise how much thinking is actually taking place. Willingham explains "your memory is not a product of what you want to remember or what you try to remember; it's a product of what you think about". It is therefore important we take his tip and "review each lesson plan in terms of what the student is likely to think about". If we are to help commit what we are teaching to students' memory to be recalled later, we need to ensure the level of thinking is high throughout. So, when reviewing your lesson plan, ask yourself the following questions:

- What is it that I want my students to remember?
- How am I ensuring that students are really paying attention to this information?
- Am I asking students to think hard about it?
- Will they be challenged?
- Are there opportunities to ask quality questions, solve problems, make meaning and make the content interesting?

And it's not just about asking more questions to set students. You need to look at everything and scrutinise it. Look at how you give definitions for example. Do you just get them to copy them out, or do you use things like "fragments", an idea from Hochman and Wexler (2017, p. 27), where you give students three words (a part of a bigger sentence) which students have to form a whole sentence around. For instance, in my skeletal system lesson, I could use the fragment "to create movement" when asking students to explain what an agonist is. They could use it at the start of the sentence, in the middle of their sentence, or at the end. The point is, it's making them think. They could come up with:

> The agonist is the muscle that contracts to create movement at a joint, such as the bicep, which causes flexion at the elbow.

It's not copying a definition; it's working out how to fit a definition and knowledge into a sentence using a predetermined fragment. Such a small change, which has such a big impact.

How else can we design lessons that ensure students are thinking hard so that content becomes memorable? In Chapter 2, I go into more detail about how to make learning stick, which includes asking how much thinking is taking place. But for now, let's visit my final planning principle.

---

6 Be responsive

Ditch the timings!

Timings on a lesson plan can inadvertently make you stick to the plan letter by letter. What is seen as a well-intentioned guide for newer teachers, can actually make the lesson feel more about doing what was planned, rather than what is right for the learners. Take this obvious example for instance. On my lesson plan we see that we had assigned ten minutes for students to answer a question. As they are working on it, we see that they are actually taking a little longer, not because they are distracted, but because they are thinking hard about the answer. Because the ten minutes is up we stop students and then move on. We now plan seven minutes for students to organise a card sort and discuss the relationship between the topics, ordering them into importance. On goes the interactive timer. Seven minutes is up and we say, "Sorry Year 9, we need to move on". We do the same for the next three activities until the lesson is done. We leave the lesson safe in the knowledge that we have covered everything we had planned. Everything went seamlessly from one element to the next. Unfortunately, we also leave with the feeling that we probably didn't cover things in as much depth as we could.

For a long time in education, there has been a myth that every lesson must demonstrate rapid and sustained progress. This myth has been dispelled in numerous quarters, but still its shadow lurks over our shoulder. As a result, it may be common that teachers feel they are expected to move on rather than taking time delving deeper into a topic. Learning takes time. To ensure things are remembered means we shouldn't rush. And timings should guide, but not interfere with that.

But if it's on the plan I need to stick to it

A plan is good to have. Whatever form your planning takes, it acts as a guide. Planning ensures you can critically think about your endpoint, working backwards to find the route there. It helps you think about the learning and keep it simple. It allows you to scrutinise how much thinking is taking place and analyse how you can help them remember what it is you will be teaching them. However, with all of that planning, students and learning can make you divert from it and require you to be responsive. A plan needs to be less rigid and more fluid. Flexibility is the key. If students find things difficult, divert from the plan and address misconceptions – it will be worth it in the long run. If students know the topic quite well – divert from the plan and introduce something more challenging. But how do we know how to do this?

Know your subject

Read up, find articles and predict what might be asked. If you were a student in that lesson, what might you want to know?

Build in opportunities to gather feedback

We need signposts in the lesson to gather (as best as we can) an idea of how students are progressing. This can help us make the decision to stick to the plan, divert from it or scrap it altogether. We'll talk more about this in later chapters – in Chapter 3 we look at questioning strategies, in Chapter 4 we look at feedback methods, in Chapter 5 we look at how to plan challenge. The key is to have these as part of your plan. Gathering formative information helps you be responsive.

Right. Simple and backwards; thinking and learning; over time and responsive

That may seem a lot to take in. Believe me it can be a complete change in your approach. It won't come easy and you may feel some struggle when changing your habits. However, planning in this way can free you up, allow for more learning and ensure that things stick. And if you don't believe me, I think John Tomsett, a headteacher and author from York, summarises this chapter so well.

> Lesson planning is so last year! Yet I can't help thinking you need to plan something before you step into the room for an hour and attempt to teach in a way that enables the students learn . . .
>
> I find planning in chunks of lessons, say six or even ten at a time, really helpful. That way you know what you want students to learn over that span of lessons and can build up their knowledge, understanding and skills bit by bit. Importantly, you can plan for mini-formative assessments to check that the incremental learning is secure; if it's not, you go back and make sure it is. Then at the end of the planned series of lessons you can use a summative assessment to gauge what the students have learned in the round.
>
> I swear by the aphorism: fewer activities; deeper learning; better outcomes. What dismays me most about planning is over-planned activity-central lessons. And timings should be banned from any lesson planning! Rather, use a blank piece of paper, know where you would like to get to, jot down a couple of ideas about resources that you might use and clarify in your mind a few routes the lesson might take, depending on how well the students progress. Think of your

lesson like a map, with a starting point, a destination and several routes to get there. Crucially, just remember, sometimes you have to abort your journey because the road is closed and you try again the next day.

To recap

- Never underestimate the importance of a good plan. I think we should scrap the term "lesson" plan and instead look at topic plans. Plan backwards so that we know the content that needs teaching, and what prior knowledge is needed to make your way to a challenging outcome. Then plan activities.

- In order to transfer information to students, lessons should be as simple as possible, but no simpler.

- Ensure every part of your lesson encourages students to think hard. Look at old tasks and see if you can tweak them to make students think about the thing it is you've taught them.

- And finally, and probably with experience, be responsive. Watch what is going on in your lessons. Ask students questions. Spot misconceptions. Divert from the plan if needed if it will help move learning forward. Respond to your students, and your students will respond as a result.

And don't, don't, don't go chasing "outstanding" lessons. They don't exist.

Note

1 A huge thank you to John Biggs for his time discussing SOLO taxonomy with me and guiding me through writing part of this chapter.

References

Anderson, L. W. (Ed), Krathwohl, D. R. (Ed), Airasian, P. W., Cruikshank, K. A., Mayer, R. E., Pintrich, P. R., Raths, J., & Wittrock, M. C. (2001) *A Taxonomy for Learning, Teaching, and Assessing: A Revision of Bloom's Taxonomy of Educational Objectives* (Complete edition). New York: Longman.

Bartle, K. (2013) The myth of progress within lessons. In: *Kevenbartle's Blog*. 12 February 2013. Available at: https://dailygenius.wordpress.com/2013/02/12/the-myth-of-progress-within-lessons/

Berger, R. (2003) *An Ethic of Excellence; Building a Culture of Craftsmanship with Students.* Portsmouth, NH: Heinemann.

Bjork, R. A., & Bjork, E. L. (1992) A new theory of disuse and an old theory of stimulus fluctuation. In: Healy, A., Kosslyn, S., & Shriffrin, R. (Eds) *Learning Processes to Cognitive Processes: Essays in Honor of William K. Estes.* Volume 2. pp. 35–67. New York: Psychology Press.

Buck Institute for Education. (2018) *What Is PBL?* Available at: www.bie.org/about/what_pbl

Coe, R. (2015) *From Evidence to Great Teaching*. Presentation delivered to ASCL Annual Conference, 20 March 2015. Available at: www.ascl.org.uk/index.cfm?originalUrl=utilities/document-summary.html&id=45878A48-32E1-48FC-8729663C8DC4E8FA

Didau, D. (2013) Fireworks teaching: Why less might well be more. In: *The Learning Spy*. July 15, 2013. Available at: www.learningspy.co.uk/featured/fireworks-teaching/

Hattie, J. (2012) *Visible Learning for Teachers: Maximising Impact on Learning*. Abingdon: Routledge.

Hochman, J., & Wexler, N. (2017) *The Writing Revolution. A Guide to Advancing Thinking through Writing in All Subjects and Grades*. San Francisco, CA: Jossey-Bass.

Isaksen, B. (2015) A lesson is the wrong unit of time. In: *Red or Green Pen: Thoughts on Teaching in a UK School*. 29 January 2015. Available at: https://redorgreenpen.wordpress.com/2015/01/29/a-lesson-is-the-wrong-unit-of-time/

Kirschner, P., Sweller, J., & Clark, E. (2006) Why minimal guidance during instruction does not work: An analysis of the failure of constructivist, discovery, problem-based, experiential, and inquiry-based teaching. *Educational Psychologist*. 41(2). pp. 75–86.

Nuthall, G. (2007) *The Hidden Lives of Learners*. Wellington: NZCER Press.

Smith, A. (1998) *Accelerated Learning in Practice*. London: Network Educational Press.

SSAT. (2018) *The Teacher Effectiveness Enhancement Programme (TEEP). A Summary of the TEEP Framework*. Available at: www.ssatuk.co.uk/cpd/teaching-and-learning/teep/what-is-teep/

Willingham, D. T. (2009) *Why Don't Students Like School? A Cognitive Scientist Answers Questions about How the Mind Works and What It Means for the Classroom*. San Francisco, CA: Jossey-Bass.

Why do they seem to remember in lessons, but then forget it in the test?[1]

You plan an amazing lesson, thinking extremely hard about what you want students to learn and how you want to deliver it. You think about the topic's key points and what students might do to pick them up. You plan your sources, activities and resources. You put a few slides together on a PowerPoint. You think of potential questions the students might ask and design some of your own.

The students walk in. They are attentive, focused and hardworking. The image displayed on the board to act as a starter seems to go down well. The students get involved in discussions, sharing ideas that show a good grasp of the topic. They answer questions and pose some good ones. As you walk around the room you see that they are writing some really good ideas. You give some individual feedback to move understanding forward. At the end of the lesson you check everyone has understood what you've covered and they all nod happily. They leave and you feel like you've had a result. The topic can be ticked off. High fives all round.

Two weeks later, the class sits a unit test. It covers everything you taught in this unit over the last six lessons. You feel confident. The students seem confident. They sit it and you collect in the papers. As you spend the next few days dipping in and out of them to mark, you begin to feel the need to scream into an empty room: "How do they not remember this? We just did it a few weeks back!"

Collectively, this class could give you a full run down on the stats of their favourite football teams, the lyrics of every song in the charts, the mobile numbers of all their friends or an overview of every episode of the latest reality TV show. How annoying!

Memory is an amazing thing. There are world memory champions who can recall the positions of hundreds of cards in perfect order. Yet students find it difficult to remember the stuff we teach them, things we are lulled into believing they know. This can be frustrating. But it is also a challenge, one that makes me curious to learn more about the brain and how we can make learning things more effective.

But we know all of this. We already do it

At an INSET day in 2016 we were lucky to have part of the "Learning Scientists" fly over from the USA and Scotland to teach us all about cognitive science, memory and how we can make things stick. It was a fascinating day. We looked at how the brain stores information in the long-term memory and at strategies to ensure it has a better chance of doing so, especially those with the potential to make a significant difference to the way we teach. However, at the end of the training a few colleagues said, "It was good but we know all of this. We already do a lot of these things".

A number of things that have emerged from cognitive science seem pretty common sense. But that is the problem. Sometimes we "sort of" do things. We are aware of current research, but do we just have a simplistic overview? We rely on snippets of information from various sources and patch them all together. As a result, a number of ineffective practices have been implemented and, even worse, some untrue theories about the brain have filtered into classrooms.

Take, for instance, Brain Gym® and the "right side/left side" theories that came into prominence in the early 2000s. Many of these are based on assumptions and myths that seem to have become "factual" as more and more people refer to them. Original pieces of research have been distorted or used inaccurately. What I'm trying to say is that as any cognitive scientist will tell you, how the brain works is actually a lot more complicated than we think.

Myths and nonsense about the brain

I'm a right side/left side brain learner

There is one belief around brain and learning that doesn't seem to go away. At training sessions, somebody always brings up the notion that we are right side brain or left side brain learners. "*But we need to be aware that some of our students are right brain learners so we need to ensure that we foster their creativity and include strategies to help them*". Or we are encouraged to use more logical and reasoning strategies for left brain thinkers. You can book yourselves onto courses and even get consultants in to help embed the idea whole-school. The issue is that what has become a common belief is actually an over-simplified and distorted version of the original research.

Sections of our brain do control different functions and processes. The right side is concerned with creativity and the left side is concerned with logic and language. Unfortunately, as too often happens, people jump on research and twist its real meaning.

The theory arose from studies conducted on a group of "split brain" patients, starting in the 1960s. Back then, a last-resort treatment for epileptic seizures was to sever the corpus callosum – the thick bundle of fibres that connect the left and right cerebral hemispheres – in the patient's brain. This successfully stopped the seizures but left patients with two brain halves that were unable to communicate with each other.

At first glance, these split brain patients seemed normal. They could walk, they could talk, but neuroscientists Michael Gazzaniga (1967) and Roger Sperry designed a series of experiments that demonstrated the impact of the split. And in doing so, they learned that certain functions are controlled by only one half of the brain.

They found that the left side of the brain is the first to deal with what the right side of the body is doing, and the right side of the brain is the first to deal with what the left side of the body is doing. If you touch something with your left hand, this information travels first to the right side of your brain. Those with an intact corpus callosum can share this information between the hemispheres, those with it severed cannot.

Gazzaniga continued this work with a war veteran referred to as Joe whose corpus callosum had been severed. In experiments where Joe would stare at a dot in the centre of a computer screen, images and words would appear to either the right or the left of it. When images or words were shown on the right side of the dot Joe was able to name them. This is because the information was being transferred to the left side of the brain, the dominant hemisphere for language and speech. When the word or image went to the left of the computer screen, that information went to his disconnected right hemisphere, not concerned with language. When this happened, Joe was unable to instantly name it. However, he could use his left hand to draw it, and then after looking at it again, could name the image because his left hemisphere was able to process it.

The research thus found that the two sides of the brain are responsible for different functions (although some are bilateral). But it is more complex than that.

Unfortunately, prompted by an article in *The New York Times Magazine* is September 1973, many people pounced on the right brain left brain theory and began the misinterpretation. Years later and we can take tests to tell us that we are more dominant right brain creative thinkers or logical left brain thinkers and begin a self-fulfilling prophecy to explain why we are rubbish at drawing because we're a left brain thinker or we're awful at maths because we're a right brain thinker.

The problem is that the theory has been debunked numerous times. For example, a study by Nielsen et al. (2013) found there was no dominant side, with some functions taking place on the opposite side we would expect. The brain works predominantly as a whole and we are whole brain thinkers. However, despite being thrown out by research, the idea will probably be around for years to come.

What about VAK and learning styles though?

This is probably the best most well-known of all of the learning theories. Early on I went for a whole school teaching and learning post that revolved around the notion of Learning to Learn (L2L). I scoured the internet for background information on what L2L was. One of the things that popped up was learning styles.

The version I read up on was a more detailed version of VAK (Visual, Audio and Kinaesthetic) and came in the form of Howard Gardner's Multiple Intelligences. The theory detailed how learners have a variety of intelligences, including Musical-rhythmic, Visual-spatial, Naturalistic and Intrapersonal. Armed with a basic grasp of the topic, I gave a presentation at my interview on how we should be designing school curriculums and lessons to help develop these intelligences so that students could learn more.

A multitude of initiatives followed. We tested students to find their dominant intelligence and what style would match it. We encouraged teachers to embed these into their lessons and ran a whole school campaign. We even talked about how this understanding could help with revision. Everything seemed to be going well. However, after a few years I began backtracking. I felt uneasy that we were encouraging students to learn in a particular way. I questioned whether learning could be compartmentalised so formally. I found the whole process of having to highlight styles/intelligence laborious and not ultimately worth the effort. I began to realise that it might be a load of nonsense.

Since my own retraction of it, a number of researchers and educators have debunked the idea of learning styles and different intelligences. A review of literature by Harold Pashler, Mark McDaniel, Doug Rohrer and Robert Bjork (2008), found no supporting evidence that learning styles benefitted learners or even existed . But what about all of the staff training we've had? Surely if a student learns in a particular way the delivery of a lesson should meet this? Well, there are three problems here.

First is the problem of categorising students. As with the right brain/left brain theory, if we begin to tell our students they learn in a particular way, they can use it as a reason why they aren't tackling a task. "I'm a visual learner so I can't do any writing in this lesson, Sir". If we are promoting the matching of styles/intelligence to instruction/tasks, we may end up with a generation of students who, for instance, aren't literate because it isn't their preferred mode of learning. That makes no sense. By tailoring lessons to follow a style are we developing students who are weak in other areas? Are we making them fixed theorists who give up on certain paths simply because they think they "aren't that person"? Are we making them less resilient because they have a fall-back excuse for why they don't do something – i.e. it doesn't match their style?

Second, if you have 30 students in your class in 7 different categories of intelligence, that is a lot of differentiated tasks you are going to have to create. In the current climate of workload and teacher pressure, time could be better spent on things that are proven to actually help students.

Third, what does catering for some of these styles/intelligences even look like? For instance, if my class had to understand the way to find the angles within a triangle, how could I do this in a Naturalistic way? If I need my students to get on and write an extended exam answer, how could I do this in a Musical way? By trying to force that style onto my lessons, am I making tried and tested instruction less effective? Should I just teach it the way I always do which always gets great results? Or should I match style to learners and risk losing the critical understanding of how to work the angles out or write a well-constructed answer? And there lies the problem. Surely the best modality is dependent on the material. Try teaching topography without any visuals. And in fact, there is evidence that people learn best when there are multiple modalities (styles), not just a single one. So, when something feels like it is a "bolt on" to a lesson and too good to be true, it's usually not worth doing.

But many will be grappling with the fact that this idea – that students learn in different ways and we therefore need to cater for it – makes so much sense. "We learnt it at university. They wouldn't lie to us, would they?" That is the difficulty. Many of us have heard these things repeatedly.

However, there seems to be no research that suggests that being taught in a preferred learning style actually improves learning. In fact, as Pashler and colleagues (2008) found out, the research that was available either didn't support the notion of learning styles or was not robust enough for any meaningful conclusions. They instead reminded us that there is research on more effective methods, such as testing (which I will talk about later), that have far more impact on learning. Once again, we need to trust the evidence.

Brain Gym®

Brain Gym® International explains that

> Brain Gym® movements, exercises, or activities refer to the original 26 Brain Gym movements, sometimes abbreviated as the 26. These activities recall the movements naturally done during the first years of life when learning to coordinate the eyes, ears, hands, and whole body.

The idea is that performing these movements at key times in learning can bring about improved results. In fact, Brain Gym® International states,

> Even though it is not clear yet 'why' these movements work so well, they often bring about dramatic improvements in areas such as:

- Concentration and focus
- Memory
- Academics: reading, writing, math, test taking
- Physical coordination
- Relationships
- Self-responsibility
- Organization skills
- Attitude

These are bold claims, though they come with the warning that it is not yet clear why these movements work so well. If you were working with a class, you might want to try a Brain Gym® movement called a "Hook Up" to get students refocused or reengaged. Maybe try this yourself right now. What you'll need to do is:

- Sit down and cross your right leg over your left leg
- Place your right wrist over your left wrist
- Curl your hands so your fingers link/interlock
- Rotate your hands inwards so your fingers point towards your chest
- Slowly bring your hands into your chest
- Breathe deeply and slowly in this position for a few minutes
- You will now be reengaged for your learning.

Sounds simple. There are other ideas too, such as utilising your brain "buttons". For instance, using your finger and thumb, feel for the hollow area under your collarbone, just off centre from your chest. If you rub this area for around 30 seconds to a minute, you stimulate the carotid artery and send fresh supplies of oxygenated blood to your brain which helps literacy. Amazing.

As part of my role in learning to learn, I bought into these ideas with classes. We would all stand up, we would do one of the Brain Gym® activities, and then get on with the learning. Part of the sell was how they could tackle classes after breaks or at the end of the day. It sounded brilliant. Except it is a myth.

A paper, "Brain Gym® Building Stronger Brains or Wishful Thinking?" by Keith J. Hyatt (2007), looked at the evidence underpinning Brain Gym, explaining that it was created by Dennison and Dennison in the 1970s and describing it as "a series of movements that purportedly activate the brain, promote neurological repatterning, and facilitate whole-brain learning" (p. 118).

Hyatt found that a number of the theories that Brain Gym® is based on have no scientific backing. For example, its creators split brain coordination into three dimensions, but there is no conclusive evidence that the brain is actually wired this way.

> Furthermore, none of the movements include an assessment activity to determine which of the three dimensions of the brain require attention and which movement would be most appropriate. It appears that an armchair diagnosis is all that is required to implement a movement regime.
>
> (p. 118)

Hyatt goes on to explain that Brain Gym® is built upon three theoretical categories: neurological repatterning, cerebral dominance and perceptual motor training. However, as Hyatt points out, "Neurological repatterning has been described as fraudulent, cerebral dominance has not been linked to learning, and perceptual motor training has not withstood rigorous scientific investigation". And a review of published research papers supporting Brain Gym® showed them all to have flaws.

Hyatt finishes by saying:

> It is time that educators and educational training institutes – whether university or other entity – ensure that practices such as Brain Gym® that have no substantive theoretical or research support are no longer used with children in the hope of ameliorating a learning problem.

(p. 123)

We remember 10 per cent of what we read, 20 per cent of what we hear . . .

Hands up if you are familiar with the Cone of Learning or Learning Pyramid, which goes a little something like this:

We remember . . .

10 per cent of what we read
20 per cent of what we hear
30 per cent of what we see
50 per cent of what we see and hear
70 per cent of what we discuss with others
80 per cent of what we personally experience
95 per cent or what we teach others
– Edgar Dale

Before we look into it in a little more detail, I want you to look at the list and answer the following questions:

- Have you seen this before?
- Have you ever believed it?
- Do you still believe it?
- When was the last time you read it or heard someone (a colleague or INSET provider) refer to it?
- Why might it be a problem?
- Isn't it curious that every level has a neat percentage?
- Do you think it's funny that we only remember 10 per cent of what we read, yet we (as educators) read a lot?
- Isn't it funny that we remember 10 per cent of what we read and 30 per cent of what we see, yet we need to see in order to read?
- Isn't it amazing that a scientist was able to create sound research experiments that completely isolated each way of remembering so they could truly test them?

- Why aren't our lessons simply full of students teaching each other over and over again if that helps them remember precisely 95 per cent of what they taught?

I admit that I was once sucked into this belief. So much so that when posters of it were put up in classrooms, I adapted how I taught and even shared this with students. I integrated it into revision programmes and encouraged students to prepare for tests this way. What is worrying is that it is still sometimes shared by colleagues. I can't blame people for this. As with other myths, when something is backed up by percentages or linked to a study, people tend to believe it. When it is spoken about over and over again, it becomes part of the education world we live in. And this myth in particular has been mentioned a lot over the years.

So why is it a myth? Well, to begin with, I refer you to the work of Deepak Subramony, Michael Molenda, Anthony Betrus and Will Thalheimer. In a special edition of *Educational Technology*, Nov/Dec 2014, they wrote a number of articles that tried to debunk the thinking once and for all.

In the first article, "The Mythical Retention Chart and the Corruption of Dale's Cone of Experience" (pp. 6–16), the authors explained that the numbers that accompany the cone/pyramid were not actually part of Dale's original diagram but was simply intended to discuss various channels of imparting information, aimed at modelling levels of abstraction. It wasn't a hierarchy, didn't value one channel over another and was never designed to explain retention or learning. However, in the 1970s, people began merging the cone and overlaying percentages on how much people remember, although the source of these widely distributed figures is not clear. Molenda and his collaborators believe that this is because internet content is not as closely scrutinised as articles in scholarly journals:

- "The data shown in the retention chart cannot reasonably be construed as research findings; they are both invalid and unreliable" (p. 7). For example, the percentages cannot be accurate and have also been altered numerous times by different authors.

- "Dale's Cone of Experience even in its unadulterated form has been misused regularly in the literature of educational technology" (p. 7). It isn't being correctly applied.

- "The retention chart has been overlaid illegitimately onto Dale's Cone of Experience; the two constructs have been fallaciously confounded, thus corrupting the original intent of Dale's cone" (p. 7). The original cone/pyramid never had percentages. They were added later, without any further research.

- "The retention chart and the corrupted cone have a murky provenance" (p. 7). No research backs up the claims of any of the sections (cone or percentages).

Nevertheless, the Cone of Learning has been shared by many people all over the world. It is shared in business, by companies, by consultants, in schools, by teachers, by INSET providers, by authors and more. As Will Thalheimer (2015) explains:

This proliferation is a truly dangerous and heinous result of incompetence, deceit, confirmatory bias, greed, and other nefarious human tendencies. It is also hurting learners throughout the world – and it must be stopped. Each of us has a responsibility in this regard.

Oh . . . so what do I actually need to know about the brain, memory and learning?

With so many myths being fed into education, it is hard to know what to believe. There is still a lot about the brain that we simply do not know yet and the newest insights into how memory work are quite complex. In 2013 I began reading a number of books, articles and research papers on the topic. On the surface, some of the things seemed pretty obvious. But what reading further into this domain told me was that things are a bit more technical than people make out. If it were that easy, we would all be teaching the same way and getting fantastic results. So what do I need to know?

Some basics

The brain is made up of numerous sections (or lobes) including the temporal lobe, the occipital lobe, the parietal lobe and the frontal lobe. Contained in the brain are vast numbers of nerve cells. According to paediatric neurologist Dr Andrew Curran, "the present best guess for the number of nerve cells in a developed human brain is probably in the region of 150 billion" (2008, p. 20). That is a huge amount of nerves contained in a relatively small space. As we begin to learn or experience things, these nerves (or neurons) begin to connect to other nerves. As we know and understand more, these connections, or synaptic connections, increase. Each neuron may eventually end up being connected to 10,000 other neurons, which in turn are connected to 10,000 others. Signals are passed between these neurons provide us with information on how to think or create body movement. The more we call upon specific neurons to complete a function or trace a memory, the stronger the connections become. But what has this got to do with teaching my Year 8 class about coastal erosion on a Tuesday morning? Well, if our job is to get information into students' memories so that they can retrieve it, make meaning of it and apply it to various situations, I'd say it's got a lot to do with it.

We are trying to help students learn new information and commit it to memory. When these isolated pieces of information are stored, we want them to be connected to other relevant pieces of information, so that students can begin to make meaning and have a better understanding of the concept. Amongst other things, this involves committing them to the long-term memory and developing things called schemas. What are these? Let me give you an example. Try this:

I want you to think of everything you can about the word **Australia**. Take as long as you need.

If you are like me you might come up with something like the following:

- It's a continent.
- Some of its many cities include Canberra, Sydney, Melbourne and Perth.
- It has a blue flag with the Union Jack on it and white stars.
- Tim Cahill and Harry Kewell played Football for them.
- The national football team are known as the Socceroos.
- We play the Ashes against them in Test Cricket.
- My hero from Australian Cricket is Adam Gilchrist.
- He was an amazing wicket keeping batsman.
- Who scored loads of runs against England.
- Australia has the Great Barrier Reef.
- Which I dream of visiting.
- But has been in the news because it is suffering from back to back bleaching.
- Which is depleting the coral coverage.
- When I was growing up, I used to watch Neighbours everyday (at lunch and again in the evening) on BBC1.
- I can still remember Harold Bishop, Madge, Lou Carpenter, Paul Robinson, Karl Kennedy and Toadfish.
- Kylie Minogue was Charlene and went on to have a music career.
- With songs like "The Loco-Motion" in the 90s.

Over the years I have been taught, or picked up, these pieces of information from various sources. Some of them came through experience (like watching Neighbours), some came from being taught. If I learnt them well enough, I then managed to commit them to long-term memory. Long-term memory has a vast capacity – how large is still unknown. The way the long-term memory works is very clever. When I learn a fact about Australia, not only is it stored, but my brain is able to connect it to another related piece of information. So when I say Australia, not only do I list simple unrelated facts, but I can describe – for example – the accent Australians have, some of the slang, and how the weather is warm and the beaches are amazing. In fact, as I write the word "beach", I am already thinking about sand, the sea, the waves and some of the amazing beach holidays I've been on around the world. From one word, Australia, I have a *schema* – an organised framework of related information. Hattie and Yates (2014) described schema as "the basic units by which we organise and structure our knowledge" (p. 130). They go on to say that "They provide the frames we need to make sense out of ideas and facts that would otherwise exist as isolated islands of knowledge".

Some schemas are extremely complex, made up of thousands of facts, information, ideas, experiences, emotions, smells, sounds. We also have very simple schemas revolving around things we don't know much about or haven't experienced much. For instance, I would struggle if asked to write down everything I know about *palaeomagnetism*. That's because I don't have a complex schema for this word. I can pick out the part "magnetism" and, using a schema around that word, work out it has something to do with magnetic fields. I could probably work out that palaeo has something to do with old and prehistoric, but beyond that I have nothing.

Schemas are malleable, which means they can change and adapt as we learn new things. This is why it's important to remind students that memories aren't fixed and learning new things allows the brain to develop further. The more things we learn, the more schemas we create or add to, the more things we are able to draw upon in our memories. This in turn makes learning new things easier. If I began learning about palaeomagnetism, I would start creating a schema about it which after a while would make learning more complex facts about it easier.

Schemas do more than just connect information. Because of them we can make meaning of situations or new things. We can use schemas to fill in the gaps of new information we are learning (provided it is similar). We can use them to understand problems and work out solutions. It therefore makes sense that we try and develop them in our memory.

But if we have a vast capacity in our long-term memory and we create schemas, how is it we forget things? One reason may be that we might not have actually *learnt* it in the first place. We are poor judges of what we think we've learnt and it may be the case that we never committed it to memory in the first place. Secondly, although you thought it was in your memory, you might have actually forgotten how to find it. There are those who think that when we don't remember something anymore, it has simply disappeared from our memory. That's not quite the case. As I said earlier, when we search for information in our memory, we make the connection to that thing stronger. The more we find it, the easier it is to find it again. And the more that it is connected to other things, the more routes we have to finding it. However, if we don't find it, that pathway may be weaker and finding it may be more difficult. It's not that it has disappeared, it's just harder to locate.

It sounds simple. Teach well enough, prompt commitment to memory, get the students to make schemas and get them to find them a lot. Easy. You would think it is so, but unfortunately it isn't. Unfortunately, the brain can make learning tricky. However, if we know more about how the brain operates in learning we can tweak how we teach to maximise it. And to start with I am going to introduce you to a major sticking point and my first principle.

1 We have a working memory and it has limited capacity

How many of you have had the following situation?

Your class arrives and promptly get sat down ready to learn. After the usual, you begin explaining the topic you are teaching. It's quite complicated but you are aware of this and take your time. You have a PowerPoint with animations that move to highlight what you're saying, diagrams to provide clarity and your wealth of knowledge to share. After about five minutes you finish talking through the topic and are met with blank faces. When you ask questions, a few of them remember some of it but many don't get it. There's the odd one that seems happy with what you've said but not enough to make you feel confident. What has just happened?

Whenever we pay attention to something and have to think about it, we use our working memory. As you are reading this chapter, the words are being processed in your working memory as it begins to make sense of the content. It's where you're holding the information you're currently thinking about. Some liken it to the RAM of a computer that deals with current processes. Others liken it to the reception/lobby in a hotel that deals with new arrivals before they are moved on to their room. It's the initial workspace in our brain that information enters before something happens to it.

The working memory is fundamental to learning. If we can get our students to pay attention to what we are saying and get them to process this information in their working memory, we are a small step to potentially getting them to learn new things. Once again, when you say it like that, it sounds simple. Well, as you see from my first example, it's not quite that simple. And here's why.

Working memory deals with whatever we are paying attention to and is the gateway to memory, but it has huge limitations. As Kirschner et al. (2006, p. 77) explained, working memory is the site of conscious processing and has two characteristics. Firstly, it can only hold information (if unrehearsed) for around thirty seconds, or until something new comes and pushes out what was there. Secondly, according to George A Miller (1956) our working memory can only store seven (plus or minus two) pieces of information at any one time. Cowan (2001) believes it might actually be only four (plus or minus one) pieces of information. Either way, it can't hold much information for very long. This was demonstrated by English teacher Lindsay Skinner at the Teaching and Learning Takeover (TLT) Conference 2016 in Southampton, England. In her closing speech she asked delegates to repeat back a series of numbers to her. They began by reciting, for example, seven. Then seven followed by two. Then seven followed by two then five. After a while the delegates struggled to remember the numbers she was saying. Then Lindsay changed from single digits to double digits. For example, she asked us to recite 11. Then 11 followed by 46. Then 11 followed by 46 then 73. This time, delegates struggled to recall this information much earlier on.

Why is this? In very simple terms, as Daniel T. Willingham (2009, p.109) states, "working memory is the site of thinking". Whenever we are tasked with dealing with a problem, something in the environment or indeed learning, the information about that particular situation enters our working memory. Here, our brain tries to make sense of what we have been presented with. If it's a phone number, it tries to hold it without it being forgotten. If it's a new word, it begins the process of trying to recognise if we have heard it before. If it is a problem, it is the site where we begin to think of a solution. Some have better working memories than others, but there is no way to increase working memory capacity. As teachers we need to be aware of its limitations.

Working memory has a lot to deal with in order to pay attention in class (see Figure 2.1). Students are not only trying to listen to what you are saying but are also trying not to pay attention to the message written on the desk saying "Craig woz ere 2014", the noise of the PE class coming back in from their lesson, the gossip they heard at break about two students. They're trying not to be distracted by the student to the right who keeps tapping her pen and the people who are walking past the classroom door. Luckily our brain helps and filters most of this out in the sensory memory, until students decide to pay attention to it.

If we give students a task and provide them with too much information, we run the risk of overloading their working memory. This is known as cognitive load. Cognitive load is "the demand for working memory resources of a particular learner by specific cognitive tasks or activities" (Lee & Kalyuga, 2014, p. 32). Cognitive load theory was developed by John Sweller (1988) and he explains the limitations of working memory and the various factors that affect cognitive load: if too much information is placed in the working memory, it begins to lose track of what it is trying to process, and things become confused and forgotten. As teachers we need to be mindful of what we ask students to do and how we present information. If we present something that is complex, or give too many novel pieces of information, the load is increased and causes the initial point of learning to be restricted (see Figure 2.2).

The theory and many of the subsequent studies on the theory can be quite complicated. A key area, though, is to understand the types of load that may be placed into the working memory. The first is called *intrinsic cognitive load*. This load "is determined by the interaction between the nature of the materials being learned and the expertise of the learner" (Van Merrienboer & Sweller, 2005, p. 150). It is also determined by

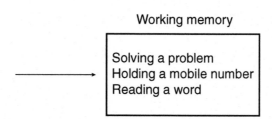

Figure 2.1 Working Memory

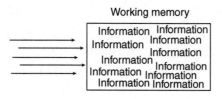

Figure 2.2 Cognitive Overload

the complexity of the material being learned and how many elements need to be processed simultaneously in the working memory. If something is new to a learner, they may face high intrinsic cognitive load. This is because they have no understanding of it and all of the various components of the topic are having to be carefully processed and attended to at the same time. That's a lot of things to process and the reason why learners struggle the first time we teach them a concept or topic.

The other type of load is *extraneous cognitive load*. This is load to the working memory caused by "undesirable instruction design [which] requires learners to engage in cognitive activities that are not related to learning" (Lee & Kalyuga, 2014, p. 33). We need to try and reduce this as much as possible as it is not conducive to learning. For instance, we may decide to show a video in a lesson to explain a concept that has both captions and narration. Along with this we also give them a worksheet to fill in. Video, narration and worksheet – surely that's helpful. Unfortunately, the students' attention is split between the three things and adds extraneous load as they try to cross reference the information with each other.

A third type is *germane cognitive load*, which is the load that is involved in the processing and construction of schemas. It is desirable for learning and should be promoted, although its place in Cognitive Load Theory has been the focus of discussion. I will talk more about it in principle 4 when I introduce you to Robert Bjork.

Ok, I sort of get it but what does this mean for me as a teacher? How on earth do I manage the various loads in students' heads?

When I started investigating this domain back in 2013, a lot of it seemed unachievable and well beyond me. What do these things actually mean? How could I control the amount of load received by students? What does this even look like in teaching? With any new change to your practice, things look daunting at first. However, there are strategies that help make processing in the working memory more efficient and indeed reduce cognitive load.

Don't shoehorn an example in to make a concept relevant

I remember when I would teach a concept and think "If I relate this to students they'll understand it better". I can vividly remember working with a maths teacher who was struggling to get her lower set class interested in perimeter and area. I suggested using various sports pitches to help make the content more real. But the moment she mentioned pitches, the students began to get distracted. Instead of thinking about area, they began chatting amongst themselves about stadiums, capacity, recent games and transfer gossip. Instead of helping students pay attention to the content, it actually detracted from it. Their working memory was filled with anything but maths.

I made a second error with this piece of advice. I assumed that the whole class knew about sports stadiums or were interested in it. I didn't think that many in the class might not like sport or know about different shaped pitches. If I had just worked with the teacher to make her better at teaching the actual concept in its best format, my advice wouldn't have made a mess of things.

Many of you will now be screaming at the page, saying that this is simply taking the life out of learning. I hope not. I am suggesting that you shouldn't shoehorn an example in or change the way you teach to make it more relevant. Use an example if you think it would really help, but be mindful that it may fill up working memory up with unwanted thoughts.

Use stories

Daniel T. Willingham (2009) explains that using stories in your lessons can help working memory: "the human mind seems exquisitely tuned to understand and remember stories – so much that psychologists sometimes refer to stories as 'psychologically privileged', meaning they are treated differently in memory than other types of materials" (p. 66). They are great at helping students comprehend information. When somebody explains an idea to me with just facts and specifics, I find it hard to understand. My working memory struggles to process it. However, when somebody explains something to me with a story of it in action, I make sense of it much more easily. The story gives you a schema, a structure on which you can begin to organise and understand new information.

Ensure there are actual challenges to solve

Without challenges or problems to be solved, the working memory is simply holding information. If the lesson has challenge (questions or tasks where students have to do something with that information) then the working memory can begin to do something with what you are teaching them and this in turn will help. So check whether challenge is there.

Clarify the problem

If we have given students a lot of information, make sure that we actually clarify what exactly it is we want them to do before setting them off. It may feel like we are making it far too easy for them, but we're not. All we are doing is ensuring that their working memory is attending to the right bits before it doesn't.

Use visuals and words during instructions

The multimedia principle (Mayer, 2014) talks about how visuals and words combined (spoken or written) are better than just words alone. By having two kinds of instruction, the working memory can process the material more effectively and reduce the cognitive load. Mayer provided a number of principles to make this more effective in order to maximise its potential.

1. Delete any unnecessary information that adds to germane load – for instance, adding interesting facts to a visual may seem helpful, but it adds to the germane load. Keep to the point.

2. Signal or highlight the important bits – provide cues to the important pieces of information which students must attend to. Highlight, underline or make the point in bold.

3. Redundancy – In things like videos and presentations, people learn more deeply from graphics and narration than from graphics, narration and on-screen text (Mayer, 2014 p. 63). Don't add more germane load by adding on screen text when you already have graphics and narration – it just causes the students to attend to too many things. (Very helpful if making a video presentation!)

4. Keep text and visuals next to each other – ensure the relevant text is next to the relevant visual. Having them separate puts strain on the working memory as they have to hold information. It also leads to split attention (see the next section).

5. If narrating, put the visuals and the narration together at the same time. Showing an image and then narrating it afterwards increases germane load.

But avoid split attention

When creating a resource or material, it may seem helpful to have a diagram with some explanations underneath. Or you may put instructions underneath an image of a model you want students to make in a resistant materials lesson. Or you've created a worked example to a geometry problem (see Tarmizi & Sweller, 1988) and listed the workings underneath it. You have accompanied an image with written instructions. What could be wrong with that? Well, what this does is create a "split attention effect". By having the visual and the written text separate, we make the student switch between the two. Lee and Kalyuga (2014, p. 35) say the problem with this is that "Searching, matching, mentally holding and integrating multiple split-source materials that need to be co-referred for full understanding may generate additional extraneous cognitive load. As a result, insufficient working memory resources are left for making essential inferences and enhancing understanding". See Figure 2.3.

At first glance, this looks fine. We are familiar with replacing a battery and could probably do it successfully. When I showed it to my daughter, she struggled to understand it, partly due to her lack of experience of changing a battery (she has no schema developed for it) but also because her attention was split. She constantly had to look down at the words and then back up at the image. Each time she had to remember what she was looking for while looking for it. She then had to remember what she was supposed to do with it. That's a lot of things to remember in a working memory and understandably caused cognitive overload.

Van Merrienboer and Sweller (2005, p. 159) referred to this when talking about the effect of process worksheets. Process worksheets describe the phases one should go

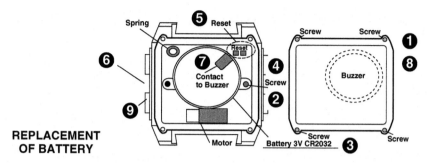

Figure 2.3 Watch Battery Guide

through when solving a problem and provide hints or rules-of-thumb that help students successfully complete each phase. But the researchers found that although intended to be helpful, they had strong effects on cognitive load and impacted transfer.

> Because the information provided in a process worksheet typically has high element interactivity, simultaneously performing the learning tasks and consulting the worksheet may be too demanding. Working memory demands may be increased further because learners must split their attention between the task and the process worksheet. It may be better if learners thoroughly study the recommended phases and hints before they start to work on the learning tasks.

One solution is to integrate the materials together in one place. See Figure 2.4, which is worth thinking about when creating your next worksheet or resource.

Break down the problem/task/challenge into stages

If the issue is that a problem, task or challenge may cause cognitive overload, one way to reduce it is to break it up into smaller elements. There is a side effect, however. By presenting the elements in isolation, you aren't asking them to interact. This means that students may have reduced understanding. It's therefore important that once students have a grasp of the various elements, you pull them back together so that meaning can be made between them all.

Example demonstrating split attention

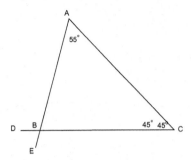

Integrated example

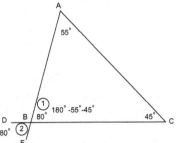

In the above figure, find a value for Angle DBE

Solution:
Angle ABC =180° - Angle BAC-Angle BCA(Internal angles of a traiangle sum to 180°

    =180° -55°-45°
    =80°

Angle DBE = Angle ABC(Vertically opposite angles are equal)
    =80°

Figure 2.4 Integrate Solutions

Use worked examples

One of the biggest takeaways from Kirschner et al. (2006, p. 80) was the use of worked examples. Unguided or discovery learning for novices places a high cognitive load on learners as they try to grapple with numerous pieces of new information. Searching for solutions also adds to this load. Being more direct and giving students a step-by-step guide on how to perform a process or work through a problem reduces extraneous load and provides an expert model for novices. Create worked examples and models and talk them through with your class.

Attention grabbers

As I mentioned in the planning chapter, Daniel T. Willingham (2009, p. 80) makes the point that if we aren't careful, our exciting, whizzy hooks to learning can be the only thing that students remember. For example, when I taught science in 2016, I did an experiment called the "Elephants toothpaste". After mixing chemicals, a huge fountain of foam appears, capable of reaching the lab ceiling. Science teacher Lindsay Phillips describes the purpose of doing the experiment:

> It can be for a few different reasons, exothermic being one of them. I generally use it to show the effect of a catalyst on a reaction – hydrogen peroxide will decompose naturally, but very slowly – the addition of the catalyst speeds it up – so much so

that the oxygen creates huge bubbles! Could also use it to show conservation of mass, covalent bonding and so on.

However, all students remember is the fact that the foam nearly hit the ceiling. What has happened is that attention has been moved away from the important concepts and directed to information that isn't so important. How many attention grabbers do you have in your lessons? They may be the problem.

Background knowledge

One of the most efficient ways to maximise working memory capacity is ensuring students have good background knowledge. As I explain in the next principle, having more knowledge makes learning new related material easier.

But how can I incorporate all this in my teaching?

Being aware of working memory limitations and cognitive load theory can make instructions more efficient. I know it seems daunting, but Drew Thomson, a head of science in North London, explains:

> I had a bit of an epiphany when first reading about cognitive load theory as it all seemed to make a great deal of sense. My teaching is certainly better as a result, with much of the change coming from improved instructional design. Now when planning lessons and creating worksheets or presentations, I take many of the cognitive load theory effects into consideration. I try to ensure that text and diagrams are as integrated as possible to minimise the split-attention effect, allowing my students more space in their working memory to process the information. When presenting, where I have an image I will typically exclude explanatory text and explain verbally. If I were to include text, students would use valuable working memory resources processing both the text and my speech, where both provide the same information, potentially leading to cognitive overload. I also take account of this, the redundancy effect, on my worksheets by stripping away unneeded information and by ensuring all that is required for a question is brought together so my students do not have to use their limited working memory resources scanning around the page.
>
> Another element of instructional design that has changed is my explanations. Given the limitations of our working memory, I have refined my explanations to minimise the amount of redundant information. This was never something I thought was a potential problem because I know that I am a good communicator, but minor tweaks to what I say can make learning more effective. I have tried to make my explanations more concise because longer and more meandering explanations can increase cognitive load, filling working memory unnecessarily. I have also planned more of my explanations before each lesson to ensure that I minimise the number of them that are imperfect, and then having to explain again, placing strain on my

students' working memory. None of this is to say that what I have done for years previously has not been effective, it is just that these minor changes can lead to my students learning better, and all without too much effort.

Hold on, I have one final question. If working memory is the gateway to learning or remembering things, why is its capacity so limited? It makes no sense. Isn't it penalising our memory?

We are still not certain about this. But as Van Merrienboer and Sweller (2005, pp. 148–172) say, its limitation might actually be a good thing as it helps us store only usable information in the long-term memory, rather than random things. Imagine how hectic our brain would be if we had endless amounts of information to process and store. Cowan (2005) also discusses various hypotheses, the first being that the actual process of firing neurones to activate information in the working memory is quite a task. If we have to do this for a vast amount of information, this information may get mixed up or suffer from interference. He also suggests that having a limit on this in our working memory means we can actually make distinctions between different pieces of information and work out associations. So fewer items might actually help us in our thought process. But we know that people with higher working memory capacities tend to do better academically. Now that's interesting.

---

2 Don't underestimate the importance of prior knowledge

If you learnt anything from the first principle, it is that working memory is the site where we hold information for thinking, it has a limited capacity and it can become overloaded if we aren't careful. Once the information is in there, it needs to move on if it has any chance to become a memory. This is where long-term memory comes in (see Figure 2.5).

The relationship between the two memory systems is incredibly important. As Kirschner et al. (2006, p. 77) state, "If nothing has changed in long-term memory, nothing has been learned", and the only way into long-term memory is through working memory. When information enters the working memory, it begins to communicate with our long-term memory to see if any prior knowledge related to it is stored there. If there isn't any, our working memory struggles to make sense of the information. Take my earlier example of the word "palaeomagnetism". When a word of that sort enters our working memory, it begins to communicate with the long-term memory to see if we have heard of it before. It looks for schema or prior knowledge. If no schema exists, we can't make meaning of it. But when we look for "Australia" in our long-term memory, our complex schema and prior knowledge allows us to reel off numerous facts and ideas.

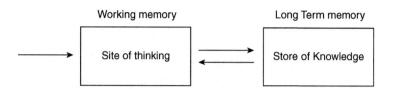

Figure 2.5 Working Memory LT Memory

Thus, the most important element is the amount of prior knowledge that we have stored in our long-term memory. Very basically, the more prior knowledge we have in our long-term memory, the easier it is to learn new things.

As Kirschner et al. (2006, p. 76) explain:

> Our understanding of the role of long-term memory in human cognition has altered dramatically over the last few decades. It is no longer seen as a passive repository of discrete, isolated fragments of information that permit us to repeat what we have learned. Nor is it seen only as a component of human cognitive architecture that has merely peripheral influence on complex cognitive processes such as thinking and problem solving. Rather, long-term memory is now viewed as the central, dominant structure of human cognition. Everything we see, hear, and think about is critically dependent on and influenced by our long-term memory.

Why is prior knowledge so vital? How exactly does it help learning?

There are many reasons why prior knowledge is so important. For the purpose of this chapter, I am going to focus on just two.

The relationship between working memory and long-term memory

As I have explained, there is a direct link between working memory and long-term memory. If you read a word or see something familiar, that information goes into your working memory. If you have information about it stored in your long-term memory, you call upon it to make sense of it. However, if it is unfamiliar, then you can't make sense of it easily because there is nothing stored in the long-term memory that helps you.

Can you remember how many pieces of information your working memory can hold? Miller (1956) believes it could be 7 (plus or minus 2); Cowan (2001) thinks it might be 4 (plus or minus 1). However, when we draw upon our long-term memory, the amount of information that can be held in our working memory is treated differently and more efficiently. Let me explain.

When we hear a number of unrelated words, our working memory stores them as separate pieces of information. For example, take a minute to learn these fourteen words without writing them down. Off you go.

Over Half Dump Drop Knock Centre Gain Fly Goal Outside On Line Ruck Tackle

How did you do? Some of you might have blitzed it, some of you might have struggled. I bet some of you tried to make a story to remember the words, others might have used simple repetition and rehearsal. If you used those techniques you would remember the words, but how much meaning would you have made? If you have any background knowledge about the world of Rugby Union, you probably remembered all of them. And if I pressed you further, I bet you could explain what each of them meant as well. How? Well, the words could be grouped, or chunked, into Rugby Union terms, as follows:

Ruck Over
Fly Half
Dump Tackle
Drop Goal
Knock On
Outside Centre
Gain Line

A person with a high level of prior knowledge of Rugby Union is able to utilise their working memory more efficiently by chunking this information. Instead of remembering fourteen separate words, their working memory can deal with them as seven pairs or even one entire entity, depending on how much prior knowledge, or schema, they have of Rugby Union. Clever!

Let's give an example from our own domain – teaching. When I introduce Year 9 students to the topic of movement analysis in my subject, there are a lot of new terms that students are unfamiliar with. For example, talking about the different classes of levers, the fulcrum, mechanical advantage, the order of levers, effort arms and resistance arms – students get very confused. There is so much new information for them to learn, understand and be able to apply. However, if a student has already learnt this in design and technology or in science, they have a base of prior knowledge. When I speak to these students, they can draw upon this prior knowledge and begin to piece the puzzle together. They can process information in their working memory more effectively because information drawn from their long-term memory makes what goes on in their working memory more efficient. Just how much information from long-term memory can be held in working memory is still unknown. All we know is that it is a lot more than Miller's or Cowan's estimates. Prior knowledge and schema help significantly to make working memory work more efficiently and reduce cognitive load.

Long-term memory and building new memories

My four-year-old is about to start school and is really keen to learn her letters and letter sounds beforehand. When we use alphabet books or phonics resources, she stares at the letters and begins to pull her "thinking" face. After a moment she looks up at me and says the relevant letter with the sound. It takes her a while but she gets there in the end.

We move to new letters and the process repeats itself. Then we start linking letters together. Once again, she screws up her face into thinking mode, begins to decipher the individual letters one by one, says them out loud and then like a light bulb, she recognises the whole word. If it's a word like dog or cat, she knows exactly what it means and could explain lots of things about dogs or cats if I quizzed her. However, if I gave her a word like trigonometry, she would struggle to work it out. She might single out each letter and sound, but by the time she got all the way to the "y" she would probably have forgotten the eleven letters that preceded it. If I gave her a short word like annex, she could probably work it out but would have no idea what it meant.

When I am reading with her – or indeed as you're reading this book – this doesn't happen. We quickly see each of the words as one complete word, decode it, understand its meaning instantly and apply it to the situation. This again is due to prior knowledge and schema: when I see a word like trigonometry, I treat it as one entire word, rather than 12 individual letters. I have used it numerous times and have built up a complex memory about it.

Expertise of prior knowledge is a huge factor in future learning. "In fact, prior knowledge is one of the most influential factors in student learning because new information is processed through the lens of what one already knows, believes, and can do" (Ambrose & Lovett, 2014, p. 7). And as Robert Marzano (2004, p. 124) states, "what students already know about the content is one of the strongest indicators of how well they will learn new information relative to the content".

When we are teaching students, those who have higher levels of expertise or good levels of prior knowledge in a particular topic will be able to process it more easily in their working memory. They can call upon relevant schema or prior knowledge from their long-term memory and use it to make meaning of new information. This information can then join existing schema and increase its complexity (assimilation). If you already have a good understanding of a topic you can place new information within the schema more easily. This updated schema can be called upon and used for future problem solving or challenges. As Marzano (2004, p. 3) explains, "Students who have a great deal of background knowledge [prior knowledge] in a given subject area are likely to learn new information readily and quite well".

In contrast, novices (or those with low prior knowledge) struggle to learn new things as quickly. This is because they struggle to understand or make meaning of new information. Like my daughter with her reading, they have to use a lot of working memory space to make sense of what it is they are trying to learn. When this information slowly makes its way into the long-term memory and schemas begin to form, new information can be assimilated (attached) or even created to help develop its complexity – which turn helps future learning. This dynamic helps explain why those from disadvantaged backgrounds, who haven't been exposed to or experienced a lot of knowledge, fall behind those from more advantaged backgrounds whose experience and exposure give them a lot of prior knowledge/schema.

So there you have it. Having prior knowledge not only helps our working memory work more efficiently (by reducing cognitive load), it also makes learning and remembering information easier. Knowing what our students already know and what they don't know is an important area in teaching. We just need to be sure they're making the connection between their prior knowledge and the new information we're teaching.

Ok. But once again, how on earth do I know what each of my students know before I start teaching them. I'm not a mind reader!

Exactly. This is an easy thing to understand but difficult to implement. Graham Nuthall (2007, p. 35–36) explains:

> Our research has found that students already know, on average, about 50 percent of what a teacher intends his or her students to learn through a curriculum unit or topic. But that 50 percent is not evenly distributed. Different students will know different things, and all of them will know only about 15 percent of what the teacher wants them to know. So, at any one time, a teacher will probably be facing a class in which about 20 percent of the students already know what the teacher is trying to teach them, about 50 percent know something about what the teacher is trying to teach them, and about 20 percent have little or no idea about the topic.

How on earth do you plan lessons to cater for everyone? How do I know how much each student knows? Where do I buy one of these crystal balls? Fortunately, there are some strategies you can use to find out how much students know about a topic before you begin teaching them:

1. **Low stakes pre-test**: At the start of every unit that my students take I set them a pre-test. One of the main reasons for this is to find out what they already know. The test can be a well-designed multiple choice mini-quiz or a short answer topic test. As long as it's easy to mark but allows us to gather some information about their prior knowledge, it is quick and simple to implement. From this you can build up a picture of what they *might* know and bare that in mind when designing lessons. It also brings information to mind which can be connected to the new information.

2. **Use concept maps or graphic organisers**: By using concept maps or graphic organisers, you can ask students to map out everything they know about a topic before they begin. Using these allows students to also highlight connections and relationships between information to give you a broader idea about what they *might* know.

3. **Challenge question**: Use a well-designed open-ended question which requires students to have an understanding about the topic in hand. Provide cues if needed and assess what they do or do not know upon reading it.

4. **What do you know about this topic?** Get students to draw or write everything that they know or can remember about this topic already. Scan the room and begin to get an insight into what they already know.

5. **Self-assessment**: By using a well-designed topic list, students can rate themselves on how confident they are with each area. Unfortunately, this needs to be carefully implemented, as students are notoriously poor at gauging how confident they are in areas; usually rating themselves higher than they actually are – especially when it only requires them to rate themselves on what they *feel* they know, rather than listing exactly what they know.

Right, I've assessed prior knowledge. Now what do I do with those who lack it? How do I build up this knowledge?

There is no quick-fire way to building up good prior/background knowledge.

Encourage them to read

Reading is one of the areas that can help build up prior/background knowledge. "Books expose children to more facts and to a broader vocabulary than virtually any activity, and persuasive data indicate that those people who read for pleasure enjoy cognitive benefits throughout their lifetime" (Willingham, 2009, p. 49). Whenever possible, find articles, reports or book extracts that can support the topic that you are teaching. Get students to read in lessons as much as possible.

Vocabulary, key words and definitions

Learning new vocabulary and definitions isn't going to turn our long-term memory into a hive of information. What it will do is help make students understand new words and concepts. For example, knowing that an acute angle is an angle less than 90° will help in maths. The knowledge may not be complex, but it will help form or be part of new schema. For students, coming across new or unknown vocabulary adds a working memory load as they try to figure out what that word means. Teaching them vocabulary first means you lessen that load.

Incorporate stories when appropriate

Without hijacking working memory, use stories to build understanding further. For example, using a 1500 m runner to explain how the aerobic and anaerobic systems create energy helps students contextualise a quite complex concept. Attaching it to something they may already be familiar with will help as long as it doesn't distract. If they aren't familiar with the example, show them.

Spend time explaining

Many a time I have breezed through a topic or concept, totally unaware that actually knowing it might help future learning. Highlight the important concepts that really need understanding and spend time doing it. Ask students to explain back to you or actively answer questions.

Organise a curriculum that builds upon knowledge

It may be detrimental to other parts of learning (see Principle 4), but organising a curriculum so that it builds upon the last topic could be really helpful in developing background knowledge. What is the most basic topic in your curriculum that everything hinges on? What comes next? What do you leave last, not because it's the hardest, but because knowing the other topics first would make it easier to understand?

Organise experiences

In her book *Overcoming Textbook Fatigue*, ReLeah Cossett Lent (2012), citing the work of Robert Marzano, says, "The most straightforward way to enhance students' academic background knowledge is to provide academically enriching experiences" (p. 43). Organising trips isn't easy, what with forms to fill out and costings to cover. However, they are worth their weight in gold. In our current curriculum we identified points in our Key Stage 4 curriculum where we could go on academically beneficial trips – not that all trips aren't academic or beneficial in some way. In the first year of our GCSE programme we have two trips, both to universities. One is to the Christmas Lectures on Sports Science at a local university, the other is to a Festival of Sport at a different university. Both offer access to experts who explain and demonstrate topics in detail and use skilfully designed examples, demonstrations and instructions to make what they are teaching understandable. Both certainly help our students build up their background knowledge, ready for us to call upon back in the classroom.

You're going to give some warning aren't you?

I am indeed: just two things to be wary of.

The first is what is known as the expertise reversal effect (Lee & Kalyuga, 2014). Very simply, when we are dealing with novices with low prior knowledge, it is important that they receive more guidance. Techniques such as scaffolding and worked examples will help novices reduce their cognitive load, deal with the information more effectively and begin to build schema. However, if you use scaffolding and worked examples with experts, it creates extraneous cognitive load as the extra instruction (which they don't need) can cause a distraction. For this type of learner, a more open-ended problem-solving approach is better as this encourages them to use their complex schema and greater knowledge.

The second warning relates to misconceptions in prior knowledge. Unfortunately, misconceptions stored in the long-term memory about a particular topic have a greater negative impact than no prior knowledge at all. When students believe something that is now part of a complex schema, they may reject, ignore or even reinterpret new information that goes against what is deeply engrained in their memory. Changing misconceptions is difficult and takes repetition, guidance and time.

But getting things into the long-term memory isn't as easy as it seems. As said earlier, one possible reason for limited working memory capacity is to stop things automatically being stored in the long-term memory. To consider getting things into memory, I need to introduce you to my third principle, which comes from the expertise of Daniel T. Willingham.

---

3 Remember, "memory is the residue of thought"

Not everything that goes into working memory necessarily ends up in our long-term memory. It can't. If it did our brains would be overflowing with every single thing that ever entered it. There has to be a filter. Remember, as Kirschner et al. (2006, p. 77) state, "If nothing has changed in long-term memory, nothing has been learned". So how do we help make the transfer from working memory to long term. We have already talked about not overloading working memory. We've then discussed prior knowledge and the importance of it on developing schema. This is something I feel I have the most control over in lessons: thinking.

So making them think about something is all it takes?

It would be naïve to believe that whatever we ask students to think about in their working memory simply stuck, but particularly when we are in a rush we can make that mistake.

I remember times when in the run up to a test or exam, I would think, "Aaah! I've only got one lesson left but I still need to cover x, y and z". I used to spend the next lesson cramming the remainder of the unit into a 60-minute performance. I would rattle through as much as I could hoping that a new concept or topic every 12 minutes would do the trick. I'd introduce it, give them an example, ask a few questions to make them *think* and then move onto the next topic or concept. I could tick them off from my planning and walk away thinking, "Well, at least I covered it ready for the test". The problem was that when I marked those tests, some students remembered a bit of what I had crammed into the lesson, but many didn't. Was it really worth rushing through it all? Probably not, as much of it was forgotten. So how much thinking and how many times do you have to cover it for students to remember it?

Graham Nuthall (2007) in his book *The Hidden Lives of Learners* looked at learning from the perspective of students rather than teachers, having observed numerous students over many years learning in the classroom. One of his most prominent findings was how many exposures students needed to have to new information if they were to learn it (in the early phases of acquiring that knowledge):

We discovered that a student needed to encounter, on *at least three different occasions*, the complete set of information she or he needed to understand a concept. If the information was incomplete, or not experienced on three different occasions, the students did not learn the concept.

(p. 63)

Nuthall and his team went on to apply this in classrooms, with the following result:

We have found that, in each classroom, with each student and each concept that was not already known, we could predict what the students would learn – and what they would not learn – with an accuracy rate of 80 to 85 percent.

(p. 63)

On the face of it, this is an amazing finding. Simply sit students down in your classroom and follow this procedure:

Mr Fawcett: Ok, so first thing we need to know about this is that to find out the gravitational potential energy of an object, we need to multiply the mass by gravity and by height of its fall. Let's think about that.

Class: Ok.

Mr Fawcett: So once again, to find out the gravitational potential energy of an object, we need to multiply the mass by gravity and by height of its fall. Everyone thinking about that?

Class: Yep.

Mr Fawcett: So as I said, to find out the gravitational potential energy of an object, we need to multiply the mass by gravity and by height of its fall. Cool. Let's move on.

The formula has been mentioned three times. Boom! Learning complete. Except, of course, it doesn't work like that. The experiences need to be different. Introducing it, discussing it, examples, demonstrations, questioning, solving a challenge, coming back to it at a later date. There needs to be variety in order that students can manipulate the information in different ways and make connections between the information they are being introduced to. They need to be doing more than just having us tell them.

Are we actually getting them to think? A lot?

One of the most significant pieces of advice in this area comes from Daniel T. Willingham (2009):

Whatever you think about, that's what you remember. *Memory is the residue of thought.*

(p. 61)

It looks on the surface a very simple statement. In fact it should be the fundamental principle behind all our planning. The level of thinking that takes place in our lessons should be high in our priorities. But getting thinking right can be hard. As we already ascertained, when students have different levels of knowledge of the topic you are teaching, it's extremely difficult to ensure everyone is being challenged enough to think.

There is another problem. Willingham (2009) warns that although the goal is to initiate thinking, the mind is not designed for thinking (p. 4). It finds it slow and unreliable. It prefers to be automatic. Just recall times when you've had to learn anything hard and remember the struggle you had. Compare that to things you now do automatically, like read this chapter.

We could just fall back and plan things to be easier for students. Remove the thinking for them because they give up too easily or moan about having to do work. However, as Brown et al. (2014, p. 3) state, "Learning is deeper and more durable when it's *effortful*. Learning that's easy is like writing in sand, here today and gone tomorrow". We need to insist that students think if they are to remember.

When we do get the level of thinking right, the brain actually likes to solve problems and experience a challenge (as long as it's achievable). It likes the reward it gets: dopamine. When dopamine is released as a positive reward during learning, it prompts the brain to take note of how to replicate this in the future.

Thinking about something also gets the brain to establish a temporary neural network to process that information. Keep thinking about something enough and you keep calling upon its neurons and neural pathway. Every time you do this, the connections get stronger. As neuroscientists say, neurons that fire together wire together. So thinking begins to create memories that can be accommodated by or assimilated into schema.

And ensuring students are thinking about what we are teaching is so important. If we are paying attention to something, the brain makes an educated guess as to what it should and shouldn't remember. As Willingham (2009, p. 61) explains, if we think about something a lot, it hedges a guess that it's important and begins to store if for the future. If we don't think about it very much, it guesses it's not important and we don't need it. It therefore doesn't store this in our memory. If we want to ensure that things do make that move into long-term memory, we need to get students to think about it so the brain knows it's worth storing.

So how do I go about ensuring they are thinking hard about something?

There are many things you can do very quickly and simply in order to check how much thinking is going on. There are also a few strategies that may require a little bit more planning time.

Input less, output more

As Robert Bjork (2012) explains, we need to try and input less, output more. That is, if I give you one example of this idea in use (input less), can your students come up with two examples (output more). If you read a chapter in a textbook (input less), can your students draw a map and outline of how that chapter was organised (output more). If I give you one question for this topic (input less), can you generate two of your own (output more). Having this as a fundamental principle in lesson planning can really help students think about the material they are learning and aid long-term retention.

Assess your lesson for levels of thinking

It sound really simple but check your lesson for how much thinking is taking place. At each stage, look through the eyes of the student and ponder, "How hard will I have to think here?" Is the task passive or will it require them to make connections, understand meaning or apply it to a situation? I had to change from "How much fun will the students have?" and "Will my students get bored of this?" to "How much thinking is happening?" Switching my question to be around the level of thinking doesn't mean lessons have to be dull or mundane.

Pitch the challenge right – could understanding what they already know help?

As Nuthall (2007, p. 35) says, every student in your class knows a different amount of what you are going to teach them. Therefore, if we set everyone the same activity, some will have to do a small amount of thinking and some a lot. Using some of the earlier ideas from principle two such as a pre-test or "Write down everything you know about ..." can help you begin to pitch challenge right. Remember, if the challenge is too high, students could experience high cognitive load or simply give up because the problem is unachievable. Make it too easy and students won't bother or learn anything. Where's the thinking in that?

Support those who need it – experts versus novices

In the second principle, I mentioned something called the Expertise Reversal Effect. If a student is a novice, we may need to provide more support through things like worked examples or other scaffolds. This minimises cognitive load and helps the process of thinking. However, experts find this level of support unhelpful as it makes them pay attention to the worked example or scaffold when they don't actually need to. It adds load. They work better with open questions or problems to solve. So when we have an idea about the prior knowledge of individuals, think about what we set our so-called "experts" and novices'.

Make meaning

Making meaning is extremely important in getting students to think. It encourages them to make sense of the information, what it means, what it links to and more. It requires them to call on schema from their long-term memory. If there is information there, it will create or strengthen connections. If there is no information there, it will begin to build up background knowledge. There are three ways to get students to make meaning that might be helpful.

Get them to make meaning of the vocabulary – I sometimes use technical terminology in a lesson and assume that students understand it. Unfortunately, if a student hasn't got prior knowledge of that word, what I am talking about makes no sense. I could get students to make a glossary but that only touches the surface. I now use a technique called the "Four Part Process", adapted from Lee Donaghy (2013) and Helen Handford. The process asks students to identify the thing being defined, add a connective/verb, define it and then apply it in a context to make meaning. The last part is the most important.

The thing being defined	Connective/Verb	Definition	Meaning

Elaborative interrogation – Asking students to elaborate on a piece of information, topic or concept is easy to implement and beneficial to thinking and learning. "Why" questions make students expand on the thing being thought about and pay more attention to it. Dunlosky et al. (2013, p. 8) explained the benefits, saying that "elaborative interrogation enhances learning by supporting the integration of new information with existing prior knowledge". We can use questions like "Why is this true?" or "Why might this act like it is?" We can take it a step further and ask students to compare with questions along the lines of "Why might x be a better answer than y?" If students have low prior knowledge, the teacher can provide further instruction or examples to help model the process.

Self-explanation – Self-explanation is one of the principles/learning strategies recommended by the Association for Psychological Science (2007) and the Institute for Educational Science (2007). As Chiu and Chi (2014, p. 91) say, "Self-explaining, or making sense of new information by explaining to oneself, helps learners construct new knowledge by elaborating upon presented information, relating them to existing knowledge, making inferences, and making connections among given information".

Self-explanation helps students see the gaps in their knowledge and then seek out missing information. In essence, the process doubles up as a self-reflection tool. It also serves as a type of revision by helping students recall what they know. Students can then adapt or correct what they know as a result.

Does it help? In a study by Chi in 1994 (cited in Chiu & Chi, 2014, p. 93), eighth graders were asked to self-explain after every sentence they read about the circulatory system. The group that was asked to do this understood more, learned better than the control group who did not self-explain, had more accurate mental models and understood complexities of the circulatory system that were not explicit in the text. Numerous other studies have had similar results.

As a teacher we can include self-explanation quite easily. Again, using "why" questions is a good starting point. Or simply asking students to explain a concept after reading or hearing about it. Getting pairs to check each other's self-explanation is quick to set up. The important thing is to ensure that students aren't simply regurgitating what they have just heard. We need to prompt them to explain with purpose. Get them to make connections, explain in a different context or with a particular purpose.

Use graphic organisers or concept maps

I used to simply teach students a topic and then ask them some questions or set them a *fun* task. These questions prompted them to do something with the information, which is perfectly fine. However, in 2009 I began using graphic organisers when I taught a new topic or concept. These are designed to help students make sense of information, concepts and instructions. They allow students the opportunity to visually arrange knowledge, ideas, relationships, similarities, differences and so on. The beauty of this type of resource is it allows students to place information on a page in a visual sense and manipulate it, rather than trying to do it in the working memory. For those students who struggle to grasp a topic, a graphic organiser can really help. For example, in Figure 2.6 you can see a basic double bubble map. Students use it to compare the similarities and differences between the aerobic and anaerobic system. They write facts about how they are different along the outer edges and write how they are similar down the middle.

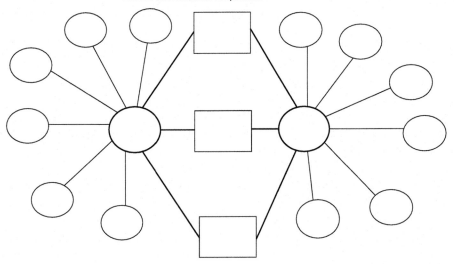

Respiratory System

Complete the double bubble diagram below to define the similarities and differences between **Aerobic** and **Anaerobic** Respiration.l

Figure 2.6 Double Bubble

By having it in a visual form, students can manipulate what they are thinking about much easier. It also gets the students to think about the information in new ways; in this instance about the similarities and differences of energy systems. There are numerous graphic organisers to use and all of them encourage students to think deeply about information.

Make sure our lesson focuses on what needs to be learnt in a way that doesn't make them remember what they did (attention grabbers)

Students remember what they do. If all they remember from your lesson is how they coloured in a map in eight different colours then they've missed the point of your lesson. Daniel T. Willingham (2009, p. 80) calls these activities attention grabbers. The lesson where we asked students to dress up as Romans sometimes means they only remember that they were asked to dress up as Romans. Even simple tasks like making a movie to show global warming can distract students' thought process from the thinking behind the video. Again, it doesn't mean remove any fun from lessons. All it means is be mindful that we should encourage the thinking first, and then add in the activity. Or, if possible, redesign the task we ask students to do so that they have no choice but to think about content throughout.

Use big questions

> Effective activities are built around big questions. Make them really important for the curriculum and the children we are teaching.
>
> (Nuthall, 2007, p. 37)

Incorporate big questions into your lessons. By having a "hook" you provide context and direct students attention towards a goal or problem to be solved. In our newest curriculum, each unit is designed around a big question. For example, one unit is driven around the different training considerations elite athletes have to consider, ranging from training methods, the training season, components of fitness, fitness testing and training thresholds. That's a lot of information so we drive the unit with the question, "What do elite athletes have to consider in their training in order to be world beaters?" Presenting it as a whole means that as we progress through the unit, each part filters back into the bigger over-arching question. It all ties in. The question or hook also gets students to think. We use it at the start of the unit to ascertain prior knowledge. We use it throughout the unit to pull everything together. And finally, we use it at the end of the unit as a question to be answered to see if students have understood what they have been taught.

Get them thinking. I can do that

So once it's in the long-term memory, is that it? Unfortunately not. There's one more element to the process you need to be aware of.

---

4 Implement desirable difficulties into your teaching to help them remember

---

Before we begin the final section, I want you to do the two activities in Table 2.1, which involve things you *might* have been taught at school. All you need to do is write down as many answers as possible.

Which column did you find easier? When I have tried this on friends and family, all of them found column 1 to be the easiest. Was that the same for you? If it was, do you know why?

When I was at school I was in higher maths. If you asked me what things I can remember from maths, I could probably tell you a number of things, including *sockatoa*. I know it's a maths term and has something to do with triangles. I apologise if you are screaming at the page saying exactly what it is, but that's all I remember. I do know that I studied it a lot at school. I must have done as it's stuck in my memory. Could I tell you what it is now, though? No. And why? Because I have forgotten it. It's actually a set of trigonometry formulae that

Table 2.1

Column 1 – Write down the answers to this first	Column 2 – Write down the answers to this last
1. What is the capital of America?	1. What is the English term for comparing one thing to another?
2. What is your mobile number?	2. What was the name of Henry VIII's only surviving son?
3. What is the largest mammal on Earth?	3. Which planets are smaller than earth?
4. Name one rank in the police.	4. Eugene Cernan was the last man to do what?
5. What is the name of the small fungus that is used to make bread rise?	5. In which country is Taipei?
6. What are the order of planets?	6. In which continent are the Atlas Mountains?
7. Who was the first person to walk on the moon?	7. What does the pink triangle signify on a map?
8. What is the largest ocean on earth?	8. A musical scale is made up of how many notes?
9. Ellen has four cats, three dogs and twelve fish. How many animals does she have altogether?	9. What is the name of the universal soul in Hinduism?
10. How many vowels are there in the English alphabet?	10. Hydrogen, helium and gold are three examples of what?
11. What vessel takes blood back to the heart?	11. What is the name of a badger's home?
12. What did the Titanic hit, causing it to sink?	12. What is meant by the term onomatopoeia?

help calculate the lengths of sides and sizes of angles in a right-angled triangle, and it's not really sockatoa, that's just what it sounds like. It's actually SOH CAH TOA. Now I've given you some information about it, could you use it to solve some maths problems? Me neither. And that's frustrating as I must have used it hundreds of times back at school.

You teach your class their first unit in your course. You teach it well. You do a unit test and the scores are pretty good. You do the same for unit two. Once again, the scores in the unit test are pretty good. You do the same for unit three and four. Teaching it well and completing unit tests on the content you've just taught. All goes well. Then at the end of Year 10, they sit a mock exam to assess how they have gotten on. The exam, this time, has questions from every unit. They did well before so all signs should be good that they'll do well now. The problem is that the test scores you get afterwards indicate that they have forgotten a lot of what you taught them. But they knew it. So why have they forgotten now?

There is a common pattern here. If you remember back to the first two principles, long-term memory has a vast capacity. To get information stored in there requires a certain number of things to happen. Once it gets in here, why is it so difficult to find them? Why do we have those *tip of the tongue* moments when we know we know the answer, we just can't remember it at that moment. Why do have things like SOH CAH TOA stuck in our heads but struggle to explain any more than it has something to do with triangles in maths? Why is it that students always forget what we teach them (when we were certain they knew it)?

Learning versus performance

As a teacher I have been drilled over the years to assess what has been learnt in a lesson there and then. I teach students something and then I ask them some questions to see if they have learnt it. They are able to give me an answer because I have just told them what to say a few minutes before. What we are seeing at this moment is easy and can be referred to as performance. We are able to see how many answers they get correct. We can see what they think during an explanation. But have they actually learnt it? Will they remember it next week, in a month's time or in their final exam? If they can remember it, we may conclude that learning has taken place. If they can't, and they have simply forgotten everything, learning didn't take place.

We can take into account cognitive load. We can take into account prior knowledge. We can think about how much thinking will take place in lessons. But if there is no change in long-term memory, learning hasn't taken place. And that is the thing that we want to happen. We want students to be able to remember things for a long time. We want them to be able to draw upon these things so that they can answer questions, discuss, evaluate, create and hypothesise. But if these things slip from memory, these outcomes can't happen. So what do we need to know about this final phase?

Storage strength and retrieval strength

Bjork & Bjork's 1992 New Theory of Disuse aimed to explain why memories may become harder to retrieve and how things. It suggests that memories aren't forgotten but are harder to retrieve. It's not that things fall out of our heads, it's simply that we can't find them as easily as we once did.

The Bjorks suggested that two factors determine how easy it is to retrieve a piece of information or memory (p. 42). The first is storage strength. Storage strength (SS) is how well learned something is. If a piece of information is learnt well it develops a high level of storage strength – it is well connected with other things in your memory. Take your address. You probably know it off by heart as it is learnt well and you've referred to it a lot: it has high storage strength. An address you're on your way to for one time only this morning will probably be forgotten in a day or so. It's not learnt well and not important: it has low storage strength.

The other factor is known as retrieval strength (RS). This is how accessible something is in the current moment. If it has a high retrieval strength you can bring it to mind easier; if it has a low retrieval strength, it is harder to recall. But retrieval strength can fluctuate up and down, depending on what we have just been thinking about or doing. A piece of information could have high retrieval strength and be easily recalled because it is recent, not because it is well learned. For example, If I told my class that in order to create short-term energy in the muscles we use the adenosine triphosphate and phosphocreatine system, releasing energy, adenosine diphosphate and one single phosphate, they may remember it there and then. If I asked them in six weeks' time, they may not. The problem is, as teachers we often rely on measures of retrieval strength (can they recall it right now?) to make inferences about storage strength (will they be able to recall it later?).

The two factors have a relationship we need to be aware of. Some things in our memory are learnt well (have a high storage strength) and because we use them regularly are easily retrievable (high retrieval strength). This is what we are aiming for. However, if we don't retrieve that fact/concept/information again, the retrieval strength around it begins to diminish and we find it harder to locate. An example of something with high storage strength but low retrieval strength might be your old phone number. You used to know it well but haven't had to think about it recently. If reminded, though, it will come back to you very quickly.

As Bjork & Bjork point out, it's not merely that *time* causes it to diminish, it's also the consequence of learning and retrieving other/new pieces of information. For example, learning your new phone number will affect the memory of your old phone number. Isn't that crazy? (p. 44).

So what about that lesson when the student gives you the right answer but a week later has forgotten it. It's probably because they never developed the storage strength of that information in the first place. It wasn't learnt well enough and never formed enough connections or became part of a larger schema. It had good retrieval strength within the lesson. Unfortunately, because of low storage strength, it lost its retrieval strength quite quickly and was forgotten a week later.

The aim, over time, is to help useful information become both well stored (SS) and readily retrievable (RS). To do this isn't easy and some of the methods may go against some of our own beliefs.

How do I build up both of these strengths? What are the best methods?

Many of our existing methods of teaching, may not actually be that good at developing both storage strength and retrieval strength. In fact, some of the things we do every day, like organising our lessons into blocked units, don't help long-term retention at all.

Some of the methods in the next section may seem to slow performance or even progress. It may look like students are struggling and things aren't working. But we need to break old habits and look at the long-term benefits. Whizzy lessons that show progress every five minutes may look good to an observer, but they don't necessarily foster learning. The methods that Bjork recommends are referred to as *Desirable Difficulties*. They are effortful and tough but help learning in the long run (i.e. increase storage strength). They may make you think about how you set your curriculum up and even what you include in lessons. They may pose some tough questions and make you ponder if you could or should do them. Stay with it, though. We may just have to make things more difficult if we want students to remember.

Space learning out

For nearly ten years I followed the same sort of process with students. I would share a concept or piece of information with students. I would then spend that lesson going over it a lot until I thought they had got it. Next lesson I would move onto a new topic and following the same procedure. The only time I ever came back to a topic was before a test, in the test itself, or in a final exam.

What I was doing was massing the practice; that is, I was teaching the topic in one lump and one go (sometimes referred to as a block). As Nuthall (2007, p. 63) stated, students need repeated exposure to the information they are trying to learn if it is to stick, and how it is spread out is the critical thing. Simply cramming that all into one lesson isn't going to cut it. What I need to do is distribute the practice, or space the learning out.

What is distributed practice or spacing then?

Spacing is when two or more exposures to information are separated in time (adapted from Carpenter et al., 2012). In research studies in this field, the gap between exposures ranges from one minute to months down the line, but all show that spacing out practice is better for long-term retention than simply massing. As educators we need to be very aware of this. Are we allowing a gap between the first time we present information and the second or third time we come back to it? Are we revisiting things later on in the term? If we aren't, we're missing a huge trick.

In the latter half of the 19th century, Hermann Ebbinghaus conducted a number of experiments on himself to better understand the workings of memory. He learnt a series of nonsense syllables and observed the results of retention. One of his main findings was that if we want things to be remembered for a longer period of time, there needs to be repetition of that information. That makes total sense. Ebbinghaus went on to look at how many repetitions were optimal. He found that if there were too few repetitions, that piece of information would not be stored deeply and would be forgotten quickly.

Most significant, for me, was how he looked at spacing out these repetitions over time. As summarised by Christian J. Weibell (2011), Ebbinghaus observed the following:

> The series are gradually forgotten, but – as is sufficiently well known – the series which have been learned twice fade away much more slowly than those which have been learned but once. If the relearning is performed a second, a third or a greater number of times, the series are more deeply engraved and fade out less easily and finally, as one would anticipate, they become possessions of the soul . . .
>
> (Ebbinghaus, 1913, p. 81)

Ebbinghaus noted that if we are only exposed to a piece of information once, that information would lose its capacity to be revived. He found that on average we forget about 70 per cent of what we learn within a few days. That's quite scary as a class teacher. However, when visiting it a second time it would be forgotten (or fade) more slowly. Do it a third time and it fades more slowly than the second time, and so on. Each time you revisited the information it was less work to retrieve it the next time. It also became easier and faster to relearn information the second, third or fourth time (see Figure 2.7).

How far apart should these gaps be? Now that is a question.

In part, the answer to the question "how far apart?" may depend on how quickly information is forgotten. The forgetting rate depends on what is being taught, how complex it is, how related to prior information it is, and so on. This is where the expertise of the teacher and their understanding of their students comes into play. Ideally, students receive their next exposure before they forget it completely. Leave it too long and things

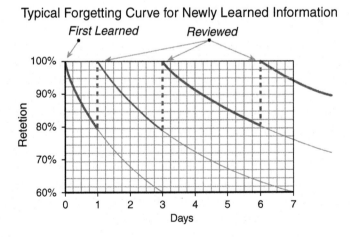

Figure 2.7 Typical Forgetting Curve

fade too much and we have to reteach it all again. Leave it too short and the information may still be too fresh in the mind to really benefit from the re-exposure.

The answer also depends on how long you want to retain the information for. Cepeda et al. (2008) used a flashcard-like web tutorial for subjects to learn obscure facts. After learning them successfully, they then had another session ranging between 0 and 105 days. Once they had completed the second session, they then had a final test after a certain delay. What they found was that the optimal gap depends on when the final test takes place. For example, if the test was in a week's time, the optimal gap was 1–2 days. If the test was in 35 days' time, optimal gap was 11 days. In other words, the longer the test delay, the longer the optimal spacing gap. Although that sounds quite complicated, it is actually quite important. If a test is quite close, leave less space between revisiting information. If the test is a long way away, space things out more.

Some studies found that very long gaps were good for memory. For example, Harry Bahrick et al. (1993) got participants to learn 300 foreign language words (three studied French, one studied German). After an intense acquisition, they began giving themselves reminders by testing themselves every 14 days, every 28 days or every 56 days.

What Bahrick found was that the person who tested themselves every 56 days did the worst on those tests. Because of the delay in sessions, that person didn't make the same progress as the others. However, the pattern was completely different on the final test that everyone took one year later: the person who studied at 56-day intervals had learned more of the foreign vocabulary than the others. In fact, the longer interval led to better memory for these words over the following five years. That isn't what I expected.

The number of sessions didn't seem to matter: 13 sessions with a 56-day interval between them led to the same amount of learning as 26 sessions with a 14-day interval between them. So less frequent exposure over a greater length of time is as effective as more frequent exposures over a shorter amount of time. Bahrick refers to the work of Bjork and suggests that what may seem to slow down progress during the acquisition phase can actually benefit longer-term retention. A 56-day gap meant the words were learnt more slowly but stayed in the memory for very much longer.

That can be quite difficult for educators to hear – especially as some schools are still focused on showing sustained progress every 15 minutes in a lesson. What it is telling us is that some of the techniques we use in lessons may only *look* like learning is taking place.

If we look at the forgetting curves in Figure 2.7, we can see that the curves get less steep as information is studied more often. If the idea is that we should be re-exposing students before they completely forget something, it stands to reason that these gaps can grow longer as information becomes better learned. This is known as an "expanding" intervals schedule. However, the research is a bit mixed regarding whether the gap should be fixed (same length of interval gap between every exposure) or expanding (the gap widens after each exposure to it). Until we know more, we'll have to use our professional judgement.

But what do the gaps actually do? Why is spacing helpful? One possible reason comes from Robert Bjork (visit his website – a treasure trove). He suggests that when something is readily accessible in memory it has high retrieval strength. For instance, let's say you've just taught students a scientific theory. If you ask them to explain straightaway what you've just said they probably can. Because it's just happened and its retrieval strength is high, its storage strength upon retrieval is unchanged. It's there on tap, the brain doesn't have to do much to find it so nothing really changes.

However, when the retrieval strength is lower and we have to think hard to find it, we get bigger gains in storage and retrieval strength. Let's say we ask the class to explain something they did in a lesson two weeks ago. Because they have had to work harder to find it in their long-term memory, its strength increases and it becomes easier to remember in the future. In simple terms, it seems that difficulty in finding information is actually good for developing long-lasting retention.

This is backed up by Brown et al. (2014, p. 82):

> Effortful recall of learning, as happens in spaced practice, requires that you "reload" or reconstruct the components of the skill or material anew from long-term memory rather than mindlessly repeating them from short-term memory. During this focused, effortful recall, the learning is made pliable again: the most salient aspects of it become clearer, and the consequent reconsolidation helps reinforce meaning, strengthen connections to prior knowledge, bolster the cues and retrieval routes for recalling it later, and weaken competing routes.

What might be worrying to teachers is that spacing can make progress look poor. If your students were tested on a piece of spaced out information they probably wouldn't do too well to begin with. And that's where some may find this concept hard to accept. In the world of accountability, progress and results, do I want my grades to look not so good in the short term? But as we've shown, when students are presented with that information again, memory gets a larger boost. Although in the short term it doesn't look too good, the benefits in the long term are handy when we have terminal tests and exams.

My head hurts! How do I apply this to my lessons?

Work out when the test is, work backwards for each topic and plan to revisit each of those topics again before mapping out the time before that, ensure the gaps between the next review gets bigger, then . . . Seems difficult, doesn't it? But remember, our goal is not to prepare people for tests but help them remember things for a long time. And if we are going to make a long-term difference, spacing could be easier to implement than you think.

Plan it into the curriculum as starters

When I first decided to build this into our curriculum, I designed a spreadsheet that listed all the topics I would teach (Table 2.2). I then tried to map out when I could recap these topics in lessons over the two and a half years. But by the time I had got half way through the spreadsheet I had run out of curriculum time to fit it all in. So, we did something incredibly obvious and used the natural rotation of the curriculum to make it work. In Unit one, we identified a couple of lessons where you could recap some of the

Table 2.2

Unit 1	Unit 2	Unit 3	Unit 4	Unit 5	Unit 6
Unit 1 recap	Unit 1 recap	Unit 1 recap	Unit 1 recap	Unit 2 recap	Unit 3 recap
	Unit 2 recap	Unit 2 recap	Unit 2 recap	Unit 3 recap	Unit 4 recap
		Unit 3 recap	Unit 3 recap	Unit 4 recap	Unit 5 recap
			Unit 4 recap	Unit 5 recap	Unit 6 recap

Unit one information in a short starter or plenary. In Unit two, those times now had things from both Unit one and Unit two. In Unit three those times had things from Units one, two and three. It now spiralled. When we had more units, we would add them in (taking a few questions out from other units). After a while you can then start missing out one unit at a time.

Another way to do it would be to use a spiralling sequence like the Fibonacci sequence. However, this can be time consuming and a bit daunting. That's where people like the Learning Scientists come in. They have a spreadsheet on their website that allows you to map in your topics and an algorithm then automatically adds an optimal spacing gap between topics, meaning you don't have to do it yourself. Amazing!

Recap tests/quizzes

Lots of teachers put tests and quizzes into lessons. Lots of teachers don't. We'll talk more about testing later but it's worth saying here that they can be a really good way of spacing topics out. For instance, every few lessons we have a low stakes-no pressure quiz. They give us an element of spacing and build up memory strength. The quizzes are cumulative and have questions from all of the previously taught topics. All we have to do is keep an eye on what questions we ask and which topics haven't been taught in a while and arrange them accordingly. Using the Learning Scientists spreadsheet or a similar programme helps us do this.

Homework

I've always struggled with rigid homework schedules. Homework in my setting works best when it is timely and fits into whatever we've been teaching (rather than just fitting in with a whole school timetable). However, using homework's for spacing can also be helpful. With limited curriculum time, why not transfer into homework the spacing activities you were struggling to fit into lessons? Plan a rota of topics, space them out and set them for your students to do over the year. Using some online platforms, these could take the form of quizzes, definition tests, concept maps and more. Many of them mark it for you – result!

So you've got spacing sorted. What next? Well, as I have just touched upon, another one of Bjork's Desirable Difficulties is testing. Whaaaaaat! Did you say more testing?

Don't be afraid of testing!

At a time when students feel like they are being tested too much, surely more testing can't be a good thing? That was my main concern when I began reading about the benefits of testing, or more specifically *retrieval practice*. But testing can take many forms.

Yes, over-testing students can be an absolute pain. Speak to any student and they'll tell you that all the mock exams and end of unit tests and the pressures of the end of year tests and actual exams mean they feel exhausted. From a teaching perspective, increasing testing means a lot more marking and nobody wants to increase workload. But testing students can act as a way to help learning and is actually a good thing. Numerous publications (Deans for Impact, 2015; Dunlosky et al., 2013; Pashler et al., 2007) recommend testing and retrieval practice as one of the best ways to learn and build memory. Let me explain.

Do they actually remember, or is it just familiar?

Whenever I ask my students to go away and revise, no matter how much I advise them to structure it using reliable strategies, I guarantee that most will spend a big chunk of their time simply re-reading their notes. The problem is that when they read this information, they retrieve it from their memory without much effort and feel they know it. It is an illusion though. For a short period of time this type of cramming can improve performance. But give it a few days or a week and much of what they had retrieved will be forgotten.

If you get students to test themselves, instead of just re-reading, the benefits would be greater. But there are problems with this. Testing is hard and requires effort; students see it as boring or harsh. They believe re-reading is better and it's hard to convince them otherwise. However much we tell our students to test themselves, they revert back to re-reading notes.

Why should I begin to love testing? I'm still not sure. It seems a bit old school

I absolutely agree. The word testing drums up a vision of students sitting in rows and doing past papers and exam questions over and over again. Everyone is in silence and all life is sucked out of the classroom. However, testing doesn't need to be like that. Making the subtle change in your mind and renaming it retrieval practice is one way to get over the hurdle. We need to take the advice of researchers and use low stakes fun tests (I'll explain what these are later). Things that make retrieving information less pressurised but are still effective. A study by Agarwal et al. (2014) found that the introduction of low stakes tests throughout the term actually lowered test anxiety when it came to the high-test stakes at the end of the term. Bet you never knew that!

We also need to tackle the fact that students fall back into old habits. We can tell them until we are blue in the face that a particular strategy works, but if it conflicts with their own perception they probably won't do it. So we need to include retrieval practice in our lessons and curriculum. Show them the benefits. Make it a habit.

And effort can also be an issue. As we have said, the brain doesn't like to think. It finds it effortful. So why would students embrace something that will make them think hard? As Robert Bjork has said in a Go Cognitive (2012c) interview, "Using our memory, shapes our memory". Making things desirably difficult will help learning. If we think of a body builder, it takes a lot of effort when weight training to build skeletal muscle. It's slightly similar for students. We need to get them to realise that they have to do difficult things if they are to remember what they have learnt. Being tested is difficult, we know that. But if learning is easy, it probably won't stick.

Go on, convince me

When we recap things in lessons or ask students to re-read their notes, students may leave that lesson feeling pretty confident. Everything you said came to their mind when you explained it and it feels quite familiar. But would they have remembered it without you explaining it or if you hadn't asked them a question? That's the problem with this type of learning. When students re-read or recap things, they develop what Brown et al. (2014, pp. 15–17) term the *Illusion of knowing*, in particular the Fluency Illusion. Students mistakenly believe they can retrieve all that information on their own. They feel they know it. They believe it is accessible in the future. However, no lasting addition to retrieval strength or storage strength has taken place.

Retrieval practice works differently by allowing students to see what they really do or do not remember. If they can't remember something in a low stakes test, at least they know that and can act to close a gap. It also allows us teachers to get some insight into what students do or do not know and adapt our instructions.

Retrieval practice also benefits long-term retention – something we need to consider with the implementation of final exams and terminal tests. In 2006, Henry L. Roediger III and Jeffrey D. Karpicke conducted two experiments that compared testing with restudying. In their first experiment they got subjects to study two prose passages 256 and 275 words in length. In phase one, subjects were given four seven-minute periods to study the passages, with a gap in between. One group would restudy the passage in their sessions, while the other group would do a recall test in theirs. They then went into a second phase where they did a final recall test five minutes, two days and a week after phase one.

As you might have expected, the subjects who simply restudied the passages remembered more in the five-minute test. They had seen the passages numerous times so had become very familiar with it. However, in the two-day and one-week recall tests, the subjects who had done recall tests in their phase one sessions remembered more than those who had simply restudied the passages in theirs. The restudying had benefitted short-term retention (five-minute test) but was not effective when the test was taken a few days or a week later. Those who had been tested in their study phase remembered more over time (and quite a bit more!). For example, after five minutes, restudy subjects remembered 81 per cent of the passage compared to 75 per cent for the retested. However, two days later the restudy remembered 54 per cent compared to

68 per cent from the retested. And a week later the restudy subjects remembered only 42 per cent compared to 56 per cent for the retested subjects (p. 251).

Roediger and Karpicke then did a second experiment to examine the effect in more detail. Using the same two prose passages, they had three groups follow one of three options. Group one would have four consecutive study periods (SSSS). Group two would have three study periods with the fourth being a recall test (SSST). The third group would have one study period and three recall tests (STTT). After this they took a final recall test.

Even though the SSSS subjects had been exposed to the passages more often and subsequently did better on the immediate final test (SSSS remembered 83 per cent, SSST remembered 78 per cent and STTT remembered 71 per cent), one week later the STTT subjects recalled more. In fact, they remembered 61 per cent of the passage compared to 56 per cent for the SSST subjects and 40 per cent for the SSSS subjects (pp. 252–253). In the initial phase of learning the information, studying it and then being asked to recall it is much better for long-term retention. Frequent restudy (or massed study) only leads to short-term retention but then is quickly forgotten. How though? The STTT group only studied the passage once? The SSSS group saw the passages more. Can that be right?

It's not an isolated result. Dunlosky et al.'s (2013) review of learning techniques also cited testing as having high utility.

But why is it effective? What does it do that other methods don't?

If I could answer that one I would. Many researchers seem to hypothesise what is happening. Robert Bjork (2012) suggests that "Retrieval altered the system". So as I retrieve something, it becomes more accessible, stronger, more recallable in the future". In fact, in Roediger & Karpicke (2006, p. 254), they explain that "McDaniel and his colleagues (McDaniel &

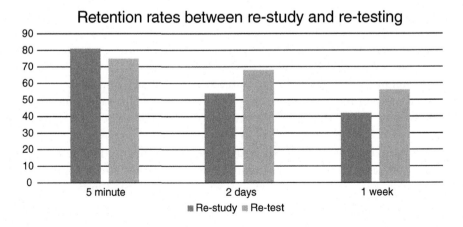

Figure 2.8 Graph of results from Roediger, H. L., & Karpicke, J. D. (2006) focus on re-study v re-testing

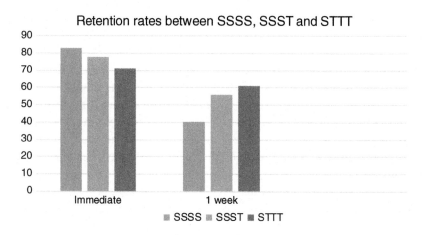

Figure 2.9 Graph of results from Roediger, H. L., & Karpicke, J. D. (2006) focus on SSSS, SSST and STTT

Fisher, 1991; McDaniel, Kowitz, & Dunay, 1989; McDaniel & Masson, 1985) have argued that testing enhances learning by producing elaboration of existing memory traces and their cue-target relationships, and Bjork (1975, 1988) has suggested that testing operates by multiplying the number of "retrieval routes" to stored events.

So how can I incorporate testing into lessons? Isn't it just going to make lessons dull and boring?

With the perception that some have around testing, it is easy to worry that it can be monotonous and boring for students. But we have to weigh up the benefits. We also have to remember that it doesn't have to be actual exams, past papers or exam questions. Tests used for retrieval practice should be low stakes and fun. They shouldn't just be used as a way to continually measure students. Here are some ideas.

Build it into your curriculum and lessons – regularly

[I]f students know they will be tested regularly (say, once a week, or even every class period), they will study more and will space their studying throughout the semester rather than concentrating it just before exams.

(Roediger & Karpicke, 2006, p. 249)

One simple way is to build mini quizzes and low stakes tests into your lessons. Starting each lesson with a quiz that recaps a topic you taught a week ago, a month ago or even at the end of last year is really helpful. It also builds in spacing. By having these low stakes tests, students can monitor where they are. This in turn allows everyone to be aware of what they think they know and what they actually know. Dawn Cox, head of RE in North Essex, used something similar with key word tests in her curriculum:

> I've used research findings and worked on creating practical strategies for trialing them in my classroom, in particular curriculum design using spacing/interleaving and no stakes testing. This has reminded me that if we don't cover and recover content with students we have an unrealistic expectation that they will remember it in their final exam. We need to actively be planning for memory and supporting students in the techniques that research suggests have most impact.
>
> At GCSE I have also embedded weekly keyword tests where students have to write keyword definitions. These support learning in several ways:
>
> - Every fortnight they are tested on the current topic, which keeps current content fresh in their minds.
> - They sit in silence to do them, which is good exam technique practice.
> - They peer mark using the correct definitions. This is an excellent way for them to think carefully about what is/isn't acceptable.
> - These keywords are used in all exam questions. If they know the definitions, they will know what a question is referring to in order to answer it exactly.
> - It models a simple technique of testing that they can do by themselves for homework/revision.
>
> I have frequently asked for feedback on these tests and whilst the word "boring" has come up, all students can see a real benefit of using testing to help them remember these words. In fact, they specifically asked for more tests. This year I have begun to interleave previous keywords into another weekly test. This makes students recall previous topics' keywords one week and current topics' words the next week. My own simple reviews of this testing have consistently lead me to believe that they have a positive impact on learning and long-term memory.

When I've spoken to teachers about doing this in their lessons one of the first concerns is where will they find the time? My answer is to replace things like starters or plenaries with them: they are more beneficial. In our department we use the first five minutes of every lesson to have a retrieval practice task, displayed up on the board in one slide. Students answer it on their own on silence and the answers are on a second slide, which helps students self mark. The whole process takes five minutes max.

Question them – a lot

You may not think it but the questions you pose are technically retrieval practice, every student in that class has to think. If you look at the questioning chapter, there are a number of strategies you can use to ensure that every student is thinking and therefore participating in retrieval practice. Make sure you pose something challenging, provide wait time, get them all to write it down and then take answers at random.

What type of test is best?

According to Dunlosky et al. (2013, p. 31), the type of test you undertake doesn't matter and it doesn't have to match the final test.

However, one thing I omitted from the earlier research experiments is that one type of retrieval practice/recall test does seem to be more beneficial than others. Can you guess what it is? What type of practice test helps students remember more later on?

I thought I would be told that maybe short-answer questions would be better as they force the student to retrieve specific short pieces of information that activated memory. Or maybe multiple choice, as you have to work out the wrong answers in order to generate the correct one and this type of effortful retrieval strengthens connections. However, it seems much simpler than this (yippee!). Many of the experiments suggest that the free recall test is one of the most effective (Dunlosky et al., 2013, p. 31).

Free recall is simply having a blank page and writing down everything you remember about a topic. Students can begin to connect things, link things, show relationships, create subheadings. When they are done they can check if they have everything or have missed things out. The process promotes a lot of retrieving but is so simple.

Other studies have found well-designed multiple-choice questions or essay-type questions to be helpful. Either way the things to ask are: does it promote retrieval, will they have to think hard, can they check how well they have done? If "yes", it is definitely worth doing. Before you move on, try to come up with five different things that you could do in your lessons to promote retrieval practice:

1
2
3
4
5

But what if they keep getting wrong answers on these quizzes, tests and practice? Won't that just demoralise them?

You are right to be concerned. The last thing we want to do is make our students want to give up because they keep flunking these quizzes. There are two things you should be aware of.

Feedback – According to Pyc et al. (2014, pp. 81–86), tests that are followed by feedback have greater benefits. They cite a study by Pashler et al. (2005) in which subjects had to learn Luganda vocabulary items. In the test trials, students were provided with either no feedback or the correct answer each time. In the final test a week later, those who were given the correct answer outperformed those that weren't. There is the suggestion that feedback to correct answers is also helpful, especially when students thought that they might have got it wrong. So either way, feedback is beneficial.

Getting answers wrong – Whilst some warn against errors in student learning, others like Clark and Bjork (2014, pp. 20–30) believe we should embrace them. Allowing errors to take place (providing there is corrective feedback) leads to longer-lasting retention of information. In a study by Kapur and Bielaczyc (2012), one group of students was in a maths class where they received direct instruction and were helped to solve problems. The other group was in a productive failure group. These subjects were given difficult problems which they were unable to solve. Afterwards, this group received corrective feedback and in a later test outperformed the direct instruction group on numerous problems.

The message is that errors and failure in these tests shouldn't be a worry. As long as we provide corrective feedback to students and show them how to produce correct answers, these tests can be very helpful.

But how much testing?

Various researchers suggest that more is better – as long as it is more low stakes rather than high stakes tests/quizzes. As we saw in the Roediger and Karpicke (2006) example, multiple tests surprisingly produced better retention over time. Use different methods, keep it low stakes and correct wrong answers and all should be fine. Testing is effortful and difficult, but ultimately it will help retention. And now to the final of Bjork's Desirable Difficulties: interleaving.

Interwhat?

Let's have a quick discussion about how curriculums are set up. Firstly, I'd like you to answer the following questions:

1) You are mid-way through the school year and you are teaching a lesson on topic X. You spend the first 25 minutes introducing the topic, showing examples, posing questions and discussing it. In the second half of the lesson you set some questions for the class to answer. What topic are these questions on?
2) If you had twelve lessons to cover four topics, each taking around three lessons to teach, how would you organise this? What would your lesson order look like?

You might be looking at question one and thinking "what?" Let me explain. Normally when you teach topic X in a lesson, after you have introduced it and taught it, you end up completing questions based on topic X. You're studying a topic so the subsequent questions are linked to it. This was my practice for a number of years. I taught my students about nutrition in sport and then set them questions on nutrition in sport. But amazingly, this might not be the best thing to do. Try to think why.

With the second question you might be thinking, "If I have to teach topics A, B, C and D – each taking three lessons – I will go AAA, BBB, CCC and then DDD".

Again, that is what I did for a number of years. It seems natural. Teach it to students in a block and they'll understand it, we can iron out any errors, solve some problems and when we're confident they've got it we can move onto the next topic. Well, once again, this may not be the best thing to do. Why might that be?

This makes no sense at all

I for one have always believed is that if I teach a topic I need to follow it up with questions which link to that topic. It also seems to make sense to teach a topic as a group and when it is done, move on. However, this type of teaching can lead to the massed or blocked practice discussed in the spacing section, where students develop short-term but not long-term memory strength (both storage and retrieval). And if we apply the spacing effect, we similarly might face a problem. Let's say we stick strictly to spacing and start a course with topic one. We teach it in the first lesson. Knowing we need to leave a spacing gap, we do not teach anything in lesson two, then go back to topic one in the third lesson. If we did this for every topic we would run out of curriculum time. And what do we do during the spacing gap of a topic? One solution is to use interleaving.

Interleaving refers to mixing the various topics together as we teach. If we used interleaving in question one, it would look a little something like this:

- Teach topic X – explaining it, showing examples, demonstrations, posing questions and everything else you would do.
- Then you would set a few questions on topic X. Maybe two or three. You would also include some questions from topic A, topic F and topic M.
- As further lessons go on, like the rest of the topics, you would put a few of the questions you need to cover in topic X into other lessons.

Wait, wait, wait! You're saying that when I teach a topic, instead of setting a load of questions on that topic like normal I only need to set a few and mix in random questions from other units? Really? But wouldn't they struggle to grasp the topic that way?

Well, actually it seems not. Let me move on to question two. It is suggested that we should do something like this: A, C, B, D, B, C, A, D, B, A, C, D, A, D, C, B. What???? Surely this way we would only just get our teeth into a topic before we have to stop and move on. My students would get so confused.

There is that. But let me explain why it might be best all the same.

Interleaving sounds unrealistic (and weird)!

I agree. Of all of the things I've looked into, this was the most difficult to get my head around and be brave about.

In probably the most referred to study on interleaving, Rohrer and Taylor (2007) conducted two experiments. Experiment one focused on massed vs spaced practice; experiment two was focused on interleaving. In the interleaving experiment, college students were taught how to find the volume of the four obscure geometric solids and then completed one of two randomly assigned practice schedules. One group had the practice problem grouped (shape A, A, A, A the shape B, B, B, B . . .) and the other had them mixed. Practice sessions for both were separated by a week, with a final test one week after their second practice session. Similar to what had happened with spacing, during the practice sessions the blocked practice students outperformed the mixed (interleaved) practice sessions. In fact, it was 89 per cent vs 60 per cent. Once again, blocking benefits short-term retention. However, in the final test, the mixed (interleaved) subjects outperformed the blocked by 63 per cent to 20 per cent (p. 492). That's huge! It seems that similar to spacing, interleaving is far more beneficial than blocked practice. However, blocked practice is common in lessons and curriculums.

The funny thing is, students prefer blocked practice. In fact, Robert Bjork (2012) explains that he found that 80 per cent of students in his study felt they learned better using blocked practice compared to interleaving – even though the results were the exact opposite. Interleaving was much more successful. The problem is once again fluency and the illusion of knowing, when blocking practice students feel familiar with information and get a sense that they've learnt it. However, they quickly forget it if they don't come back to it. Interleaving feels effortful and is a struggle. But it seems this struggle is an essential part of learning.

But why is it better? What's happening?

Some of the effects are actually quite similar to spacing. People like Bjork (2012) suggest that it works because it requires learners to constantly retrieve strategies, information and schemas. As we have seen, this retrieval strengthens pathways and accessibility so information becomes more retrievable in the future. It creates a natural spacing that allows this to be done on a regular basis.

Researchers have also said that interleaving also does something else. Constantly recalling different topics makes us better at working out strategies. It helps us problem solve because we can compare and see similarities and differences. That's an essential skill. It also helps students to see links between topics, which can be a struggle for some students within a huge curriculum.

Ok, I'm slowly being convinced. How should I do it?

Don't spin plates! – It is important to point out that we shouldn't be flicking between topics every few minutes. That will obviously confuse students. We should spend proper time on a topic before moving on to a new one.

Mix problems into your lessons – Don't just have questions in your lessons from that specific topic. Include two or three and then have questions from other topics in there. Students will find it difficult, but that's the important part.

Weave in topics – If you have a well mapped out curriculum you might be able to see where an old topic might link into a new unit. If you do, try and link them in. In our Training for Sport unit we bring in old topics of gender, age, diet and principles of training. They aren't in that unit but link very well.

Mix starters up – As we said in spacing, why not spend the first five minutes of a lesson, or even the last five minutes, practising problems from previous topics. This is a form of interleaving because different topics are being presented in the same lesson. As with retrieval practice and spacing, this will build up the strength of that memory in the long term.

Ensure your resources are mixed up – A lot of schools now create their own unit resources instead of using textbooks. Textbooks generally have a chapter on a topic followed by questions on that topic. This is blocking and makes it hard to interleave. If you create your own resources you can interleave and mix questions/problems up after each chapter.

Use cumulative tests – If you have an end of unit test, instead of only having questions on that unit, make them cumulative. Include questions from older units and mix the order up. Don't block questions, interleave them. If you're going to include questions on cells in science, have them as question 1, 7 and 15 – not question 1, 2 and 3.

And if you really want to be brave – Take the example from my second question. If you have four topics to teach, each takes four lessons and you have twelve lessons to do it, try going for an order like A, C, B, D, B, C, A, D, B, A, C, D, A, D, C, B. We're not currently at that stage in my school but it is next on my list.

My head hurts

Sorry. What learning about these things has done is inform me that what feels natural for a teacher and student might not be the best way. But a wealth of research backs up these claims.

They may also seem difficult to incorporate into curriculums or lessons. Some of these things, like spacing, interleaving and retrieval practice, take some planning. However, as Hin-Tai Ting, a maths teacher from London explains, it can be done:

> Focusing on the different ways of minimising cognitive load made my explanations much clearer than before. It was satisfying finally to see pupil after pupil follow my instructions and get questions right.
>
> Yet I was in for a rude awakening. Despite the big difference that I'd seen in lessons, I was still dissatisfied with my pupils' assessment results. Even when most of test questions were identical to questions we'd done in class, a large proportion of the class would answer them totally incorrectly.
>
> I realised performance in lessons simply wasn't the same as long-term learning and memory. My usual strategy of "recap it the next lesson and move on" simply wasn't enough. This led me to more research into cognitive science, and specifically the ways of improving retention and depth of learning. Interleaving, spaced practice and continual low-stakes testing popped up. These were harder strategies to implement immediately, since they required going beyond single lessons to looking at the whole teaching curriculum – that's probably why I hadn't made much use of them before. But seeing my pupils' results, I knew that I had to start implementing them.
>
> I'm incredibly fortunate now to work at a school where the whole department plans the entire curriculum with spacing, interleaving and retrieval practice in mind.

One example of how we do this is that we have weekly quizzes to give pupils retrieval practice on the entire week's teaching, as well as weekly revision lessons on topics that we've covered in previous terms and years. The curriculum sequence is also a thing of beauty: topics placed in order to ensure maximum complementary practice, and interleaving of topics within topics wherever possible. It's been a lot of team work, but the difference in the pupils' maths is extraordinary – every day I'm blown away by what they can do and retain.

To recap

- We have a working memory and it has a limited capacity.
- Don't underestimate the importance of prior knowledge.
- Memory is the residue of thought.
- Implement desirable difficulties into your teaching (spacing, interleaving, retrieval practice . . .).

Note

1 A huge thanks to Veronica Yann and Pooja K. Agarwal for reading this chapter and giving me their professional opinion, guidance and direction.

References

Agarwal, P. K., D'Antonio, L., Roediger, H. L., McDermott, K. B., & McDaniel, M. A. (2014) Classroom-based programs of retrieval practice reduce middle school and high school students' test anxiety. *Journal of Applied Research in Memory and Cognition*. 3. pp. 131–139.

Ambrose, S. A., & Lovett, M. C. (2014). Prior knowledge is more important than content: Skills and beliefs also impact learning. In: Benassi, V. A., Overson, C. E., & Hakala, C. M. (Eds) *Applying Science of Learning in Education: Infusing Psychological Science into the Curriculum*. pp. 7–19. Available at the Society for the Teaching of Psychology web site: http://teachpsych. org/ebooks/asle2014/index.php

Bahrick, H. P., Bahrick, L. E., Bahrick, A. S., & Bahrick, P. E. (1993) Maintenance of foreign language vocabulary and the spacing effect. *Psychological Science*. 4(5). pp. 316–321.

Bjork, R. A., & Bjork, E. L. (1992) A new theory of disuse and an old theory of stimulus fluctuation. In: Healy, A., Kosslyn, S., & Shriffrin, R. (Eds) *Learning Processes to Cognitive Processes: Essays in Honor of William K. Estes*. Volume 2. pp. 35–67. Hove: Psychology Press.

Brain Gym® International. Available at: www.braingym.org/index

Brown, P. C., Roediger, H. L., & McDaniel, M. A. (2014) *Make It Stick*. Cambridge, MA: Harvard University Press.

Carpenter, S. K., Cepeda, N. J., Rohrer, D., Kang, H. K., & Pashler, H. (2012) Using spacing to enhance diverse forms of learning: Review of recent research and implications for instruction. *Educational Psychology Review*. 24. pp. 369–378.

Cepeda, N. J., Vul, E., Rohrer, D., Wixted, J. T., & Pashler, H. (2008) Spacing effects in learning: A temporal ridgeline of optimal retention. *Psychological Science*. 19. pp. 1095–1102.

Chiu, J., & Chi, M. (2014). Supporting self-explanation in the classroom. In: Benassi, V. A., Overson, C. E., & Hakala, C. M. (Eds) *Applying Science of Learning in Education: Infusing Psychological Science into the Curriculum*. pp. 91–103. Available at the Society for the Teaching of Psychology web site: http://teachpsych.org/ebooks/asle2014/index.php

Clar, C & Bjork, R (2014) When and Why introducing Difficulties and Errors Can Enhance Instruction. In V. A. Benassi, C. E. Overson, & C. M. Hakala (Eds.). *Applying science of learning in education: Infusing psychological science into the curriculum*. Retrieved from the Society for the Teaching of Psychology web site: http://teachpsych.org/ebooks/asle2014/index.php. pp. 20–30

Cowan, N. (2001) The magical mystery four: How is working memory capacity limited, and why? *The Behavioural and Brain Sciences*. 24(1). pp. 87–114; discussion pp. 114–185. Available at: www.ncbi.nlm.nih.gov/pmc/articles/PMC2864034/

Cowan, N. (2005) *Working Memory Capacity*. London: Psychology Press.

Curran, A. (2008) *The Little Book of Big Stuff about the Brain*. Carmarthen: Crown House Publishing.

Deans for Impact. (2015) *The Science of Learning*. Austin, TX: Deans for Impact.

Donaghy, L. (2013) Red scare unit – Lessons 1 to 3. In: *What's Language Doing Here?* November 10, 2013. Available at: https://whatslanguagedoinghere.wordpress.com/2013/11/10/red-scare-unit-lessons-1-to-3/

Dunlosky, J., Rawson, K. A., Marsh, E. J., Nathan, M. J., & Willingham, D. T. (2013) Improving students' learning with effective learning techniques: Promising directions from cognitive and educational psychology. *Psychological Science in the Public Interest*. 14(1). pp. 4–58.

Gazzaniga, M. S. (1967) The split brain in man. *Scientific American*. 217(2). pp. 24–29.

Go Cognitive. (2012a) *Robert Bjork – Input Less, Output More*. Available at: www.youtube.com/watch?v=SSr6kjgdOqE

Go Cognitive. (2012b) *Robert Bjork – The Benefits of Interleaving Practice*. Available at: www.youtube.com/watch?time_continue=321&v=l-1K61BalIA

Go Cognitive. (2012c) *Robert Bjork – Using Our Memory Shapes Our Memory*. Available at: www.youtube.com/watch?time_continue=67&v=69VPjsgm-E0

Hattie, J., & Yates, G. (2014) *Visible Learning and the Science of How We Learn*. Abingdon: Routledge.

Hyatt, K. J. (2007) Brain Gym®: Building stronger brains or wishful thinking? *Remedial and Special Education*. 28(2). pp. 117–124.

Kapur, M., & Bielaczyc, K. (2012). Designing for productive failure. *Journal of the Learning Sciences*. 21(1). pp. 45–83.

Kirschner, P., Sweller, J., & Clark, E. (2006) Why minimal guidance during instruction does not work: An analysis of the failure of constructivist, discovery, problem-based, experiential, and inquiry-based teaching. *Educational Psychologist*. 41(2). pp. 75–86.

Lee, C. H., & Kalyuga, S. (2014). Expertise reversal effect and its instructional implications. In: Benassi, V. A., Overson, C. E., & Hakala, C. M. (Eds) *Applying Science of Learning in Education: Infusing Psychological Science into the Curriculum*. pp. 31–44. Available at the Society for the Teaching of Psychology web site: http://teachpsych.org/ebooks/asle2014/index.php

Lent, R. C. (2012) *Overcoming Textbook Fatigue*. Alexandria, VA: Association for Supervision and Curriculum Development.

Marzano, R. J. (2004) *Building Background Knowledge for Academic Achievement: Research on What Works in Schools*. Alexandria, VA: Association for Supervision and Curriculum Development.

Mayer, R. E. (2014). Research-based principles for designing multimedia instruction. In: Benassi, V. A., Overson, C. E., & Hakala, C. M. (Eds) *Applying Science of Learning in Education: Infusing Psychological Science into the Curriculum*. pp. 59–70. Available at the Society for the Teaching of Psychology web site: http://teachpsych.org/ebooks/asle2014/index.php

Miller, G. A. (1956) The magical number seven plus or minus two: Some limits on our capacity for processing information. *Psychological Review.* 101(2). pp. 343–352.

Nielsen, J. A., Zielinski, B. A., Ferguson, M. A., Lainhart, J. E., & Anderson, J. S. (2013) An evaluation of the left-brain vs. right-brain hypothesis with resting state functional connectivity magnetic resonance imaging. *PLoS ONE.* 8(8). pp. 1–11.

Nuthall, G. (2007) *The Hidden Lives of Learners.* Wellington: NZCER Press.

Pashler, H., McDaniel, M., Rohrer, D., & Bjork, R. (2008) Learning styles: Concepts and evidence. *Psychological Science in the Public Interest.* 9(3). pp. 105–119.

Pashler, H., Rohrer, D., Cepeda, N. J., & Carpenter, S. K. (2007) Enhancing learning and retarding forgetting: Choices and consequences. *Psychonomic Bulletin & Review.* 14(2). pp. 187–193.

Pines, M. (1973) Two astonishingly different persons inhabit our heads. *The New York Times.* September 9, 1973, p. 278. Available at: www.nytimes.com/1973/09/09/archives/we-are-leftbrained-or-rightbrained-two-astonishingly-different.html?url=http%3A%2F%2Ftimesmachine.nytimes.com%2Ftimesmachine%2F1973%2F09%2F09%2F90478788.html%3FpageNumber%3D278

Pyc, M., Agarwal, P., & Roediger, H. (2014). Test-enhanced learning. In: Benassi, V. A., Overson, C. E., & Hakala, C. M. (Eds) *Applying Science of Learning in Education: Infusing Psychological Science into the Curriculum.* pp. 78–90. Available at the Society for the Teaching of Psychology web site: http://teachpsych.org/ebooks/asle2014/index.php

Roediger, H. L., & Karpicke, J. D. (2006) Test-enhanced learning: Taking memory tests improves long term retention. *Psychological Science.* 17(3). pp. 249–255.

Rohrer, D., & Taylor, K. (2007) The shuffling of mathematics problems improves learning. *Instructional Science.* 35. pp. 481–498.

Subramony, D. P., & Molenda, M. (2014) The mythical retention chart and the corruption of dale's cone of experience. *Educational Technology.* 54(6). pp. 6–16.

Sweller, J. (1988) Cognitive load during problem solving: Effects on learning. *Cognitive Science.* 12 (2). pp. 257–285.

Tarmizi, R. A., & Sweller, J. (1988) Guidance during mathematical problem solving. *Journal of Educational Psychology.* 80(4). pp. 424–436.

Thalheimer, W. (2015) Mythical retention data & the corrupted cone. In: *Work-Learning Research.* January 5, 2015. Available at: www.worklearning.com/2015/01/05/mythical-retention-data-the-corrupted-cone/

UCLA: Bjork Learning and Forgetting Lab. *Research.* Available at: https://bjorklab.psych.ucla.edu/research/

Van Merrienboer, J., & Sweller, J. (2005) Cognitive load theory and complex learning: Recent developments and future directions. *Educational Psychology Review.* 17(2). pp. 147–177.

Weibell, C. J. (2011) Principles of learning: 7 principles to guide personalized, student-centered learning in the technology-enhanced, blended learning environment. In: *Principles of Learning.* Available at: https://principlesoflearning.wordpress.com

Willingham, D. T. (2009) *Why Don't Students like School? A Cognitive Scientist Answers Questions about How the Mind Works and What It Means for the Classroom.* San Francisco, CA: Jossey-Bass.

Asking more questions is better. Isn't it?

Mr Fawcett:	And that's why we need to ensure we have adequate carbohydrates in our diet. But why is it not advisable to have food before we exercise? Jack?
Jack:	Sorry, what
Mr Fawcett:	I asked why is it important that we don't eat before we exercise?
Jack:	But we do don't we?
Mr Fawcett:	How do you mean?
Jack:	We need to eat to get energy.
Mr Fawcett:	Correct, but why shouldn't we eat before we exercise?
Jack:	Er . . . because we'd get a stitch.
Mr Fawcett:	Not quite. What about you, Emily?
Emily:	Is it because our food won't be digested and we might feel sick?
Mr Fawcett:	Ok, so our food won't be digested and because of that it may make us feel sick or uncomfortable. So what else is going on? [Emily raises her hand]
Emily:	Doesn't the blood pool?
Mr Fawcett:	Not blood pooling, its blood shunting. What is blood shunting? [No hands are raised]
Mr Fawcett:	Come on, we did this in Year 9. What is happening to our blood when we've eaten and we then exercise? Ethan?
Ethan:	I don't know?
Mr Fawcett:	Sally?
Sally:	I'm not sure?
Freddie:	Doesn't it want to go to our muscles?
Mr Fawcett:	It does. But where is the blood going to? Where should it be going? What part of our body has the greatest need? Anyone? [Awkward silence. A hesitant hand raises.]
Natasha:	Doesn't the blood want to go to our stomach to break down the food but instead it goes to our muscles?
Mr Fawcett:	Yes. The blood would normally want to go to our stomach to digest the food. But as we are about to exercise, the blood is redirected away from our stomach and to our working muscles as they demand a greater and more immediate supply of oxygenated blood. Good answer, Natasha. Right, now we've all got it, let's look at how we would create a nutrition plan for a long distance runner.

The art of the question

As long as I can remember, I have asked questions. In many of the schools I have worked in, questioning has been universally agreed to be one of the most prominent parts of our teaching repertoire. Many tips between colleagues have been shared on the topic. Many an INSET day or staff training session has been dedicated to improving it. Levin and Long (1981, p. 29) found that we ask on average around 300–400 questions a day with (in one study) the average question being fired every 43 seconds. Robert Marzano et al. (2001, p. 113) in his book *Classroom instruction that works* claims that 80 per cent of teacher instructions involves asking questions. And it's not just when we are providing instruction or reviewing content with a whole class. We ask questions to check understanding. We ask questions to organise students. We ask questions to ensure they are listening? We ask questions to develop answers . . . But is all questioning good? Does asking questions actually tell us anything? Does asking more questions make our teaching better? Does asking questions improve learning? Does it matter what types of question we ask? Would it make any difference if we stopped asking questions?

I'd like you to take a look at the questioning exchange in the first example. If you were in the lesson tasked with giving feedback, what would you say? What are the strong parts and what needs improving? What are the obvious blunders? Is the questioning actually improving the learning taking place?

The example is typical of exchanges I've seen as teacher, trainer, observer and coach, although the range of questioning varies from no questions at all being asked to so many being asked that hardly any work was completed by students. It is something we do repeatedly, forms a part of feedback in lesson observations and may be driven as whole school CPD. But is it worthwhile and are we doing it correctly?

During my early years of training as a teacher I would probably have said that questions were vitally important, without understanding the full complexities of how to ask them. And although my views have become more refined, I still believe that questioning is a vital part of the process of both thinking and understanding, which are intricately intertwined. At its finest it can produce a symphony of thinking, discussions and curiosity. It helps us gauge levels of understanding and respond where necessary. If skilfully utilised it allows students to explore, investigate or manipulate information. It can help strengthen the retrieval or facts, figures and content. It can open dialogue between individuals and encourage students to go beyond the level of learning expected. It can leave students thinking about the topic well beyond the time the question was asked.

There is a problem though. Just as in other areas of teaching, the technique is only useful if used effectively. This chapter will look at questioning in more depth and see if what we ask, how we ask it and what we do with answers can increase its impact on learning.

But questioning can be so painful at times, with poor answers, awkward silences or the same students answering

You are right. Questioning can spiral out of control and leave a lesson in disarray. A former colleague once said that if questioning goes bad in your classroom, nine times out of ten it was probably because of the way we worded it or the culture we created. If she's right, what things might we be doing wrong? Do any of the following seem familiar?

The high achievers club – Mainly due to the worry that taking an answer from a low achiever would slow down the pace of a lesson, teachers can go preferentially to a higher achiever as their answers are generally more accurate and more time efficient. But how do we then know what the low achievers know? What message are we sending?

Quick, what's the answer? – I'll talk more about this in a moment. You might be surprised at the average length of time we leave between asking a question and taking an answer.

Guess what's in my head – That moment when *you* know the answer but a class full of bewildered faces stare on at you. Stephen Lockyer, a deputy head in Kent, told me we should "Try to actively avoid the game I call 'guess what's the answer in my head' – for example, in a lesson seeking adjectives, try not to come up with one yourself for the class to work out. It is learning admin". It can be frustrating but an answer that may seem blatantly obvious in our head may be a million miles away from the answer in theirs.

Well actually the answer is . . . – If a student gives a partly correct answer, do we correct it for them? Do we fill in the gaps in their understanding? Do we finish the sentence off? If we do, who is doing most of the work?

IRE – Initiate, response, evaluate. In a nutshell it is those moments in a lesson when we pose a question, one student answers it correctly and we instantly move on because we think if they've got it, so must everyone else. But one person's answer isn't a reflection of every student. A risky gamble.

The hands-up kids – Is having students putting their hands up in lessons an issue? I'll discuss this more later on in the chapter.

Er, I don't know – How do we respond to students who don't know the answer. Is it because they weren't listening, can't be bothered or genuinely don't know? Do we persist or give up and move onto someone else? It can be a tricky one to deal with.

1, 2, 3 questions – Sometimes we begin asking a question, only to think of a new one mid-way through that. Then when we've done that, we add a little extra. Before we know it, the one initial question has become two, three, four or more. So which one do the students have to focus their attention on?

Rephrasing – Asking a question and then immediately rephrasing it because we're not sure students understood it doesn't sound like a big deal. Surely, we're just trying to clarify it for them and make it easier? However, a rephrased question can suggest that there are two different questions being asked (not what you had intended). Not a big deal but something to be mindful of.

How familiar are the things on this list? None of them are huge. None of them destroy a lesson. But being aware of them and why they may reduce the effectiveness of questioning and discussion is a powerful thing

But asking questions is a good thing, isn't it?

The answer is yes and no. There are teachers in some quarters who would say that the whole process of asking questions is an inefficient use of a lesson. And they have a point. How many times does a conversation take twists and turns with students going off at tangents? How many times do we simply think at the end of it all, "I wish I just told them the answer"? How many times do you wonder how you can actually assess what students have said? Wouldn't it be more efficient *not* to ask questions? S. Pavar, a science teacher from London, really got me thinking whether we should abandon verbal questioning altogether when she said, "Classroom questioning and answering for assessment rather than discussion is a waste of time". I asked her to expand:

> Classroom questioning models cannot be used as tools for assessing understanding. At best they help discussion. This is due to the limited cognitive load that human working memory (short term memory) can manage and its reliance on memorised knowledge also known as long term memory.
>
> This is because they are restricted by a limited time for responses and small sample of students questioned. Furthermore due to the constraints on working (short-term) memory it is not possible for conceptually deep and technical questions to be satisfactorily answered by students in a Q&A – this excludes nearly all Science and Maths answers in secondary school as they require calculations and diagrams to illustrate their answers if anything more than a banal or non-trivial response is required. If you want to assess students understanding, assess them via a written test where they cannot rely on notes or peer help, but they do have sufficient time to manage the constraints and limits on working memory. Also match the test to the content of the course so they get a chance to be assessed on all parts of the course and not some random selection. Then match their responses to the specification/course content to reveal the gaps in their knowledge – that need to be subsequently fixed.
>
> Restrict classroom questioning to helping a discussion occur and avoid the illusion and hubris that you are assessing the knowledge and understanding of the class or individual students.

A lot of the questions we pose are there to assess what the students do or do not know. Teach a topic, ask some questions, listen to responses and make an assumption that they have learnt something or not. But by doing this we are possibly limiting the depth of response, and the time needed to create that response. If we pose challenging questions, do students actually have the capacity in their working memory to be able to produce well thought out answers? Can they effectively process all of that information into something that really reflects their understanding? In the pursuit of really challenging students, some of the questions we pose can be quite complex. Yet the limitations of students' working memory mean that trying to formulate an answer entirely in their head in a short time can actually be very difficult. Maybe we should even steer clear of questioning students for that purpose and, as suggested Pavar, only use questions to prompt discussion. There's also the argument that questioning to check understanding is a poor proxy for learning. One or two responses can't show what a student fully understands. Maybe there's an argument to remove questioning in lessons altogether.

However, many voices stress the importance of asking questions. Articles, books and papers regularly point to the work of Walsh and Sattes (2005), who found asking questions is better than not asking questions. Gall et al. (1978) found that those who were asked even low level questions learned more than those who were not asked any questions at all. Strother (1989, p. 324) found that "students who regularly asked and answered questions did better on subsequent achievement tests than students who did not".

We need to be careful about simply dismissing questioning. Yes, there are pitfalls in the process and more efficient things we could probably do in lessons, but questioning does offer so much. Maybe we should be mindful of the negative aspects of questioning and think about simply asking questions in a better way. To begin this I would like to introduce my first questioning principle.

---

1 Questioning should be challenging and allow time for students to create exceptional answers

---

In the schools I have worked in, we've dedicated a lot of time to the quality of answers that students write in their books. In response to an exam question, we can read what the student has written, analyse it, make notes on it, provide feedback and correct grammatical errors. On paper we insist that the answer is high quality. But do we have the same expectations of the verbal answers that students give? We have already indicated some of the problems that can arise with questioning, but that is no reason not to aim high, and this can begin with questions that challenge.

But what is a challenging question and should I just ask more of them in lessons?

Pitching questions at the right level is never easy. Make a question too difficult and you lose the class. Make a question too easy and what exactly will you learn from the response? There are many helpful tools – taxonomies, grids, questioning shells, questioning stems. They all give the user guidance on how to manipulate a question into one worthy of asking. Like everything, understanding why one question may be better than another is the key.

Is it better to ask challenging (higher order) questions or easier (lower order) ones? Well, it depends on the students you work with. In a well-cited research paper, Gall (1984, p. 42) concluded: "About 60 percent of teachers' questions require to recall facts, about 20 percent require students to think, and the other remaining 20 percent are procedural". She went on to say that "researchers have concluded that young students and low-income students – who are learning basic skills – benefit most from low-level questions; whereas middle and high school students appear to have higher achievement when exposed to more higher-level questions". This is the key point. It's not simply that asking a greater number of higher order questions in your lessons is better. In fact, doing this with novices will probably be counterproductive. We need to be flexible and adapt in response to the class. If the students are novices or working on a topic they have little understanding of, lower order questions would be better. If the class is quite knowledgeable, asking a greater number of higher order questions would be better. If you've read *The Hidden Lives of Learners* by Graham Nuthall (2007, p. 35), you'll also realise that on average, students know about 50 per cent of what we are going to teach them, but the amount differs from student to student. We need to be aware that every lesson will have a mix of novices and experienced students and our level of questioning should reflect this. You can't have a one size fits all approach.

But what exactly is a challenging question? On the surface the answer seems obvious. If it's difficult it must be challenging. If it makes them really think it must be challenging. If it's high up on a taxonomy it must be challenging. However, as I've pointed out, what may be challenging for one student isn't for another. According to Nancy Gedge, a consultant teacher at the Driver Youth Trust,

> I would suggest it depends on your knowledge of the learner. Your questions stretch and challenge according to them. So a seemingly simple question is a real stretch for one child, in a way that isn't for another. The skill of the questioner is to pitch it right.

Peter Blenkinsop, an educational consultant from North Wales, agrees:

> A question can be challenging for one learner and not another. Challenge will be to do with the gap between what the child knows and what they need to know next. A question will be challenging depending on how much prior knowledge is used to answer the question.

Right, now we've sorted that one, all we need to do is know exactly what each student's prior knowledge is on each topic we teach and then ask each of them a question that pushes their varied levels of understanding.

We need to be constantly engaging with them. The conversations, varied forms of assessment and even (dare I say it) the times we question them all help build up a picture. Challenging questions therefore need to be responsive. How we question needs to adapt as the lessons flows and in response to what students say. How can we do this?

Know your subject inside and out

As teachers we are all (I hope) experts in our subject. Sometimes, though, school continual professional development focuses purely on generic teaching and learning. For instance, if there is a perceived weakness with planning across a school, the senior leadership team runs workshops on how to plan better. Important and well intentioned as this is, is further developing our subject knowledge sometimes neglected? Do we just assume that teachers are reading up on their subject in their own time? This is relevant because one of the best ways to manage questions productively is to know the topic inside out. Having a rich vault of knowledge means that we can constantly add more layers to the questions we ask as responses unfold. If a student is struggling, we can call upon examples that provide clarity. If a student is doing really well, we can make more complex points and extend their understanding. Expert subject knowledge allows us to scrutinise answers, insist on domain-specific terminology and drive learning forward. It allows us to know what needs to be made clear, evidenced and explained. And as Lee Donaghy, a history teacher from Birmingham summarised, "*It allows you to know what to ask, not just how to ask it*".

We all have weaker areas in what we teach. Becoming expert in as many areas as possible is incredibly important and should be continual, hence proposing that schools make this part of our routine professional development.

Work out the sticking points

As we become more experienced in our subject we begin to recognise points in a topic where students get stuck. Those lessons where misconceptions creep in or students simply don't get it. Complex topics, abstract theories or conflicting views, we all know the times when this happens. As well as refining how we explain these topics, we can also think ahead to the questions we might ask during these pinch points. Having something like "Why isn't x then a consequence of y?" at our disposal allows us to keep the lesson moving forward.

Use taxonomies as a guide

If you've gone through teacher training you've probably heard numerous references to taxonomies such as Bloom's. Created in 1956 by a team including Benjamin Bloom, it was designed to categorise educational goals. Since its creation there have been subtle changes to the names of the various stages, but it is essentially built on the same foundations (see Anderson et al., 2001). Many refer to it in terms of levels of thinking, ranging from the (perceived) low level categories such as remembering and understanding to the (perceived) higher end such as creating and evaluating. Bloom's taxonomy is a good starting point for questioning. At each level you can create question prompts that allow you to be mindful of what you ask at each stage. For example:

Remembering/knowledge – The remembering level is concerned with knowledge of facts, terms and concepts. It is the fundamentals of a topic that are associated with recall. At this level the taxonomy helps us to pose questions such as: What is . . . ? When did . . . ? Can you select . . . ? Which one . . . ? Because it looks at information recall, and many of the questions are closed, it is perceived to be a lower level of thinking.

Understand/comprehension – This is concerned with being able to explain ideas, topics and concepts. It is where facts are expanded upon and now have meaning. We can pose questions such as: What ideas show . . . ? Can you explain . . . ? How would you summarise . . . ? What is the main idea of . . . ? It encourages students to understand information and be able to demonstrate it.

Apply/application – Here we look to solve problems in new situations by applying the facts and knowledge we have learnt, in a different or new way. We aim to develop ideas, build upon answers and see things in context. We can ask questions like: How would you use this information to solve . . . ? What would happen to this if . . . ? Can you show how . . . ? How could we apply . . . ? We're now beginning to develop a broader picture of the information in action.

Analyse/analysis – The stage asks us to look for connections among ideas. We make inferences and find evidence. We unpick how ideas work. Questions can include: Why do you think ....? What evidence can you find ....? How is this related to ....? How could we categorise this ....?

Evaluate – We aim to justify, make judgements or present and defend opinions. We evaluate the validity of ideas or quality of work against criteria. We can pose questions such as: What is your opinion of . . . ? Do you agree with . . . ? How would you evaluate the . . . ? What evidence helped you to that conclusion? Why was this idea better than . . . ? It forces you to scrutinise ideas, opinions and information.

Creating – Here we use old concepts to create new ideas. We compile ideas together in a new way or look for solutions. We use what we know to provide alternatives. We can pose questions such as: How could you do this different? Is there another way to . . . ? How would you improve . . . ? How could we adapt this to prevent . . . ? Can you design a different method that . . . ? We look beyond what is presented to us and see if there are new ways to work. We aim to answer problems with innovative ideas.

Bloom's would seem to be a very handy tool for teachers (see Figure 3.1). It provides an excellent reference point and gauge for the types of questions we use in lessons. The hierarchy of the taxonomy also makes sense. We obviously need to spend time knowing and understanding things before we go on to use this information to apply, analyse, apply or create new ideas. Our questioning can go hand in hand and tie in closely. I would argue that keeping a taxonomy like Bloom's in mind can be really helpful when planning questions for lessons or responding to answers. Would asking a closed knowledge question at this moment help my class remember the key point? Are we at a stage where I could stretch them with an evaluation question and see if this point is appropriate? But like anything, there can be pitfalls in the way we interpret it or use it. We can get so locked into the pursuit of the higher levels that we discount the importance of the lower ones. We can think that if we're throwing out lots of higher order questions, then our lesson must be great. If we ask too many lower order ones, then we can't be doing a good job. However, James Theobold, an English teacher from Hampshire, shares the same concerns.

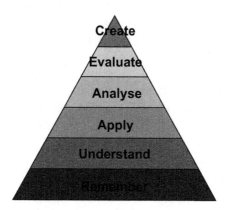

Figure 3.1 Bloom's Taxonomy

Bloom's taxonomy is, to me, a hugely problematic schema for teachers. The presentation of the skills as a hierarchy, in which remembering and understanding are seen as "lower order", creates the conditions for us to see the "higher order" skills of creating and evaluating as more desirable. This then often translates to teachers spending more lesson time on getting pupils to work on the latter. I think this presents a fundamental misunderstanding of the relationship between these skills.

In suggesting that creating and evaluating are "higher order", we are implying that they are harder. I'm not entirely sure that's true. In order to create, we need knowledge to create with – a composer needs to know (remember) and understand: notes and chords of various instruments, music notation, music theory, musical history and genres, harmony, polyphony, form, instrumentation, orchestration, not to mention a knowledge and understanding of the topic or theme of the music (e.g., Holst needed to know about the planets; Vivaldi, the seasons, etc.). It takes years to learn all of this stuff, and significantly less time to create the final composition.

I contend that much of what we are told is "higher order" is in fact a result, or a utility, of remembering and understanding. I think that, by teaching pupils content, by building their knowledge base, by making sure they can remember things, by ensuring they understand concepts, the "higher order" stuff will actually become much, much easier for them. Indeed, those "higher order" skills often involve the brain just making short cuts using the hard-earned knowledge – that which was acquired through so-called "lower order" thinking.

Whilst all the skills on Bloom's taxonomy are desirable, we should actually invert the hierarchy: if we dedicate the majority of time on knowing and understanding, I think we'll find that creating and evaluating are actually functions of this knowledge.

As James points out, a lot of the higher order things we ask our students are based on a solid foundation of facts, information, definitions and concepts. We need to be less concerned with progressing as fast as we can and more about ensuring our students know things well enough that they can manipulate them in meaningful ways. Sometimes the things we teach are really difficult. Checking students fully understand concepts before you move on can eliminate a lot of problems further down the line. Use the taxonomy in a non-linear way and be prepared to come back down it if you feel a misconception is taking place. If the answer to an *analysis* question isn't correct, following it up with the quick use of a *knowledge* level question can identify where the error is coming from and help you correct it. Bloom's and similar taxonomies can be a great guide.

Plan some quality questions and have strategies to follow them up or adapt them

When trying to define what a challenging question is, Harry Fletcher-Wood, a history teacher and associate dean at the Institute for Teaching, summarised his thoughts by saying:

> I don't think it's easy to distinguish between higher and lower-order questions: what's higher order for one student may be lower-order for another who has understood the topic deeply already.
>
> For that reason, I think it's vital that we don't just make do with a single question: if students get our first question right, a follow-up question can ask them to improve on their answer or develop it further (and if they get it wrong, an easier question may help them break it down). I also find targeted questions quite troubling: we do students no favours if we always ask easy questions to students we see as low attaining – students will surprise us.
>
> If we're looking to ask a more difficult follow-up question, we might want to ask students to reason more deeply, explaining their thoughts or the situation: "Why would this be the case? Why do you think that?" We might also want them to make connections: "How is this example similar or different to the examples we looked at in our previous lesson? How is it similar to the topic we studied in Year 7?"

"Follow-up" questioning strategies are fantastic tools for your class teaching. Remembering to pose questions in a particular order takes practice, but once embedded, it can allow you to quickly respond to an answer and amend the level of challenge. For those who are struggling, we can follow up with questions that clarify and support. If students are doing well, we can move them forward through increasing the complexity of what we ask. To get you started, here are three simple strategies:

Ask why? – If all else fails or you have a mental block, follow-up questions with "why?" can be extremely simple. It asks students to go into more depth, or explain their reasoning, or provide evidence, or show they understand the point in detail. It can get repetitive, doesn't fit in every scenario, but can be a good go to question as we begin to refine our follow-up strategies.

Use Bloom's – One of the quickest and easiest strategies ties in with Bloom's. As was mentioned, having Bloom's in mind allows us to pose and respond with ease during the questioning process. As Fletcher-Wood suggests, if we ask a question at an *understanding* level, we may follow up by asking students to *apply* what they've said with a question like "What happens to this if . . . ?" If they respond to an *analyse* question well, we may follow up with an *evaluate* question. Simple and quick, but requires us to fully understand the taxonomy and have question stems to hand.

ABC questioning – As I have pointed out, questions posed in lessons often follow the sequence of what researchers call IRE (initiate, response, evaluate). How many times do we ask a question, one student responds, we evaluate the quality of their answer, we move on? What this does is make the quality of that students answer the judgement for moving the lesson on. What it doesn't do is allow us to follow up that answer with more depth, scrutiny, opinion or level of challenge. A great way to combat IRE is through ABC questioning. The strategy works by asking a question, taking a response and then asking another student to "Agree" with what has been said. At this stage, if we just ask students to agree, they may find it quite easy. "Do you agree with what Tom has just said?" can result in another student replying with just a yes or no answer. One teacher I have worked with takes the answer and then asks every student to raise their right hand if they agree with what was said, and raise their left hand if they disagree. Every student has to raise a hand. This then allows the teacher to pick a student at random and say "Emily, you indicated you agree with Tom's point, why?" We begin to have more depth and reasoning coming through.

Once that answer has been discussed, we can ask another student to "Build" upon it. Every answer can have the structure, the terminology, the accuracy, or relevance of evidence built upon. We can strive to make responses more academic, which is what this part of the process does. "Ollie, Emily has just talked about how we can use some metals as a sacrificial anode. What can you add to that?" At this stage Ollie can build upon the answer explaining why "some metals" would actually be zinc, and the reasons why that would be a good material for being a sacrificial anode. Here Ollie is choosing to build upon the content. There are numerous things that you could focus on here, but the underlying process involves more depth of answers.

The final stage involves offering the opportunity for anyone to "Challenge" what has been said. This is crucial as students may not agree. This is where we really stretch the thinking. Were there any errors? Did the answer miss anything? In our example, some might challenge Ollie by saying that Zinc isn't the only material used as an anode, that magnesium and aluminium might also be used. Rather than it being a free for all, the process encourages a rational approach to rebut, disagree, oppose or offer a different perspective. The process of reasoning also helps students understand a variety of viewpoints or even consider an alternative answer that might not have been perceived initially. Depending on the quality of the answer, the ABC process can begin again.

ABC questioning works because it's simple, has an order and is incredibly inclusive. Answers can be directed at any student and all students are engaged in the process. The level of challenge in the follow up question can be amended by the teacher and misconceptions can quickly be addressed.

Socratic questions – The Socratic questioning technique is one that has come to prominence over the last few decades. It is a tool that can be used as a teacher to question, as well as a tool to help students ask better questions. From a teacher's perspective, the technique allows an initial answer to be repeatedly followed up with a series of probing questions. Its aims are to unpick the surface of a topic and (as best as possible) see what students know about the information being discussed. In some literature about the technique, it asks the teacher to adopt the role of a novice who knows little about the topic, forcing the students to explain it in more depth to help us understand.

There are various stages or lines of questioning that you could take. Each has a series of prompt questions that can be used to probe further.

1. Questions to clarify:

    -   Can you explain this further?
    -   What do you mean by that?
    -   Why do you say that?
    -   Can you explain that in another way?

2. Questions that probe assumptions:

    -   Why do you hold that assumption?
    -   What could we assume?
    -   Is this always the case?

3. Questions that probe information and evidence:

    -   What led you to that belief?
    -   How do you know?
    -   Is there good evidence to hold that belief?
    -   How does the information apply to this?

4. Questions about viewpoints:

    -   What is the alternative?
    -   What might other people think?
    -   Why might someone disagree with this?
    -   How have you chosen this viewpoint?

5. Questions for implications and consequences:

- What effect would that have?
- How might x effect y?
- If this does happen, what might occur as a result?

6. Question the question:

- Why have I asked you this?
- Why is this question important?
- What do we need to know to be able to answer this?
- What is this question asking of us? Can we break it down?

The Socratic technique requires skill and practice. It requires you to be expert enough in your topic to respond to questions and pose new ones. Its ability to probe allows you to really challenge students. However, as teachers, we must be aware of the pitfalls of this method. The technique provides prompts and helps us to plan questions that we may ask. In terms of usefulness, this makes it a helpful tool for us. As always though, if students don't have a secure grasp of the concept, misunderstandings can easily creep in and misconception become engrained. The fact that due to the teacher acting as though they don't understand the topic, puts the ownership on students to provide the answers. Immediately we may recognise that this could lead to shallow answers, awkward silences or even the line of questioning going massively off track. At this point we need to ask ourselves would simply telling them the answer, or using specific closed questions, or even another technique, be more time efficient and less damaging for what is being learnt. Maybe. Be aware of the types of questions, how to pose them and plan some into your lessons. Just be mindful of the pitfalls.

Pose-Pause-Pounce-Bounce – This technique is very similar to ABC questioning. It has been around for a number of years and also tries to tackle the bad habit of IRE questioning. Dylan Wiliam (2009) referred to it as a step away from Ping Pong IRE style, where questions go back and forth between teacher-student, and a step towards Basketball style questioning, where other students become involved. William describes seeing it used in a classroom where the teacher simply posed a question. She then paused (counting under her breath) to allow students to develop their own answers. After that she pounced, asking a random student what they thought. She then bounced it to one of their peers by asking if they could add, change, and develop what had just been said. Similarly to ABC questioning, it provides a memorable strategy that we can use day in and day out to develop answers.

Right is right – This Doug Lemov (2015, p. 100) technique comes with the rationale that "When you respond to answers in class, hold out for answers that are "all-the-way right" or all the way to your standards of rigour". The technique is designed to ensure that we don't credit partial answers with "That's right" or "Good answer" when in fact it isn't 100 per cent accurate. It sets the benchmark high. In his writing, Doug highlights the importance of knowing what an accurate answer actually is when planning our lessons. What terminology should be used? What is the accurate definition? What is the source that definitely backs up the answer I'm looking for? Knowing these in advance can help us when it actually happens in class. We can mentally compare it to the precise answer, and then work with the student to help them reach it.

Doug also talks about designing our own "back-pocket" phrases to give us a stock of things to say to *encourage* students to get themselves to the right answer. Things like:

> Ooh, you're very close but there's still some elements of your answer missing.
>
> The first part of your answer is right, but what is a clearer or more accurate example you could use?
>
> You're on the right lines but now reword it so it uses the technical words we've learnt.

These positive yet honest follow ups help you to create a culture where the drive to high standards and improving answers is conducted in a safe environment.

Stretch it –

> One key differentiator of teachers with high academic expectations is that once students get the answer right, they're not done teaching. Instead, the learning process continues, and they **Stretch It**, making their classroom a place where the reward for right answers is harder questions.
>
> (Lemov, 2015, p. 108)

Doug Lemov (2015) again. In this chapter I've talked about adding more challenge to questions. I've talked about techniques like ABC or taxonomies like Bloom's. But what happens when a student gives you a word perfect A* answer? Many of us would think the challenge was met so it's time to move on. Doug argues that actually, there's always something we can do to develop answers further. He offers six bits of advice on how to continue to stretch any response:

Ask how or why? – As simple as that. When an answer is given, ask how they arrived at that conclusion or why it is factually correct.

Ask for another way to answer – If there are multiple pathways to a right answer, ask students to see if they can work out the other routes. If they know more than one way to get to that answer in the future, they'll be able to provide the answer more efficiently.

Ask for a better word or more precise expression – Ask students to change the words they use in their answer to more academic ones. Are there any news specific words we have learnt that we could include? Could we remove redundant words and make the answer more concise?

Ask for evidence – Ask students to provide evidence to support their conclusion. Can they build up supporting arguments? Can they accurately make reference to materials or sources?

Ask students to integrate a related skill – Can they use a new word by explaining what it means, changing the tense, adding an adjective?

Ask students to apply the same skill in a new setting – When they have mastered an answer, can they apply what they've said in a new example or scenario? Can they see how it may transfer over?

There is an argument that this could never end and we could keep adding more and more challenge to our questions and answers. Obviously, we need to know when to move on. However, if we only follow up questions with those who have answered them incorrectly, what message is that sending those who always get it right? Ensuring that we have strategies for every student in our class is important. It establishes the culture and ensures everyone knows that they can be even better.

If it's difficult, get them to write it down

There are two reasons for this. As Pavar says, our working memory can find processing challenging questions tough due to its limitations in capacity. It's even more difficult for a child or novice lacking the long-term memories or schema to make this an efficient process. So asking outright challenging questions can be a barrier for some students. Should we therefore stop asking them? I don't think so. However, it would be wise to at least give students the opportunity to write their answers down first so that they can process all of the information. The beauty of this is that it's simple to implement. Pose the question and insist that they write their answer first. Not only will this help processing, but it allows them *time* to think of an answer.

The quality of some students' answers is poor, it's much easier and quicker to pick the hands up kids

I once wrote a blog post of things I have changed in my teaching that have made the biggest impact. I then took to Twitter and asked something similar: what in your teaching has made the biggest difference? *Teach like a Champion* author Doug Lemov replied saying that using "wait time" after posing questions was his. This on the surface may seem a pretty obvious thing. We pose a question, we give some time for students to think of an answer, and then we ask them for it. But it is never as simple as that. Research (e.g. Walsh and Sattes (2005)) has found that teachers usually wait less than a second between posing a question and taking an answer. What chance does that give students to create a high quality answer? What message does it send to the students who can't even comprehend the question in that time while all around them hands are flying up?

We all fall into this situation at some point. I certainly have – wildly firing out questions and taking answers from those who were ready to respond the first. I knew that some students never answered but never really understood why. I simply presumed they weren't as bright or weren't listening. I'd moan at them to get more involved but didn't facilitate an environment for that to happen. I probably switched a lot of individuals off.

Seeking an immediate response is a relatively easy thing to rectify. By increasing the time between question and response we create a culture for better answers to flourish. And it doesn't just support those who struggle – it benefits everyone. It gives novices of the topic time to understand what is being asked of them, retrieve it from their long term memory and then create an answer. If they don't know the answer it gives them time to find it. If they can't find it, it could be time they use to generate a question for the teacher to help them get the answer. For those students who do know the answer straightaway, giving time before a response is taken can lead them to form better answers with a higher academic structure and content. It's a win win for all parties.

So what is the best "wait time" (as it is referred to)? The general guidance seems to be anything from three to ten seconds. Some even suggest as long as 15 seconds. Any less and students don't have adequate time to formulate a good response. Any more and we begin to get nervous with that awkward silence. Even with ten seconds some teachers begin to worry. What do we do in that time? What if the students are just spending that time daydreaming? What about the pace of my lessons? If I keep leaving ten seconds after every question I'll run out of lesson. These are all relevant worries. But how much time do we spend correcting poor responses after leaving no wait time? Or even worse, without wait time, how many of our students just drift through lessons knowing they can't answer immediately like the others so simply don't?

Helen Rogerson, head of science in a Gloucestershire secondary school, decided that wait time could be beneficial in her lessons and began using it back in 2010.

> I started using wait time for two reasons. Firstly, that I have been told and read that it is a good strategy to include more students in questioning sessions and it helps improve the quality of responses, but second because I teach some students who slow processing. I noticed in one on one situations that waiting for an uncomfortable length of time with these students did result in them answering the question correctly. I had to implement this in whole class situations and it would benefit everyone. I continue to use it because it does encourage more students to think about the question and raise their hand, and the quality of the answers are increased in terms of both clarity and content.

So ask yourself the following questions:

- Do I always leave wait time after posing a question?
- Do I?
- Is it longer than three seconds? Is it anywhere near ten seconds?
- Is it? Always?
- Why might I not leave wait time? What are my worries or concerns?
- What would that extra 10 seconds do to student responses?
- What do I do in those 10 seconds?

Implementing wait time is relatively easy. There are a number of strategies. As is the theme throughout this book, keep it simple and pick a method that you know you will embed and make a habit. One which has to be the simplest of all is simply sharing the fact wait time is coming and counting to ten in your head:

So Year 9, you'll have 10 seconds to think of this. What are the immediate and long-term responses to a volcanic eruption?

Or

Was there a point at which the break from Rome became inevitable? You'll have fifteen seconds to think of the answer. No talking at all. Off you go.

Just making students aware that the wait time will occur and you don't want students to chat is really powerful. It explains the expectation and sets the routine. The insistence on them doing it individually and in silence ensures that they formulate the answer themselves. Cristina Milos, a teacher from Italy, goes a step further. She advocates that students write their answers down – writing again! – prior to them being shared:

> Questioning is so embedded in the teaching-learning process that we cannot imagine a teacher who isn't asking questions. Whether we ask evaluative, generative, diagnostic or other types of questions, it is clear that we need to focus on different aspects of the questioning process. These can be related to the purpose of questions (e.g. to check for understanding vs. to increase challenge), the expected answer (e.g. brief vs. more complex), the target student or group being questioned, the frequency of questions, their sequencing within the lesson and so forth. Many teachers, myself included, can fall into different patterns of questioning and it is quite difficult to become aware of them. One such default move is to pose questions to more students or to the whole class in the hope that would engage everyone and allow students to initiate the response right away. But this can have negative effects so I changed my approach: I simply asked students to write down their answers before sharing with the rest of the class.
>
> This is much more effective for a few reasons. First, writing down your answers forces you to concentrate and clarify your thinking unlike most oral interactions where the process is more flexible through back-and-forth explanations or other cues. Secondly, it allows more time to reactivate one's mental schema and thus to make more connections between pieces of knowledge that would otherwise be omitted in quick, oral responses. Thirdly, writing invites to better elaboration so both content and form come into focus. Moreover, some students process information more slowly than others so this would give them the opportunity to actively contribute without the pressure of speed that usually develops in oral interactions. In addition to this, I wanted to discourage students' tendency to narrow down the potential answers as it happens in group brainstorming where the group-think effect is well-known. This also encourages the introverted students to engage in answering without the anxiety usually felt when other students dominate the oral exchange. Lastly, it is a good tool to assess individual levels of understanding instead of relying on quick, less elaborate, and often similar answers from a group.

Asking that answers be written down gives us an effective strategy to use during the ten-second wait time. One that will actively improve the quality of answers.

Once the routine of wait time is embedded, you may begin to wonder what else you could do in the 10 seconds to help students who may need support. Some will still struggle to formulate an answer. This is where you can take an active role. You can develop the technique further by helping them understand how to create a better answer. You still need to be aware that any input here could distract or interrupt the thought process, but a few pieces of advice at this critical time could pay dividends. Help them model the process, point out sources that could help them or even encourage them to rehearse what they are going to say. Insist on them striving to make their answer as academic/high quality as possible.

Wait-time pointers

Give them prior warning – *"You'll have ten seconds to think of a high quality answer to this question . . ."*

Model the process – *"So, first think about what the term carbohydrate loading means and then think about why a marathon runner would need it?"*

Check off raised hands – *"We've got two hands up, now four, five, eight hands . . ."*

Insist on silence – *"No talking at all. I want everyone to be thinking about their answer"*

Rehearse what you are going to say – *"If you have time left, practise or rehearse it in your head. Does it sound right?"*

Give them advice – *"In the time you have, if you don't know the answer, check back through your books or use the second paragraph of the text I gave out"*

Once this is embedded, once you have fought off all of the impatient individuals who insist on shouting out the answer, once you have become comfortable with the silence, you'll find that the quality of answers improves. And if it doesn't, remind the class that everyone needs to use the wait time effectively and set them off again. I guarantee the second time round the answers will be better.

This section has focused on the use of challenging questions and wait time. But with this increased challenge, won't more students avoid contributing out of worry they'll get it wrong? Won't increasing the level of challenge see us relying on the same students to provide answers? Won't the wait time simply be a chance to daydream for those who feel they have no chance of putting their hand up. The answer is probably yes. If we push people to their edge of their comfort zone they may shy away from contributing out of fear of "looking stupid". We therefore need to make sure that every student is involved in the questioning process and feels safe to make a contribution. This brings me to my second principle.

2 Questioning should encourage every student to think

At the start of this chapter I talked about potential issues with questioning in the classroom. Of these, three of them revolved around only certain students participating in the questioning process: the hands up kids, the go to kids and the high achievers club. In one study of fourth to eighth graders, target students talked more than three times as often as their classmates; 25 per cent of the students never participated at all (Sadker & Sadker, 1985). One teacher, quoted in the excellent book *Working inside the black box: Assessment for learning in the classroom* (Black et al., 2004), described how thinking by every student was probably missing from their classroom:

> They and I knew that if Q&A wasn't going smoothly, I'd change the question, answer it myself or only seek answers from the "brighter students". There must have been times (still are?) where an outside observer would see my lessons as a small discussion group surrounded by many sleepy onlooker.

(p. 11)

Questioning can be inconsistent. Even when we create the best questions to ask students and combine them the various wait time strategies, do the following things still happen?

- We take answers from the few students who put their hands up.
- We take answers from those who we know might know the answers.
- We go to our go to kids.
- We take "I don't know" as an answer.
- We avoid challenging "I don't know" as an answer.
- We reword questions when nobody shares an answer.
- We have to repeat the question with the bemused student who wonders why you have picked them.
- We accept poor answers.
- We finish answers off for them.
- We answer the whole question for the class.
- We wonder why we even asked them a question in the first place.

Next time you question in your lesson, have these in your mind and see if you notice them happening. If that's a struggle (and it would be for me), how about asking a colleague to watch your questioning and see what is causing students not to be fully engaged. Recording your lesson is also a great way. You may cringe at the thought of watching yourself back, but it allows you to not only watch what you're doing but also analyse what the students were doing during your questioning to help work out why they might or might not have been involved.

My students hate the thought of being questioned, though

As good as our questioning might be, students don't always actively participate in the process. This could be down to one of the following two (unscientific) theories.

Confidence

There are students who sit in your lessons who may fit into one of these categories in Table 3.1. Some students will know the answer and be immediately confident to provide one if asked. Some will not know the answer but will be brave enough to give it a good go at providing it, even if they're wrong, just to be involved. There will also be those who know the answer but will cringe at the thought that you may ask them. They will actively avoid eye contact and hope that you skim past them and ask someone else. These students know the answer but hate the thought of providing it. Lastly, we have those who don't know and aren't confident. They are happy to be onlookers. It doesn't mean they're not listening or uninterested in the answer. They simply don't know and don't want anyone to know that. Now, this is a hugely unscientific theory and probably misses out all the complexities of student differences, self-esteem and behaviours. However, I notice these types of student all the time. Even the most top-set, high achiever children can fall into one or other of these categories. Whether it's because they're introverts or extroverts, confident or unconfident or what Carole Dweck (2006) refers to as fixed or growth mindset learners, we need to be aware these groups exist and we need to work out how to involve them all in the questioning process.

Interest

Some of you may have looked at those categories and said "That probably happens in top set classes, but I have a class with a range of able, less able, well behaved and simply not well behaved students. Some don't know the answer because they weren't even listening". To explain it again (in a very simplistic way), I will use another framework. It's not perfect and in no way intended to label students; it simply highlights reasons for lack of involvement.

In this framework we have those students who don't listen because they aren't even interested. See Table 3.2. They don't contribute because they're "not bothered". This is a difficult group to crack because there are many underlying factors both inside and

Table 3.1

Know the answer. Confident	Don't know the answer. Confident
Know the answer. Not confident	Don't know the answer. Not confident

Table 3.2

Involved and willing to contribute.	Involved but not willing to contribute.
Not involved but will try to contribute if asked.	Not involved and not interested in contributing.

outside of the classroom that you may have to contend with: poor language skills, low reading age, little parental support being some of those. We may sometimes avoid them in the process in order to avoid confrontation or silly responses. However, there are things we can do to slowly bring them into the conversation and engage them in questioning.

How on earth do you crack that culture, though?

There is no one way, even if colleagues or consultants tell you there is. It is like everything else, a process of chipping away and forging your own culture. It's about trying one thing at a time. Explain to the class why you're doing it is a sound piece of advice. Years ago I would get an idea and deploy it stealth like into my lessons. The students knew something was different but never why. Now I explain why I work in a particular way so they understand the reason for it: "This is how I work, these are the rules for when we do this and this is how you will learn more by doing it". Once you have used a method, ensure that you evaluate it. If it doesn't work, ask why before you dismiss it. Be open minded and aware.

However, there are some ground rules you could put in to place that will improve the questioning culture in your classroom. Have a look at this list.

- Set the expectation that answers are just as important as written work.
- Ensure that everyone knows that they are all expected to make a worthwhile contribution.
- Foster the idea that getting an answer wrong isn't a bad thing.
- Have the time and patience to see a good answer come to fruition.
- Challenge those who won't give answers.
- Challenge those who mock their peers for poor answers.
- Allow time to for students to work through an answer.
- Value the process of asking/answering questions.
- Ensure that everyone listens when someone is speaking.

Many of the things on this list may be in place in your classroom. The key to success is being consistent. If we interrupt a student rather than let them finish, they might not contribute again. If we shut down or dismiss an incorrect answer without valuing the contribution, they might not contribute again. If we let people take over answers or make remarks, they might not contribute again. If we insist on this, a cultural shift in your classroom may happen, and they might just actually want to contribute again.

Involving them all

One of the simplest ways to involve all students is to simply take away the option to contribute or not. You may think that's a bit harsh. Putting students on the spot may seem cruel, especially for those who aren't confident. However, an old colleague reminded me that questioning happens so frequently in lessons. If we allow people not to get involved then how do we know what they're thinking? How can we check their understanding? Do we allow them to not answer questions in exams? How will we nip misconceptions in the bud before they get engrained? Involving everyone in questioning has to be worthwhile.

There are many tools and strategies. At one end of the spectrum we have the very tech savvy piece of software called Plickers. A teacher writes a series of questions into the app. Each question has a series of choices for the answer. Each student has a piece of paper which has a unique QR style code on it. Students rotate the image to provide their answer – so if the think the answer is B, they hold the image sideways (for example). The teacher then holds up their tablet or smartphone and the camera scans the room and displays each student's response live on the screen. It's a nifty bit of kit and definitely gets everyone involved. However, I'll begin with a method that involves no resources at all and can be used instantly.

No hands up (but with hands up)

Insisting that students do not put their hands up to answer a question can be a very uncomfortable strategy to roll out. It can go against all of your training. But why would you insist on not taking hands? Well, a number of blogs, books and educational speakers over the years have pointed out that with raising hands, only those involved in the process benefit. Dylan Wiliam (2011) explains that:

> when teachers allow students whether to participate or not – for example, by allowing them to raise their hands to show they have an answer – they are actually making the achievement gap worse, because those that are participating are getting smarter, while those avoiding engagement are forgoing the opportunity to increase their ability.
>
> (p. 81)

By going to the "hands up kids", as I referred to them earlier, we allow those not involved to not be involved and therefore increase the chance that they are not learning. By insisting that nobody puts their hands up, the teacher controls who they ask and when they ask them. Keeping it random means that there is no chance that students know who is next. And why is this important? Because it means that every individual in the class has to be listening and thinking about the question – they may be called upon to share an answer. Combined with wait time it can be an incredibly powerful tool.

Keeping it random is an important part of the process. Some would say that random is inefficient as it can pull out poor answers and slow down the process. There is that. There is the argument that having the teacher choose who to ask in a non-random way means that they can keep pace, target questions and differentiate where necessary. Again, there is that. But random selection has its place. It means we can call upon students we might not have heard from before. It means we get an insight into a student's thoughts that we might not have got before. Also, that really difficult question answered by somebody other than the high achiever or go to kid might actually surprise you.

But keeping it random can be difficult. Firstly, some people insist on technology and random selectors. Simply input your class names into a giant spinning wheel graphic, click a button and off it goes. A few moments later, the name of a student is displayed on the board and you pick them. The name is then removed from the spinner and next time it chooses someone else. Simple. But does the technology benefit the process? You have to find the app. Then you write in the names. Then you have to load it up in the lesson. Then you have to come out of your PowerPoint, maximise the app to full screen on your projector, ask the question and then put the PowerPoint back up. And will students remember the spinny thing rather than the important question that got asked? An easier and quicker way is to just point. With your finger. Towards a student. The second thing to be aware of when trying to be random is that sometimes our bias and old habits mean we gravitate back to our "go to kids". We try to be random but we randomly didn't ask Luke (who was looking out of the window) the hardest question. Weird that we posed it to Amy, who knew the answer perfectly. Being aware of this – and being brave to ask questions in a genuinely random order – should be enough.

Why have I called it "No hands up (but with hands up)"? Imagine this scenario. Rachel is a switched-on girl who loves your lesson. You come in one day and say "Guys, I'm using a no hands up rule from now on and taking answers at random". You pose a question. As the group are new to this, most of them put their hands up. You remind them of your rule. Hands go down and you ask at random. You don't choose Rachel. You ask another question. Fewer hands go up. Rachel's is still one of them. You remind them again of the rule. You pick at random. Again, not Rachel. This goes on for a few more questions. You still haven't picked Rachel. The lesson finishes and Rachel, who was so keen, hasn't shared her ideas. She leaves frustrated and her view of your lesson has changed.

Sometimes the students put their hands up because they really want to contribute. If we ignore them for the sake of following a strategy, do we risk disengaging them? Stuart Lock, a headteacher from Cambridgeshire, allows hands up in his lessons but still chooses at random. The hands up gives him information about who knows what. Shaun Allison, a deputy headteacher from West Sussex agrees: *"it's useful to know who thinks they know the answer, even if you don't pick them to answer"*. Having hands up allows you to quickly gather information on whether taking answers might be worthwhile. Having no hands raised may mean they simply don't know and the following probing of answers could be painful.

For this reason, I advocate a mix of both. Pose challenging questions, implement wait time and then take no hands up answers first. Randomly take a few responses and then allow those who really want to contribute to do so. Let them raise their hands and explain their thinking. Or you could use some of the wait time strategies, like counting the number of raised hands as they occur – insisting you will begin taking answers when you have 15 hands up, for example. Simply remind them that you will pick at random.

Mini-whiteboards

Mini-whiteboards rose to prominence after AfL (Assessment for Learning) became a priority in education. And a set of mini whiteboards can still be a fantastic tool in the classroom. Students, each armed with a board and a pen, write down their answers or ideas in response to a question. Already the strategy is employing two bits of advice from this chapter: provide wait time and encourage students to write their answers down. After the wait time is up, students hold up their answer. This could be a definition, a multiple choice response, a diagram of a processing model or a chemical reaction. The best bit is that you now have a class-full of responses that you can now Add, Build, Challenge, or Pose-Pause-Pounce-Bounce with. You can ask individuals to elaborate, redraft answers or upgrade terminology. Those who have written nothing can add to their board as their peers provide answers, and you can then ask them what do they know now. They are inexpensive, involve no tech and will work as long as the pen lids stay fully clicked on after use.

You might take mini-whiteboards for granted. Phil Stock, a deputy headteacher from London, doesn't. In his 2017 blog post titled "Show Me: Maximising the Use of Mini Whiteboards in Lessons", he points out some important protocols to make their use in lessons really effective. For instance, do you have a standardised response format? So that, on a specific command, every student knows to show you their answer, written in the same format? Phil has a 3-2-1 countdown and insists that students fill the board with their answer – he needs to be able to scan them quickly and read them all. Another rule is making answers one or two words maximum. I know there are times where I've got students to write whole sentences, and then made them wait in an awkward silence as I tried to read them all. Not cool.

The key as always is follow up. What do we do if most of the answers are wrong? What do we do if only two students got the answer wrong?

You have 30 seconds – Bounce

There are times when you pose a question and students have to work out an answer, in silence and on their own, when answers aren't very forthcoming. That's when a technique like Bounce comes into play. Shaun Riches, a director of learning at a secondary school in Hampshire, used this technique brilliantly in a lesson I observed. He had followed a number of strategies in the build up. He had posed a really thought provoking question, insisted on wait time and then asked for hands up to gauge who might have an answer. Unfortunately, only two students raised their hands. This could be attributed to them not using the wait time effectively, not being able to write own ideas or even not listening in the first place. In any case, Shaun asked them to discuss the question with a partner for 30 seconds, after which he would take hands up again. During the 30 seconds, with a sense that Mr Riches was looking for a better response than a moment ago, students discussed their answers. When the time was up, the response was overwhelming. More students had an idea to share and this allowed Shaun to call on an individual at random and then follow up with other questioning strategies.

Snowballing or Think, Pair, Share

Sometimes students simply can't formulate an answer by themselves. This might be because they don't have the schema or prior knowledge to create one or perhaps they weren't listening in the first place. They are probably reluctant to get involved. Two very similar strategies (Snowballing and Think, Pair, Share) build up the answer from individual to whole class. In each method there is an element where the students must think of the answer on their own. In this time they must have something meaningful to contribute to stage two. This is where the individual now works with a peer (the "pair" stage). Here they share each other's thoughts and collaboratively refine it to produce a better answer. From here we go up another level and possibly join into a four. Again, we refine our answer and pull in a number of viewpoints we might have missed. Finally, at the share stage, each student now has an answer which they can present if called upon. Hopefully their initial answer at the first stage has been critiqued and refined to produce a response they feel confident to say in front of their peers. Their answer has "snowballed" and grown in quality. There are words of warning, though. Peer input can vary. Some are relied upon because they are the more able and end up doing all the thinking. Some can be too dominant and not allow all viewpoints to be considered. Then there are those who at the start get a part of the answer wrong, and this misconception spreads unnoticed by the teacher until it comes out at the final stage of the process. Be aware of this, plan to avoid it happening, and the technique can successfully encourage participation.

Write the question somewhere

With working memory having its limitations and some students attention span not as expected, individuals may simply forget, or even not have heard the question being asked: you call on a student to answer only for them to not know what you're talking about. You have to remind them of the question at the end of the process, rather than at the start. I've seen teachers make the question visible so it can't be avoided. Some display it on the board, others insist the students write it down. Don't allow students to miss what is being asked of them and use that as an excuse when they don't have anything to contribute.

Having challenging questions, providing time to formulate answers and now creating an environment where everyone feels they can contribute is certainly a step forward. But what if after all this the answers they give still aren't up to scratch? This brings me to my third principle.

> 3 Questioning should allow us to model and construct exceptional answers

As already mentioned, one of the main things I have focused on over the years, whether as an individual or in a whole school capacity, is how students *write* exceptional answers. We spend hours talking about grammar, sentence structure, exam technique and what various command words mean. We get students to write answers, act upon feedback, redraft or make improvements. But can we say we do this with the quality of verbal answers? Probably not in as much detail. However, as Cristina Milos once told me, "*Students need both oral and written modelling. Be consistent in asking for good answers – that will create a class culture of excellence*".

Once students feel they can share, we need to ensure that what they share is of high quality. There are challenges, though, as there are a number of reasons why the quality of answer varies from student to student. Different levels or language skills, different levels of knowledge or simply different levels of confidence mean that an answer can range from a thing of beauty to something difficult to understand. But as teachers we have to give as much attention to what students say as to what they write.

Answers come so frequently and quickly I don't have the time to correct everything

We ask so many questions in lessons and we don't get just one answer for each. So imagine if it's true that we ask over 300 questions a day .... We need methods that set the standard before questions are answered, so that we have fewer corrections to make during the process.

Before

Have rules in place for sharing good answers.

On walls in schools across the globe are lists of classroom rules. Reminders of how to get unstuck, how to settle or how to work. Rules ensure a benchmark is set to a high standard from the start. If anything slips below this we can challenge it and correct it. The same can be used for verbal answers. If we make our expectations clear from the onset, we can eliminate some (not all) of the errors that may creep in. If we insist that answers are given in a particular way, it acts as a reminder or prompt to the student. The rules can cover numerous things from the simple to the complex. They could include:

Rules about voice:

- Ensure that everyone can hear *what* you are saying
- Make sure I speak at a *pace* that everyone can process what I am saying
- Try not to mutter or hesitate throughout my answer

Rules about body language:

- I will try and maintain eye contact when giving an answer or speaking to others
- I must make sure my body posture is positive so others will want to listen (not slouched when giving an answer, swinging on my chair, fidgeting/distracting)

Rules about technical/structure:

- I will ensure I use the correct pronunciation of key words
- I have thought of an excellent way to start my answer
- I use specific terminology as much as possible in my answer

General rules:

- I must be prepared to elaborate if asked to by my peers or the teacher
- I mustn't use slang
- I am not allowed to say "I don't know"

Rules or protocols aren't anything new, yet they can get forgotten if we don't build them into our daily routine. Have a maximum of five: more can lose their power. When they are used every day, as Louise Hutton, head of RE in a school in Hampshire, does, they set high expectations with all students. They also reinforce good habits, which hopefully get adopted. This is her simple but effective list:

1. Every answer should be worth listening to so never accept mediocrity.
2. No student can opt out of providing an answer
3. Every answer should be loud enough so people can hear
4. Every answer should answer the question asked
5. Every answer should be in full sentences
6. Every answer should use the correct academic vocabulary
7. Every answer should be prepared to be challenge

What might your rules for answering questions be?

Answer stems.

Sentence starters or writing stems have become a great tool with written answers. They help students begin their writing and some provide a prompt of what to include. They can be adapted so that they support those who struggle as well as stretch those to improve the academic quality of their answers. Something similar can be used with verbal answers. If we have pre-planned a number of key questions before the lesson, we can anticipate what type of answer we may be greeted with in return. By doing this we can imagine the response we would ideally like and then design some stems to help students. When students respond, we can share the stems and insist that students either use one of them to initiate their answer or create one of a similar standard. By doing this we are modelling what an excellent answer looks like. Students can physically see the structure and subtleties required to generate answers at this level. After a while, we can begin to remove the scaffold and become more adaptive as the lesson unfolds. Phil Stock, an assistant headteacher in London, also uses answer stems to help scaffold excellent responses from his students.

> I tend to just jot down a few sentence openings whilst I am questioning students. So for a recent unit on the Odyssey, I would write openings for students to use like:
>
> - Odysseus's heroism is conveyed through ...
> - Odysseus's heroic qualities are displayed when ...
> - Odysseus acts heroically when ...
> - The heroic features of Odysseus are shown in ...
> - In book VII Odysseus appears heroic when ...
>
> In an ideal world I would plan these out, but it tends to be responsive and designed to frame better initial oral then written responses.

The next time you plan a lesson, think of the questions that are critical for what it is you are teaching. For each question, write down some exceptional responses. Use these as a guide, prompt students to use them and then discuss why these are answers that we should all be striving to create.

Prompts

After you have posed the question, there is a perfect opportunity to prompt students to create exceptional answers. It comes during wait time, when you can use two strategies that have been outlined: model the process and give advice. Both are great at getting the thought process rolling. Simply saying "Remember to include x in your answer ..." or referring students to a part of a text will help them begin to formulate a response. It reminds them of the importance of content and directs them to include it in their answer.

Write it down

As already mentioned, giving students the opportunity to write their answers down before they share them can not only ease the limitations of the working memory and reduce group think, but also allow students to focus on how/what they will say. If some individuals struggle to find the words when put on the spot, having a few notes, bullet points or key words to refer to can help improve the quality of what they say.

Answers range from "I don't know" to sheer brilliance. Most are fine, though, as I sort of know what they're saying

I too was a teacher who let students off with answers which weren't technically correct, but I kind of knew what they meant. I accepted bit part answers because they were on the right lines, or I simply finished them off or reworded them myself. One of the biggest things I've seen go unchallenged is when students say "I don't know". Many who say this genuinely don't know. We can look back and think whether the challenge was right, whether we used wait time well or whether we could have prompted them better. A lot of the time I have seen this response from students who simply don't want to share an answer. James Hughes, a PE teacher from Hampshire, observed the following in his PGCE year:

> It became apparent that students would give the response "I don't know", having been asked a directed question. This at first seemed quite a fair response, having not raised a hand or without the pupil self-volunteering a response to the question. Having reflected upon the lesson, and subsequently revisiting similar questions with the same pupil, the "I don't know response" seemed far too easy and I began to question if the pupil was getting away with what was either a genuine response, shying away or laziness, but perhaps a combination of them all.
>
> I wasn't satisfied with the response, and set about changing how I dealt with the situation when it occurred. Initially this was providing a pause after the "I don't know", in the hope the pupil would come up with an idea. But still, the pupil felt that this was an acceptable response. I then challenged the pupil, and rephrased and diluted the question to one that seemed different or easier, but actually, the question remained the same. Further still, I stated that "I don't know" can no longer be used, after all, it doesn't make for a great exam paper response. All pupils in the class began to realise and come round to the fact that something, a single thought is better than those three words. The pupil who used the response on multiple occasions suddenly began to think, and visually engage more when class discussions were occurring. Later in the lesson I came back to the pupil, who gave a fantastic response surrounding the benefits of a long distance runner benefitting from a lower body fat percentage. Within follow up lessons the pupil who would shy away from an answer, began raising their hand, willingly wanting to contribute or add further to other answers provided by fellow classmates. More so, during the packing away of books and resources, the pupil came to me with questions surrounding the topic, adding further thought to the answer provided ten minutes prior. I undoubtedly saw a change in the pupil in questions behaviour within lessons with greater willingness to contribute and provide ideas drastically increasing. I am glad I challenged the pupil on the "I don't know response", as I am still yet to find it appear on a mark scheme.

Challenging this type of answer can be quite daunting. We could be calling out a student and risking confrontation. We might be impacting an individual's self-esteem. We probably think it's easier to let it go and move on. If we do, though, what message does this send? Does it say that we're happy to not take answers, which might encourage others to do the same? Does it give the message to that child that it's ok not to answer as it's not important? Maybe it does. The point is that we are there to help every student learn. We need to find out why they "don't know". Challenging it in a friendly and supportive way sets the precedent that "I don't know" isn't an option. I saw this done well in a geography lesson. A student gave the response and the teacher saw that they genuinely didn't know what to say. They then took answers elsewhere, reinforcing key points and insisting people made note of these in their books. The teacher then returned to the initial student and asked a slightly different question. Instead of getting them to simply repeat an answer from another student, they asked them what they knew now that they didn't a moment ago. For me this not only highlighted the fact that a student has to be involved in the process but also showed the importance of questioning for learning.

During

When we've embedded the rules, given answer stems, prompted, encouraged them to write something down and challenged the "I don't know" kids, we then have the outcome: the actual answer. Even after all the strategies are in place, we can still improve the quality of an answer by helping students refine what they say and how they say it. Having high expectations of what verbal answers should be allows us to react and respond to what we are hearing as we hear it.

Format matters

> Help your students practice responding in a format that communicates the worthiness of their ideas.
>
> (Lemov, 2015, p. 116)

When an answer is shared it is done in the public domain. It can't be hidden on a piece of paper. In the open forum of a classroom, everyone paying attention will hear the answer and be analysing or evaluating what has been said. Great answers can help clarify meaning or application. Poor answers can cause confusion or create misconceptions. Challenging answers in front of an individual's peers can be either a positive or a negative experience. If a child is open to suggestions, they will happily improve what they have said. If you hit a nerve when analysing their response, you may encounter conflict or reduce the student's motivation. Get it right and you can help every student see that what you're doing is helping them provide answers in a more academic and structured way, using terminology and examples to show clarity in their thinking.

Format matters is a technique from the now-familiar Doug Lemov (2015). Doug highlights the importance of correcting the way students present their answers. If it is presented in a format not fitting for the class, it can be dismissed by the audience even if it has good points. If we allow students to use slang or poor grammar when speaking, at some stage they will be in an environment where those listening will stop doing so because it does not meet the demands of that environment. You wouldn't use slang words, for instance, when presenting to prospective investors in your job. For Doug, this should be no different in the classroom, and the classroom is no better place to practise this. Doug provides helpful guidance by encouraging us to focus on three things as we hear students speak:

- Grammatical format – Correcting slang, syntax, usage, and grammar. Helping students to, as Doug puts it, use a "language of opportunity".

- Audible format – As Doug puts it "If it matters enough to say it in class, then it matters that everyone can hear it". We need to help students ensure they project their voice so that everyone not only hears, but wants to listen.

- Complete sentence format – Helping students, using methods like our answer stems, put together complete sentences in our lessons. Provide the prompts and set reminders that complete sentences are the norm.

Putting the theory into practice may be the daunting next phase in the process. As mentioned, we sometimes worry how correcting answers may be received by students. Doug again offers some important advice. The main message from his book is to keep your intervention minimal. If a student uses the wrong grammatical format, quickly interject and repeat what was wrong. Failing that, begin the correction for the student and allow them to finish the sentence as it should have been said. If a student isn't loud enough and people can't hear, simply saying "voice" makes students realise they need to raise the volume. If a student gives only half a sentence, simply saying "complete sentence please" means the student repeats what they have said, including everything that was missing in their first attempt. Be confident in challenging students. Let them see you are doing it to help them.

Live write answers (and collaborate to make it better)

When you pose a question that will require a Herculean effort to answer, arm yourself with a board pen. When students finally begin to share their ideas and answers, simply annotating what they have said on the board can provide an excellent platform for modelling a refined answer. Note down excellent terminology and poor terminology. Write down excellent ways that they have opened their answer or list a weak example they've used to provide meaning. As this builds it allows you to revisit what has been said with the whole class. Ask the class what they think of the quality of the answer. Build a culture of collaboration where peers helping each other benefit outcomes. You can then use your expertise to probe the inclusion of some words and question why others were omitted. It allows you to rearrange word order and tackle the grammar usage. Doing this in front of the class provides both a model and insight into what high quality looks like. A strategy to be used on occasions.

Elaborate, question and all the usual things.

Me (via Twitter): How do you get students to generate better verbal answers in your lessons?

A hell of a lot of teachers responded: I ask more questions, interrogate and ask them to elaborate.

The best answer came from Jo Facer, a head of English in London, who simply responded: "*Just through questioning, like you would anywhere. Can you explain that? What do you mean by that? Could you use a more precise word? What's an idea you could link that to?*" I have been lucky to sit in Jo's classroom and see her skilfully pose questions to her students. Every student who responded in that lesson, and they were many, did so in a very eloquent and academic way. And the secret? Well, as you have just read, there isn't a secret. It was simply questioning or elaboration. But was it that simple? In the lesson I saw, I really don't think Jo gave herself credit. While Jo was questioning, she was making reference to specific parts of a text, explaining the meaning of some very academic terminology and putting things into context using well-spoken answers. She was (probably unconsciously) modelling and providing students with the tools to create excellent answers by the way she was speaking to the class throughout. But Jo was correct in her assessment that by asking students to elaborate, answers were indeed becoming better. In the daily rush of a lesson, do we have the time to elaborate? Do we get stuck in the IRE zone? Hopefully not. Elaboration is simple to use and reminds me of the famous Rudyard Kipling quote:

I KEEP six honest serving-men
(They taught me all I knew);
Their names are What and Why and When
And How and Where and Who.

---

4 Questions should be diagnostic and provide (as far as possible) information on what has been learnt

---

There is an argument, as already seen, that questioning is a waste of time for assessing understanding. However, many of the questions that we pose in lessons are done to get an answer from a student that shows what they know, what misconceptions they have and what they have learnt. What's the harm in that? Well, the problem could be how the student created that answer, whether it's a true reflection of what has been learnt and what judgements we make once we hear it.

At the ASCL conference in 2015, Rob Coe of Durham University talked about his poor proxies for learning. He introduced us to six of these proxies, the following being his final one:

- (At least some) students have supplied correct answers, even if they

  - Have not really understood them.
  - Could not reproduce them independently.
  - Will have forgotten it by next week (tomorrow?).
  - Already knew how to do this anyway.

Questioning in a lesson may feel like we are assessing what is being learnt, but it isn't actually a very good indicator at all.

Dylan Wiliam (2011) also highlighted downsides with IRE questions (pose a question, take a response, assume that response represents the class, evaluate it and move on). He warned of the dangers of making one student's answer the benchmark for whether the students have got it or not. What if that one student gave a lucky answer or was the only one in the class who knew it?

There is one final point we should also be aware of. As already mentioned, Soderstrom and Bjork (2015) highlight the difference between learning and performance. Performance is based on what has just been learnt in your lesson. It's the here and now. Learning is what has been learnt and retained over time. It is durable, flexible and has a lasting change in long-term memory and schemas. If we teach students something new, then immediately ask them a question, we may be tricked into thinking that they've learnt something if they get it right. What we are doing is simply gauging their *performance*. The big question is whether they remember it in a week, a month or six months down the line.

The theme throughout this book is to be aware of *reasons* why some things work and others don't. It's therefore important to know that questioning as a measure of understanding has its limitations. It's up to us to minimise these limitations.

But how? You just said that questioning doesn't show us exactly what they understand

True. It doesn't show us exactly was has been understood or even learnt, but it can help us build up a picture. There are three approaches that can allow us to assess understanding a bit better.

Driving questions and pre-tests

I have mentioned the work of Graham Nuthall (2007), who found that students will already know, on average, about 50 per cent of what you intend to teach them. This 50 per cent is distributed between different students and in different amounts. So if we are to really understand what students have learnt in our lessons, we need to know what they know already (or at least get a better idea). One way of doing this is to use Driving Questions, which come from the work of PBL (Project Based Learning) – although the version I will talk about has been adapted for a specific use. At the beginning of a project, the teachers pose a question to drive the learning forward. This question would be what the class would be trying to answer using what they learnt throughout the term. With a slight adaptation, I used the idea to not only hook students in to a normal everyday lesson but also find out a bit about what they know before I started teaching it. For example, in a GCSE unit a while back I asked:

> Have developments in science and technology in sport helped or hindered sport? Have they gone too far? Will they?

This is a fairly big question and one that over the series of lessons will help put into context what I will teach. Posing it at the start of the very first lesson also allows me to ask, "What do you think?" Students are allowed time to ponder the question and try and answer it. They do it in silence and they write down their thoughts. When the time is up, I go round the room and take responses. It works really well because I immediately find out that some students know very little about developments in this domain in sport. They aren't aware of aerodynamics, carbon fibre and new training facilities. For these students I now know a bit more about how I should tailor my lessons. Then I have those who instantly begin discussing whether Formula 1 cars or their drivers are responsible for who wins. Is it the technology or the driver skill? Now I realise that these students know a little more and can pose questions for themselves.

For those who think this is too open, too sporadic in getting students answers, too vague or way to inaccurate, I have also begun implementing multiple choice pre-tests at the beginning of units. I create a ten-question test that covers the variety of topics to be covered in the next few lessons. Students again answer them prior to any teaching and I gather a bit more information to help tailor my lessons. There may be the chance of guessing (as with an MC question) but having a confidence score, an option of "I don't know this" or even a space for students to elaborate underneath minimises this somewhat.

Hinge questions

A maths teacher brought diagnostic questions to my attention. In his lessons he would use a tool that posed a multiple choice question onto the board that every student had to read, think about and provide an answer to. Students simply had four options per question and had to raise the number of fingers for the response they would select (three fingers if they thought it was option three). The teacher would scan the room and when every hand was raised they would reveal the answer and use the average student response as an indicator of whether students were "getting it".

Dylan Wiliam (2011) refined this further with his "hinge point questions". These are diagnostic questions that we pose at critical times in a lesson to check that what has been taught has been understood. They too are multiple choice and students raise their hand to respond to their chosen option. Designing good multiple choice questions is a real skill. Harry Fletcher-Wood has written some excellent blog posts on how to do it. The key is that the question needs to encompass what was just taught. The options need to be challenging enough to provoke thought, but not too difficult that students are left confused. Getting the balance of these is no easy thing. I would suggest creating a bank with your department to pool expertise and critically analyse the quality.

Dylan offers the following two principles:

> First, it should take no longer than two minutes, and ideally less than one minute, for all students to respond to the question; the idea is that the hinge-point question is a quick check on understanding, rather than a new piece of work itself. Second, it must be possible for the teacher to view and interpret the response from the class in thirty seconds (and ideally half that time).
>
> (p. 101)

You don't need to memorise what every individual has signalled, just quickly see if there is a significant number of students who got the answer wrong. If this is the case you will need to reteach and address misconceptions. You might also want to see if there are any patterns from previous hinge questions with similar students continually struggling. These will be the ones who need more personalised support.

Interleaved questions

One of my biggest takeaways from cognitive science has been Robert Bjork's Desirable Difficulties. In addition to retrieval practice and the spacing effect, there is one that has already been referred to called interleaving. The process involves introducing questions from previous lessons or schemes of work into the lesson in hand. If we are currently teaching topic H, we can ask questions from topic B or D if they tie in suitably. The beauty of doing this is that you are checking a week, a month or six months down the line whether students still remember what you taught them. In a lesson about training methods, pulling in a question from the nutrition unit three months prior forced students to think about things they hadn't done for a long while. You may wish to plan these in advance, looking for potential links. Or you may wish to use your expert level of subject knowledge and simply respond to the direction of the conversation. Either way, mix up what you ask and see if students have really learnt anything.

To recap

- Questioning should be challenging and allow time for students to create exceptional answers
- Questioning should encourage every student to think
- Questioning should allow us to model and construct exceptional answers with students
- Questions should be diagnostic and provide (as far as possible) information on what has been learnt

---

References

Anderson, L. W. (Ed), Krathwohl, D. R. (Ed), Airasian, P. W., Cruikshank, K. A., Mayer, R. E., Pintrich, P. R., Raths, J., & Wittrock, M. C. (2001) *A Taxonomy for Learning, Teaching, and Assessing: A Revision of Bloom's Taxonomy of Educational Objectives* (Complete edition). New York: Longman.

Black, P., Harrison, C., Lee, C., Marshall, B., & Wiliam, D. (2002) *Working inside the Black Box: Assessment for Learning in the Classroom*. London: nferNelson Publishing Company.

Bloom, B. S. (Ed), Engelhart, M. D., Furst, E. J., Hill, W. H., & Krathwohl, D. R.. (1956) *Taxonomy of Educational Objectives, Handbook I: The Cognitive Domain*. New York: David McKay Co.

Coe, R. (2015).From evidence to great teaching. Presentation delivered to ASCL Annual Conference, 20 March 2015. Available at: www.ascl.org.uk/index.cfm?originalUrl=utilities/document-summary.html&id=45878A48-32E1-48FC-8729663C8DC4E8FA

Dweck, C. (2006) *Mindset: The New Psychology of Success*. New York: Random House.

Fletcher-Wood, H. (2018) *Collection of Posts on Hinge Questions*. Improving Teaching. Available at: https://improvingteaching.co.uk/?s=hinge+questions

Gall, M. D. (1984) Synthesis of research on teachers' questioning. *Educational Leadership*. 42(3). pp. 40–47.

Gall, M. D., Ward, B. A., Berliner, D. C., Cahen, L. S., Winne, P. H., Elashoff, J. D., & Stanton, G. C. (1978) Effects of questioning techniques and recitation on student learning. *American Educational Research Journal*. 15. pp. 175–199.

Lemov, D. (2015) *Teach Like a Champion 2.0: 62 Techniques that Put Students on the Path to College*. San Francisco, CA: Jossey-Bass.

Levin, T., & Long, R. (1981) *Effective Instruction*. Washington, DC: Association for Supervision and Curriculum Development.

Marzano, R. J., Pickering, D., & Pollock, J. E. (2001) *Classroom Instruction that Works: Research-Based Strategies for Increasing Student Achievement*. Alexandria, VA: Association for Supervision and Curriculum Development.

Nuthall, G. (2007) *The Hidden Lives of Learners*. Wellington: NZCER Press.

Sadker, D., & Sadker, M. (1985) Is the OK Classroom OK? *Phi Delta Kappan*. 66(5). pp. 358–361.

Soderstrom, N. C., & Bjork, R. A. (2015, March) Learning versus performance: An integrative review. *Perspectives on Psychological Sciences*. 10(2). pp. 176–199.

Solution Tree (2009) *Solution Tree: Dylan Wiliam, Content Then Process*. Available at: www.youtube.com/watch?v=029fSeOaGio

Stock, P. (2017) Show me: Maximising the use of mini whiteboards in lessons. In: *Must Do Better … Thoughts about English Teaching and Education in General*. 21st October 2017. Available at: https://joeybagstock.wordpress.com/2017/10/21/show-me-maximising-the-use-of-mini-whiteboards-in-lessons/

Strother, D. B. (1989) Developing thinking skills through questioning. *The Phi Delta Kappan*. 71(4). pp. 324–327.

Walsh, J. A., & Sattes, B. D. (2005) *Quality Questioning: Research-Based Practice to Engage Every Learner*. Thousand Oaks, CA: Corwin Press.

Wiliam, D. (2011) *Embedded Formative Assessment*. Bloomington, IN: Solution Tree Press.

Other reference

Shreedar Pavar's quote was based on the work from "The science behind this approach can be found in the book Cognitive Load Theory" (Explorations in the Learning Sciences, Instructional Systems and Performance Technologies) Hardcover – 26 Mar 2011 by John Sweller, Paul Ayres, Slava Kalyuga (Author)

For all the time and effort, is feedback actually worth it?

The problems surrounding feedback and how we give feedback more impact

---

I have always had a bit of a problem with marking books (that's a very generous way to put it). As far as I was concerned, the amount of time it took to do did not justify the outcome; it seemed arbitrary. Instead of real impact, it seemed like a huge amount of input for a low output. A spectrum of pen colours, red pen slathered over work utilising an entire language of marking codes, the same five or six targets copied across their books that they inevitably wouldn't read... I think I truly felt defeated by the whole thing when I was told that I needed to use my "verbal feedback given" stamp to prove I was talking to my pupils about their work. It felt like evidence was more important than the technique itself. The impact on workload was crippling, not just on my time but on how futile I felt the task at hand was; it felt impossible.

(Calum Lacey, a geography teacher in Hampshire)

In 2016, I ran an intervention programme for Year 11 GCSE students who were the most in need of support in the run up to their exam. It matched mentors (volunteers from the world of business, armed forces, leisure) with these individuals. We hosted its launch night in the evening so that parents, students and mentors could all attend without impacting work commitments. When it ended I made my way back through school, expecting to bump into the odd cleaner and site staff preparing to close up for the night. To my surprise, I walked past three classrooms in which teachers were busy marking exams, assessments and books and making copious feedback comments. School had finished many hours before but these members of staff were painstakingly scouring every bit of work to ensure that students were making progress. Not because it was school policy that staff worked themselves to the bone to prove they were doing their job, but because of something much worse.

Many strategies and approaches have come in and out of education over the years. In my eyes, none have been as talked about and glamorised as marking and feedback. I put both in the same bracket as they go hand in hand, with many teachers referring to them as almost intertwined – "You need to check books in order to give feedback and you can't give feedback unless you mark their books" – even though we all know feedback is more complex than this. The issue of feedback, and indeed marking, has gathered size and pace, inadvertently making workload an issue in schools. A number of things have contributed to this.

John Hattie and Helen Timperley's article "The Power of Feedback" (2007) and Hattie's "Visible Learning for Teachers" (2012) suggest forcefully that feedback could be a useful tool for moving student learning on. Other publications have also concluded that feedback is something we should invest our time in.

Beware of myths, good intentions and whisperers

I will be the first to admit that when I first started teaching, marking books and providing feedback wasn't high on my priority list. I knew I had to do it, but it felt exactly like that – because I had to rather than because it was beneficial. I would spray the page with ticks, crosses, the occasional "well done" and a final "Make sure you use a definition next time" type of comment. Anyone that looked in them books would see that I had provided feedback but that's as far as it went.

When I set out on this journey of reflection, feedback was one of the first things I realised I just didn't do properly. I felt ashamed that I had completely missed the point. I began reading articles, research and publications to see where I had gone wrong. There was a flow of blog posts and websites from well-meaning teachers and educators on how to "solve" feedback and make us all better. The problem with us educators is that we are magpies. We see the next shiny thing and adopt it into our teaching repertoire. Before we realise it we begin using ideas based on myths, good intentions and whispers.

Myths stem from what people read and interpret in their own context. Some would call this confirmation bias where we interpret new evidence as confirmation of one's existing beliefs or theories. For instance, we know that feedback has learning gains so some see that as a remit to increase the amount of feedback we give. School policies are built around the premise that because some book or research paper has said that feedback is beneficial, we need to give as much feedback as possible. Myths brought about an abundance of ideas, strategies, stamps and different colour pens. We expect staff to feed back on anything and everything. And it all needs to be evidenced. Things become distorted and, like one giant Chinese whisper, what the research actually says isn't quite the same as the message given to staff. The myth has become embedded.

Then come the good intentions. Take triple impact marking. In 2012, I came across an idea on social media about tackling students lack of engagement with written feedback. Why give feedback if students do nothing with it? Triple impact marking sounded promising. You mark a piece of work, provide feedback, the students respond to this feedback and then you respond to their improvements – hence "triple impact". All of a sudden it became a thing that teachers did in some schools. Feedback policies were rewritten to include it and people waxed lyrical about it. What could go wrong?

The problem was that schools began expecting dialogues to appear in students' books. Conversations going backwards and forwards between learner and teacher. People wrote comments, which were responded to, then a new comment appeared, which again was responded to, and then a new comment was written . . . . Marking had become not triple impact but quintuple, nonuple, quattuordecuple and maybe centuple impact marking. A well-intentioned idea had spiralled out of control. And ask yourself, how much impact did these comments have further down the line? And how much had a teachers' workload suddenly increased?

Last comes the whisperers. These are probably the worst of all because they claim something that probably isn't true and we know isn't going to work, but because it is accompanied by "but Ofsted expect to see it" we worry that we need to follow the advice. "Ofsted expect all of us to evidence that verbal feedback is given" led to a whole market of bespoke stamps being created. To its credit, since 2014 Ofsted has endeavoured to crush such misconceptions. But some of these whispers still prevail in classrooms and corridors. It's easy to plant the seed but difficult to uproot the tree. We need to look at feedback with a fresh pair of eyes.

So what is feedback?

Strictly, marking and feedback are two separate things. Unfortunately, many people refer to marking as feedback, and the pressures that go with marking then influence our view of feedback. I was one of those who put both in the same box. If I set a student some work which they completed, then marked it, gave it a tick and wrote, "Well done. Try to use more specific references to how media use hype, bias and sensationalism next time", I had done my job. Work set, feedback given, learning had taken place, big high five to me. The problem is that this isn't effective feedback. Not even slightly.

So what is feedback and why isn't it just marking? The *Oxford Dictionary* defines feedback as "Information about reactions to a product, a person's performance of a task, etc. which is used as a basis for improvement". It can also be referred to as an action that changes future actions. If we look at it in a very simplistic way, it's the information we give an individual about the work/answer/idea that they have given in an effort to improve it and change future actions.

The process seems obvious but making it as effective as possible requires thought. At its best it can resemble a map, providing clear references to where we have been, where we are, where we are going and what the immediate landscape may be like as students continue on with their journey. It can take many forms, both verbal and written. Any provision of feedback by a teacher or even a peer is aimed at helping that individual move the learning process forward. We use it numerous times in a lesson and it impacts many of our students. Usually (as stated by both Wiliam (2011) and Hattie (2012)), it combines a strong goal or learning intention with clear success criteria. This is vital as students need to use this feedback to see what the aim is and how to get there. When there is clarity in the task, the power of the feedback is improved.

Over the years, educators and teachers across the globe have developed methods of providing feedback to students which they find work. There is no doubting that feedback is one of the most important components of teaching. We use it every day, in various forms and in response to various situations. According to Hattie (2012, p. 266), if used well it can have an effect size of d=0.75, which is twice the average impact of other classroom methods. However, as Hattie (2012, p.129) states:

> Feedback is among the most common features of successful teaching and learning. But there is an enigma: while feedback is among the most powerful moderators of learning, its effects are among the most variable.

So why is the impact of feedback so varied? Why is it that, sometimes, though we provide detailed feedback about a piece of work or learning, it fails to improve? Why is it that after meticulously providing feedback in an effort to move learning forward, it is not acted upon? There is clearly a chink in the system and identifying it in our own teaching, and then addressing it can ensure our effort is not wasted. Well, as usual there aren't any miracle cures. How we give feedback in one lesson may not suit the next. How we provide feedback to one student in a class may not be helpful to the person sitting next to them. There is a lot to master.

What might I be doing to cock up feedback?

Before we get started, I'm going to go back to my example in the last sub section. As you read the following, try and pick out what might be wrong:

> If I had set a student some work which they completed, then marked it, gave it a tick and wrote, "Well done. Try to use more specific references to how media use hype, bias and sensationalism next time", I had done my job. Work set, feedback given, learning had taken place, big high five to me. The problem is that this isn't effective feedback. Not even slightly.

Any ideas? From looking at numerous student books over the years, this is pretty standard stuff. However, as teachers we can unintentionally fall into the following traps.

Feedback is not the end of the line

If we are not careful, feedback can become the end product of a piece of work. It becomes the final thing we do as teachers when the learning process is over. How many times over the years have I asked students to submit a piece of work on which I write the only piece of feedback? How many times have students handed in homework and received a comment but never acted upon it? This summative method of providing feedback is the first stumbling point in the whole process. By providing feedback only at the end of learning, students do not have an opportunity to act on it.

Timing of feedback?

When to give feedback has been a conversation I have had with a number of teachers over the years. Should we do it straightaway or leave it till later? The more I read about the timing of feedback, the more I realise that it's not clear cut. One thing for sure, though, is that feedback shouldn't only be assigned to the end of a piece of work. John Hattie (2012, p. 137) argues that we should provide feedback "that is 'just in time', 'just for me', 'just for where I am in my learning process' and 'just what I need to help me move forward'". There isn't a magic formula: we need to be allowed to do what we do best; know our classes, be responsive and use gut instinct as to when we need to interact.

However, there are some interesting explorations into the timing of feedback from the likes of Carless (2006), Hattie and Yates (2014b), Butler, Karpicke and Roediger (2007) and Hays et al. (2010). Although not referring to exactly the environment that we find ourselves in on a daily basis (a busy and unpredictable classroom) and sometimes conflicting, there are some worthwhile points.

One is whether to provide feedback immediately or after a delay. Hattie and Yates (2014b, p. 52) suggest that for novices in any domain, immediate feedback is more beneficial. While they are early in the process of learning, having instant feedback can help them make sense of a topic and get to grips with it more easily. As a learner goes on and becomes more knowledgeable, "immediate feedback becomes less critical. Immediately experienced feedback can even discourage the emerging self-correction process (Mathan & Koedinger, 2005)". When they become confident with the topic (at an intermediate or expert level), students can begin to self-monitor and reflect on what they have learnt themselves.

It seems that the timing of feedback may also be influenced by whether an answer was correct or incorrect. For example, Hays et al (2010, p. 797) found that providing immediate feedback immediately when an item was recalled *correctly* yielded no long term retention benefit. They then referred to Pashler et al. (2005), who found that immediate feedback after an *incorrect* response improved final recall by 494 per cent. That is huge! It suggests that if an answer is incorrect, or a misconception arises, it's beneficial to provide feedback (or further instruction) there and then. Stop it becoming part of their memory before it's too late.

However, Butler, Karpicke and Roediger (2007, p. 274) cite Kulhavy (1977), saying, "Incorrect responses must be allowed to dissipate or they will interfere with the learning of correct responses". They found that delayed feedback provided greater learning gains than immediate feedback. Hays et al. (2010) picked up on this, attributing similar benefits to delayed feedback as spaced retrieval practice.

Leaving the feedback until later is another opportunity to retrieve the content, build stronger connections and embed it in long-term memory.

Not confusing at all … . Providing immediate feedback to novices is very helpful. There is little benefit in providing feedback after correct responses compared to the huge benefits of providing immediate feedback to incorrect (or low confidence) responses. The message is to tackle misconceptions as quick as you can, before they become engrained. Sometimes, however, with complex or engrained mistakes, a delay helps students forget the misconception and makes replacing it with the correct idea easier. And remember, both papers found a delay in feedback acted as a form of spaced retrieval practice, which only helps long term memory retention.

Although research might seem a bit mixed in terms of timing, there is a warning about when you *shouldn't* give feedback. In lessons I would teach the class the particular topic or concept I wanted them to learn. I would model, explain and give worked examples of how this concept worked. From here I would set the class a task to complete and set them on their way. I would then do one of three things. Option one was simply waiting. I would let them get on with their work while I made myself look busy by sorting the resources ready for the next section. Option two involved me walking around the room. Literally just walking around the room to show I was still present. Option three – within about 30 seconds of saying "Right Year 8, off you go" I would begin to develop a sense of guilt that the class had been working for 30 seconds without me doing anything. What would happen if somebody came into my classroom and I was just standing there *letting them get on*? What kind of teacher would they think I was? Why was I not earning my wage every second of the lesson?

Hattie and Timperley (2007, p. 104) point out that feedback can only build on something: it is of little value when there is no initial learning or surface information. My students had only been working for 30 seconds yet I had let the myths and whispers get the better of me and jumped in to offer help. When I do this, students simply look at me and say either they're okay, working well or "Sir, I haven't even had time to finish writing the title". As Wiliam (2011, p. 111) points out, "The timing of feedback is so crucial. If it is given too early, before students have had a chance to work on a problem, then they will learn less". How much of the problem had they even thought about before I jumped in? Probably very little.

We need to dismiss the myths and whispers and be brave enough to allow learning to take place. Leaving the class to work isn't being lazy, it's giving students the opportunity to learn and work out what they don't know. There will be times when we set a task and immediately have a student saying they're stuck. In this instance the principle is the same. Rather than giving them the answer, clarify task and get them to carry on. They need to learn before feedback is provided.

Providing more and more feedback – it's good though, isn't it?

Even though Hattie (2012) states that feedback has an effect size of d=0.75, it is worth remembering that its effects are extremely varied. Some forms of feedback yield impressive benefits, others may even damage learning. It therefore isn't safe to say that providing more feedback is better. In doing so, we risk increasing workload for teachers without any real return.

One area worth focusing on is how much feedback students need. In the early stages of learning a new concept, different students may need slightly different amounts. If we look at the students in front of us as novices (new to the topic, little understanding), intermediates (know some of the topic, have encountered it before) or experts (know the topic very well indeed), we will be aware that we can't have a one-size-fits-all approach. What may help one group may hinder the other.

Hattie and Yates (2014b, p. 50) say that we need to treat these three levels differently. They highlight that novices (or beginners) "need feedback based on content knowledge while striving to build basic knowledge and vocabulary". They would probably benefit from the most amount of feedback as they acquire knowledge. The feedback we give them needs to be corrective and very specific in terms of correct or incorrect. It needs to be clear to avoid misconceptions becoming embedded. But if there are real misconceptions, feedback might not be helpful at all. Further instruction or examples may be more beneficial (Hattie & Timperley, 2007, p. 91). The authors then suggest that feedback can tell students whether they are heading in the right direction: "They will appreciate also a level of encouragement in confidence building. They require teachers' recognition that they are genuinely getting somewhere along the path to greater understanding". They also mention cognitive load (see Chapter 2), pointing out that at this stage, novices are using a lot of working memory when learning – something we need to consider in our feedback. If we go into too much detail or make our feedback overly complex, we may cause cognitive overload and unintended stress. A final point they make is that we need to ensure that we don't highlight "glaring omissions relative to what is known by other people". Self-esteem at this early stage of learning is key and our feedback needs to be specific but not public.

Hattie and Yates (2014b, p. 51) then discuss feedback to intermediates. These learners will have potentially moved onto extending initial ideas by seeing relationships, elaborating concepts and applying knowledge. The amount of feedback needed isn't as great as novices as they have a grasp on the fundamental content. Feedback here needs to assure "that they are applying the right methods and strategies in the right place". Intermediates need feedback on whether their application and inferences are correct. They benefit from "positively phrased suggestions for alternative strategies (for instance, 'strong use of adjectives in just the right spots', 'good use of the acceleration principle, but other principles could play a role here', or 'a beautifully well-constructed argument, but have you thought of what this implies in the future?')". Intermediates are making the move from recall to application and therefore need feedback to ensure that they are putting this into context and explaining topics beyond isolated concepts. Feedback can be slightly reduced.

At an expert (advanced) level, feedback should be designed to support self-regulation. The amount of feedback here can be reduced compared to novices and intermediates as they learn to monitor their own progress. It should help students produce work of a high standard. The use of "elaborated conceptual feedback" is key and helps develop future learning. See Table 4.1.

Table 4.1

Learner level (Hattie and Yates terminology)	How we should provide feedback
Novices (Beginners)	• Higher levels of feedback • Based on content knowledge • Based on basic vocabulary • Corrective feedback • Explain correct v incorrect/right v wrong • Encouragement • Simple and specific to avoid cognitive overload
Intermediates (Intermediates)	• Focus on linking ideas and relationships between concepts • Assurance that they are using the right strategy and method • Check inferences are correct • Worked examples are helpful • They appreciate positively phrased suggestions • Feedback on the correct application of knowledge
Experts (Advanced)	• Less feedback • Aim for feedback that promotes self-regulation • Recognise efforts to extend and apply knowledge • Guide towards the highest level possible • Elaborated conceptual feedback

One final point: Hattie and Yates (pp. 47–48) use the analogy that feedback should be like computer games or GPS; i.e. something that provides timely feedback, monitors your progress, helps you get to where you are and supports you when facing challenges. However, Didau (2015, p. 251) adds a word of warning: "Our well-intentioned efforts to let pupils know exactly what they should be doing next might short-circuit learning. The 'gap' between where we are and what we should do next might be important. If someone fills the gap, we don't have to think. And if we don't have to think, we won't learn. Could filling this gap too quickly be counter-productive?" He adds, "The problem is I get *too much* feedback. I know where I am, where I'm going and what I need to do *all the time*. I never have to struggle. And because I never struggle, I never learn". Didau warns that too much feedback may turn students into "crazed feedback junkies" (p. 254) who crumble when feedback isn't available. Maybe allowing an element of struggle is desirable.

My feedback is great (Oh no it isn't!)

I started an INSET day on feedback in 2017 with the following questions:

1. How would you rate the quality of feedback you give?
2. How do you give feedback?

3. How much time does it take you to give feedback? In books?
4. What do the students think of your feedback?
5. Do they act upon your feedback?
6. Does your feedback move student learning forward?
7. Who is working harder? You or the students?
8. How would you like to give feedback?

The particular questions I want to focus on now is question 1 and question 4, to see if there is a difference between the two. When I first began teaching, I assumed the feedback I gave students was adequate and did the job. I assumed students read it and got the idea of what I thought about their work. I believed that I was doing what other teachers were doing and that my feedback was fine. However, if it was ok, why weren't students acting upon it? Why were the same mistakes cropping up again and again?

David Carless (2006) addressed the quality of teachers' (tutors') written feedback, sending a questionnaire to over 460 staff and 1,740 students in Hong Kong universities. One of the questions was whether "Students were given detailed feedback that helped them improve their next assignments" (p. 10). Sixty-six per cent of the tutors said they did this often or always (the highest two possible responses). On the face of it this would suggest that tutors thought their feedback was good. However, only 12.6 per cent of students agreed that the feedback from tutors was indeed detailed and helpful. That is a massive difference between the perception of tutor and student. In his paper he then goes on to unpick the reasons for this gap. What was so wrong with the tutors' feedback that meant it wasn't helpful? What might we learn from it?

One of the many issues highlighted was the clarity of written feedback. Carless cites Higgins (2000), saying, "Many students are simply unable to understand feedback comments and interpret them correctly" (p. 4). There is a worry that at times we write in an academic way that is beyond some of our students. Granted, this is a university research paper, but it is a reminder to read our comments through the eyes of a child. It is important that we know the students we work with and what level they are working at. If you remember the advice for novice to expert learners given earlier, does the feedback match appropriately and provide clarity?

Carless (2006, p. 13) also noticed that students felt feedback was related only to that piece of work and was difficult to transfer to future assignments. If we look at my original feedback example where I wrote, "Well done. Try to use more specific references to how media use hype, bias and sensationalism next time", the problem here might be that students would not have a *next time*. If this was the last piece of work on this topic, there would be no opportunity to make these improvements and something more general, something that could be transferred, would be more useful.

A final point is that to provide high quality written feedback to every student in a class takes time. As Carless (2006, p. 11) suggested, "the student perceptions were probably more accurate because large class sizes and lack of time make it difficult for tutors to provide detailed feedback". After writing the second comment in our twentieth Year 8 book and it's already gone past 7pm, maybe the quality of our feedback suffers. Written comments take time and students say that they aren't always helpful. Could there be a better way? More on this later.

Whole school or department driven?

One of the biggest problems with feedback is whole school policies. With the best of intentions, a number of schools I know have prescribed what each teacher in each department must do in terms of giving feedback. All staff are expected to give verbal feedback like this, and written feedback like that. The issue is that what is needed in an art lesson is completely different from what is needed in a maths lesson. Instead of having a restrictive whole school policy, we should perhaps move to whole school *principles*, with each department making it bespoke. What would make feedback effective in your department and your subject?

Faulty interpretations

There are times in the learning process where giving feedback may actually not be helpful. All of us have probably had a conversation similar to this. You walk over to a student who is working and check their work. You realise that they have missed out the key point from their answer and in fact have mentioned things not directly linked to the question. You have a chat, provide feedback and inform them you'll check in on them again in a moment. When you come back, they haven't added much to their answer and what they have is again not what the question required. You try again to provide more feedback but simply draw a blank. You then ask, "Do you actually understand this?" to which they reply "Nope".

You may remember Hattie and Timperley (2007, p. 104) arguing that feedback has to build on something. In the example here, did the student actually have any prior knowledge of the topic? If not then the time we took to give them feedback was wasted. Hattie and Timperley (2007, p. 82) go on to say that feedback "is most powerful when it addresses faulty interpretations, not a total lack of understanding". In this instance we should sacrifice feedback and instead give further instruction. If a student has no idea what the topic is, how can they be expected to act upon advice?

Praise or no praise?

Students like to receive praise. Hattie and Timperley (2007, p. 97) write,

Sharp (1985) reported that 26 percent of the adolescent students in his sample preferred to be praised loudly and publicly when they achieved on an academic task,

64 percent preferred to be praised quietly and privately, and only 10 percent preferred teachers to say nothing at all.

Other studies have similar findings. And in lessons, when we give feedback, we can usually find ourselves praising students. For years I would always begin with a "Well done . . ." or "That's amazing . . .". It's not a big deal and it can't cause any real problems. Can it?

There is a wealth of research out there (for instance, Lipnevich & Smith, 2008, p.8) that finds that "a feedback message containing praise enhances motivation and leads to improvement in individuals' performance (Cameron & Pierce, 1994; Dev, 1997; Pintrich & Schunk, 2002)". Studies have concluded that the use of praise reinforces desired behaviours and increased task attention. If a student has produced a good piece of work, praise may encourage them to do similar things in the future. It may also motivate students to work harder.

On the other hand, numerous studies have raised a number of concerns or issues. Praise on its own has very little impact as it provides no constructive instruction to the learning or task. Mixing praise with other comments can also reduce the impact of feedback. Hattie and Timperley (2007, p. 96) refer to Wilkinson (1981), who completed a meta-analysis on teacher praise and concluded that it bears little, if any, relationship to student achievement (overall effect = 0.12). Kluger and DeNisi (1998) reported a similarly low effect size for praise (0.09) and found that no praise has a greater impact on achievement (0.34).

So praise can also have a detrimental effect. It seems that the giving of praise can actually distract students from the comments that they are receiving. The thinking is that praise focuses students' attention on themselves, rather than the task in hand.

Wiliam (2011, p. 109) talks about an experiment by Ruth Butler in 1987 where she looked at 200 fifth and sixth graders in eight classes working on specifically designed thinking tasks. Part of this study, involved looking at the role of praise in feedback. She found that the provision of written praise had no effect on achievement. In fact it was the same as giving no feedback at all. This is startling.

Some argue that praise affects students' self-perceptions. Some want to be seen as a good student, others want to avoid being a good student when praise is present in the classroom. These social, or semiprivate worlds (Nuthall 2007, p. 84), are incredibly powerful and difficult to break into. If a student is embarrassed to be praised in front of their peers for social status reasons, they may avoid producing good work so they don't get labelled a nerd, geek or worse. We therefore need to be mindful of who we give praise to.

Tied into this is the fact that sometimes we praise underachieving or struggling students more. This can ultimately lead to praise being given out when it isn't really deserved, or even worse, praise being seen as false so future praise has even less impact. How many times have I praised the work of a usually reluctant/disengaged child who has picked up a pen and written a sentence, even though this isn't anywhere near the quality I expect. I praised in the hope that this would motivate them. Unfortunately, it usually does not. I remember when one of my Year 10 tutees went completely off the rails at school and got in a lot of trouble. This was a student capable of A* grades. When we finally got to the bottom of it, he told us that "naughty" students or students who did little work got more praise than good students. So should we simply ban praising students? That would be pretty harsh. Instead we need to consider what and how we praise.

One of the breakthroughs for me was the work of Carol S. Dweck (2006). Her work on mindset theories has seen her propose the idea that people, including students, have either a fixed or a growth mindset. Fixed mindset individuals believe their intelligence is fixed and success is an affirmation of that intelligence. Things like effort and challenge are avoided, and obstacles cause them to give up easily. They feel threatened by the success of others. On the other hand we have growth mindset individuals who believe that intelligence can be developed. They have a desire to learn, they embrace challenges, put in effort and learn from mistakes. They enjoy the challenge of learning and find lessons from it. If we are showering students with praise about their intelligence, Dweck suggests that we are supporting fixed mindsets. By focusing on intelligence and praising it we might be drawing attention to it and teaching them to become one. What Dweck insists on is that we don't praise ability and intelligence. Instead we need to praise things that students *can* control, like effort or process.

In her book, Dweck talks about a study she conducted with hundreds of adolescents. They were all given an IQ test. Some of the students were praised for their ability after the test whereas some were praised for their effort. Although both did pretty well in the test, students who had their ability praised (Well done, you must be smart) began displaying fixed mindset traits. When these students were given choice later on, they rejected challenging new tasks. As Dweck explained, students didn't want to do anything that could expose their flaws and call into question their talents. When the students who received praise for their effort (You must have worked really hard), 90 per cent of them embraced the more challenging tasks that they could learn from. Dweck followed up with more hard problems to solve. The ability praised (fixed) students begun doubting their ability and performed worse. In contrast, the effort praised (growth) students applied more effort and showed better and better performance.

So what does this mean? In a nutshell, praise can be good at raising motivation and reinforcing behaviours. Using it in our feedback can be helpful in moving learning forward. But we need to be aware that a wealth of research shows that praise can also have a negative impact on learning. Praise with feedback can at times be the same as giving no feedback at all. So maybe we need to think about the work of Dweck and be mindful that if we are to give praise with feedback, that praise is directed at something the students have control over, such as effort or process. By attributing praise to how hard a student has worked ("It's really great to see how much effort you have put in") or the way in which they have done it ("A really fantastic way in which you have structured your . . ."), the student can do something about it. They have control over the amount of effort they put into future tasks. They also have control over the strategy, method or way in which they complete a task. We also need to use praise sparingly and direct it at those who genuinely deserve it.

Grades or no grades?

If giving praise has caused you to have a few conflicting thoughts, giving grades may give you a few more. Praise can be easily be tweaked and adjusted. Grades are more difficult and more contentious.

Before we start, I would like you to answer the following questions as honestly as possible. If you have an answer like "Well it depends", go with the most common thing you do.

When you mark students work, exams or assessments:

1. Do you provide written comments?
2. Do you provide grades or scores with these comments?
3. Do you think it is better to provide comments?
4. Why?
5. Do you think it is better to provide the grades or scores?
6. Why?
7. What is more helpful for students? Just comments, just grades/scores, or a combination of grades and scores?
8. Why?

We'll come back to this these questions in a moment. In the meantime it is worth looking at what grades actually tell us. It seems that our education system has become infatuated by grades and scores. Everything we work towards in schools ends up with students sitting an exam in order to get a grade. There is much to debate about whether this type of system is the best system for education, but that is a whole other book. What is apparent is that grades are prominent in learning. Students want to know them to see where they are at. Parents want to know them to see where their students are at. And schools want to know them for numerous reasons, including where students are at. It therefore feels like we are in a cycle where we need to share grades and scores when we feedback to students. However, as Nuthall (2007, p. 30) discusses, grades aren't actually great at telling us things. If two students get the exact same grade on a test, does this reflect what they know? One student may know lots about the formation of NATO: its membership and purpose but very little about the formation of the Warsaw Pact: membership and purpose. The other student may know these things the other way around. By giving a grade it doesn't address the differences in the students' knowledge – instead it just groups them together and says that they scored the same. Many teachers recognise this and if they have to use grades, do so in a more meaningful way.

So if grades are to stay, we need to be aware how they impact the quality of feedback. Go back to question 7: *What is more helpful for students? Just comments, just grades/scores, or a combination of grades and scores?* Which do you think is better? In (1987) and (1988), Ruth Butler conducted two studies looking at the different types of feedback and their effects on learning. In both studies, unsurprisingly, giving comments as feedback was better than giving grades only or no feedback at all (it raised achievement by around 30 per cent). That makes sense. Grades tell you nothing, no feedback tells you nothing, therefore comments to support learning help you improve. However, what was surprising is that grades combined with comments, which is used quite frequently in schools, actually had the same effect as no feedback or grades alone. This for me was a real eye opener. As Dylan Wiliam (2011, p. 109) summarises, "Far from producing the best effects of both kinds of feedback, giving scores alongside the comments completely washed out the beneficial effects of the comments". So grades can have a huge detrimental effect on the well intentioned feedback we give.

This could link back to the last section on praise. By giving grades are we actually fostering a fixed mindset culture? How many times do we give out grades only for the following thing to happen – students compare grades with their peers. All of a sudden the opportunity for moving forward is restricted as students look for social status. So do we need to give grades or scores immediately? If we're spending time providing both (i.e. comments and grades) in our feedback, is it actually a waste of time? The message I get from this is to stay well clear of grades at the first presentation of feedback to students. All we need to do (as advised by Carless earlier) is ensure that the comments we write are at the correct level and clear enough for our learners.

But students are part of the process as well

No matter how high quality our feedback is, it will have little effect unless students are engaged in the process. We could write the best comments in the world, speak to them at a really engaging level, but if they choose to ignore feedback or fail to act on it, that's an opportunity lost.

In 2012 I conducted a feedback-related survey of students across Year 7 to Year 11. In total I surveyed 100 students, posing questions such as:

- How do you receive feedback in your classes?
- What type of feedback do you receive from your teachers?
- Generally, what is the quality of the feedback that you receive from your peers (friends)?
- What does the feedback you receive usually tell you?
- On average, how frequently do you receive structured feedback? (By structured I mean more than just a quick comment).

- What do you normally do when you receive feedback?

- How could we give you feedback more effectively so you would use it to improve your learning?

Questions were accompanied by a variety of response options. A follow-up interview of a sample of students allowed me to unpick their views in more depth. These aren't the best worded questions and the survey wasn't conducted in a strict research manner, but it did produce some fascinating insights into why students weren't engaging in the feedback process. Comments/criticisms included:

- Emphasis on grades – What we got was more important.
- Unsure of what the feedback meant.
- Fear of failure.
- Lots of feedback must mean my work wasn't good.
- Poor feedback from my peers – It's too general or we just make it up.
- No time for improvement.
- We only get feedback at the end of a topic.
- Too much writing.
- Too much in one go.
- Too long between feedback (One book had a gap of 93 days between any written feedback).
- Prefer verbal feedback.
- Forget verbal feedback.
- No follow up.
- It feels a bit robotic – We all get the same suggestions/comments.
- Let me learn it first – Teacher asks me too soon (although we could work quicker).

Knowledge of this sort enables you to develop more understanding and ultimately better tackle the issues that arise.

Verbal feedback

In my school survey this issue came up a lot. Students commented on how they preferred verbal feedback as it was given specifically to them in a face-to-face situation. Students were able to ask questions and seek clarity if needed. However, many students said that although they liked this, when the teachers moved on to speak to another student they frequently forgot what was said to them. There are other considerations here. Carless (2006, p. 9) indicated that "whilst tutors may view oral comments as feedback, students may not recognise this form of feedback as much as written comments". Maybe what we tell students doesn't sink in because if it isn't on paper students aren't sure if it is simply a conversation or a suggestion. They may miss that it was actually feedback designed to help them improve.

Too much feedback on work = work must be bad

This is a common theme with students. As soon as one student mentioned it, others began agreeing. One student in the survey said, "If there's a lot of writing on my work it must be bad and I therefore don't read it". Students buy into a culture that only poor work receives mass feedback whereas good work receives minimal (sometimes only a grade). Wiliam (2011) discusses a student saying, "When you get a lot of feedback on your work, it means it wasn't very good". She went on to indicate that good work receives a high grade and a little comment like "Good job", whereas less successful work is returned to the students with lots of annotations from the teacher. As Wiliam points out, used in this way "feedback really is punishment" (p. 129). When I tracked back through my books I saw I was guilty of this quite frequently

Peer feedback

A well-known (but hard to find) quote from Graham Nuthall claims that the majority of the feedback that students receive is from their peers, yet most of this is incorrect. At first I didn't believe this and thought that the figure far too high, but observations in the classroom do indicate that students ask each other for help or direction far more than they ask you. The problem as Nuthall points out though is this information is usually wrong. In my survey I found some students gave an answer to their peers just to shut them up. Nuthall is probably highlighting how some students have the best of intentions but still give wrong information. If this is going on, maybe we need to have a rethink about peer feedback.

Robotic feedback

For simple efficiency we teachers usually give out generic feedback statements or comments to groups of learners. If we didn't, we'd be marking and providing feedback for days on end. But students check with each other and if they find that other students have the same worded comments, all of a sudden it becomes impersonal and loses its impact. They think, if we haven't put in the effort, why should they. This is a tricky one: unless we increase our work load (which I don't recommend), is there a way we can tweak this so students do feel it is there to help them?

We don't do anything with the feedback

When I discuss feedback with colleagues and other teachers, I always show them a photo of how good the feedback I am giving is. Teachers read the comments and agree that the feedback is quite helpful. I then show them the photo which has been zoomed out. The gap beside the written feedback reveals that nothing has been acted upon by the student. If it took me two minutes to write that comment, and I did this for 30 books per class, three classes at a time, that's three hours of written comments that haven't been acted upon. Carry that over the year and I would argue I could have been doing something more beneficial. In my own survey I found that feedback was given but there were no opportunities to follow it up. It was there, they read it, but that was it. This completely devalues the effectiveness of such feedback and, over time, students become desensitised to it. Why should they ever read feedback if there is never an opportunity to act on it? It becomes a redundant task. Feedback should be part of the learning process and embedded in a culture of the classroom. If we don't value it, students won't either.

So if there is so much that can go wrong, is it actually worth giving feedback?

If we go back to the quote from Hattie earlier, feedback can have a huge impact on learning gains. The EEF has it as providing eight months' impact if used effectively. If that is correct, it can be a powerful tool. But knowing some of the pitfalls, how should we go about giving feedback? For me, three principles stand out and have transformed how I deliver feedback.

---

1 Feedback must cause thinking

If I had to reduce all of the research on feedback into one simple overarching idea, at least for academic subjects in a school, it would be this; feedback should cause thinking
Wiliam (2011, p. 127)

Nothing I have ever read about feedback has changed my thoughts and beliefs as much as that statement. In fact, I would say that of all of the things I have used to refine my teaching, it would be one of the most valuable. A lot of our comments or feedback can be very passive. "Well done, I like the way you included a diagram to support your explanation" rewards something that a student did, but it isn't challenging the student to make improvements. It isn't adding anything to the learning process. And isn't that what feedback is supposed to do? Offer suggestions in a challenging way that make students improve?

Maybe the word feedback itself is to blame. Maybe the fact we are looking *back* is the problem? Over the years I have heard, and even advocated, adapting it to *feedforward*.

This at least gets you to think about providing comments to look ahead. Unfortunately, habits are hard to break.

Feedback needs to help students see what they have done well, what misconceptions have cropped up and how they could make improvements to drive learning forward. It needs to direct student's attention to the areas that they need to develop. After this, it needs to make them think: as already discussed, if students have to think about something really hard, there is a better chance of it sticking in the long run. Feedback should take note of this.

But I thought that's what my feedback did anyway

And so did I. I really thought in the early days of my career that my feedback was alright. It was a pain to produce but it pointed out things students needed to do. The issue was that there was no thinking required by the students. My stock feedback comments always included "Make sure you . . ." and then usually ended up with me telling them exactly what they did wrong. Students would read them, think, "OK, I'll do that" and believe that their learning had been improved. Unfortunately, in the next piece of work, assessment or test, the same mistake would crop up again. So how can you ensure your feedback actually causes thinking? The main thing is to keep it simple. Anything too complicated will either become confusing or increase your workload.

Mark in class with the students

Hannah Bushnell, an English teacher from Southampton, made me feel completely stupid when she suggested I mark in class with students. How obvious! What Hannah suggested was to go around the class and check work at random. You won't be able to get around everyone in a lesson but you can at least work with a number of students who may need it. As you read over their work, you simply acknowledge the good bits (a tick or a code which I will discuss later) and then provide a prompt question, which they need to respond to, or underline an error that they have to work out and correct. You then move on to check other students' work and do the same. After a while, revisit the students you have spoken to and have that discussion with them. See if they now understand. See if their work has improved. Challenge them on the spot and decide whether they need more feedback or more instruction. Make them think. Rather than leave it and allow misconceptions to develop, marking in class with students can be extremely helpful. And the best part of it is you can engage with them and respond with further questions, discussions or clarifications. One simple strategy can open up a whole avenue into their learning.

Show call

This technique comes from Doug Lemov (2015, p. 290). After reading an amazing blog post by headteacher John Tomsett (2015), I decided to invest in a visualiser/camera to demonstrate my thought process with exam structure. The process of metacognition was powerful and really let me scrutinise what questions meant, what

I would personally focus on and how I would go about answering it. The visualiser revolutionised my teaching. However, it wasn't until I came across the technique "Show Call" that I really considered how I could use this piece of equipment to enhance my feedback.

In the technique, a teacher assigns a task for students to complete. They work the room and look over what students have written. They then select a piece of student work at random and display it under the visualiser. Already I can hear some of you thinking "What, they just put any kid's work up onto a big screen. My students would hate that!" I had similar concerns. However, once the work is under the visualiser, the teacher can pose a number of questions to the class to demonstrate technique, structure or content.

With this process, you can allow students the opportunity to discuss the work and talk about its strengths of it and how to improve it. You can discuss good habits that you want all the class to pick up and highlight mistakes that might have been evident in other students' work as well. By correcting it as a class, involving as many students' thoughts as possible and using skilful questioning, you can provide whole class feedback that really works. Students then simply redraft their own work based on the points and suggestions that were discussed. It challenges them and gets them thinking about how to improve.

Feedback questions

My favourite method of all came through simply tweaking what I wrote on students' work. Previously, similar to what I had seen others do, I provided comments like the following:

"I like how you have explained how forces on a floating object allow it to float. Next time ensure you use the term upthrust and include the value (N) in your answers"

"Great explanation of the Khalsa but next time you should use more examples of the 5Ks"

On the face of it, there's nothing wrong with this sort of feedback.

But of course, both pieces of feedback are simply offering a form of praise and then telling students what they need to do next time. It's telling them what to include and where to put it. And that is the issue – the simply telling. How much cognitive thought will the student have to use? Probably not much. So how would you reword the two pieces of feedback here to make them think?

One way is to turn feedback into a question. By simply adjusting the language we use we can engage student more cognitively. Instead of telling students that they need to use the term upthrust in their answer, you could ask:

"What is upthrust and how does it help an object float in water?"

This simple adaptation requires the student to think about a concept that they have not talked about. And using this technique is really simple. When marking work, if you notice that there is a piece of information missing or an incorrect statement, simply put a number next to it in the margin. At the end of the work pose a question related to that section. When students read their feedback they are forced to think about what was missing, what might be the correct response and then in a gap provided, answer the feedback question. The feedback has prompted both thinking and action.

There are downsides with this, though. First, remember that if a student demonstrates that they have no understanding of the topic, no feedback question will help them. In that situation the student will require further instruction. Make a note of who to chat to next lesson and do it. Second, writing these questions does take time, even though you only need to write one or two per book. The flip side is that if you were going to write a comment anyway, it's not a lot of work to change it from a statement to a more productive question.

Equal challenge

As we saw earlier, students can equate lots of feedback to poor work. Even if this is not the case, when one student has a lot of feedback and another doesn't, it is assumed by the former that their work must have been rubbish. If it wasn't, why have they got lots of teacher scribbles over it? One way is to ensure that every student gets the same amount of feedback. For example, if we use feedback questions, then ensure that every student, no matter what standard of the work, gets two questions. By doing this every student is on the same playing field. But what if students work is excellent? What if they have answered the question really well?

In this case it is important to remember that everything can be improved or stretched. But how? There are a number of ways to ensure your feedback gets even the most able students (I hate that term!) thinking.

1. Ask them to think about subject specific terminology and accuracy of definitions – Have they used the correct technical terms? Have they ensured that definitions are word perfect? If not, ask them to make their answer better by refining the two.

2. Ask them to think about structure – Is the sentence they used structured in the correct format? Does it follow a framework that would make the answer more academic? Have they included all of the components of an exceptional answer?

3. Ask them to remove redundant words – A tip from a journalist I once worked with was to refine sentences down to the most clear and informative format they could possibly be. Her advice was to remove excess "it, that, but, and ..." and try and use one word that could express the same as what you have written in five or six.

4. Link in other topics – Having the SOLO taxonomy in the back of my head has been really helpful here. The highest level asks students to think of a topic in an abstract or extended way. Although not exactly how it was probably intended, I always think about posing feedback that asks them to bring it other topics. So for instance, in a piece of work looking at weight training, I may ask students a question on how diet, or the principles of training, or gender or physique might influence how they

train. This is forcing them to recall prior knowledge and explain the relationship between numerous topics.

5. Ask them to use the concept in another context – Can this answer be applied in another topic, example or situation?

6. Ask them "What would happen if . . . ?" – The best example I have seen of this is when a teacher was explaining what happens when volcanoes produced lava (it cooled and formed more rock). They then asked "But what would happen if water erupted from it?" Students may then talk about erosion. Twisting the concept makes students think hard.

7. Ask them the next level up – I have heard a number of GCSE teachers say that at times, when applicable, they reword feedback to include some A level content for those who have done really well. Instead of saying "Well done. Great work", they push them further with even more challenging feedback.

All these suggestions ensure that even those who have completed work to a high standard are still forced to think when receiving feedback like their peers.

Target feedback

In 2016 I had a SCITT trainee called Josh Chandler teach some of my Year 8 science classes. Like many trainee teachers, he was very receptive to advice and ideas for getting better. One of the things he really developed was the way he gave feedback. Simply through discussing this overarching principle that feedback should cause thinking, he tweaked his practice to do just that. Josh used something probably well known to many of you in the form of targets and colour codes. Such a simple idea had every student working their socks off once they got their books back.

Josh knew what some of the common pitfalls would be in a topic and had prepared target questions ready to be used in the follow up lesson. As he marked books, he either put a T1 (target 1) or a coloured dot next to an incorrect section of their work. Each colour or target code linked to a question which Josh displayed on the board. As students looked over their books, they would read the section the code was next to, read the relevant target question on the board and then answer it in their books. Similar to feedback questions, the feedback made them think and produce an adapted answer linked to the error. What is different though is the fact that this process was quick for Josh to complete and didn't add to his workload compared to writing comments in each book. See Figure 4.1.

All of these methods force students to think hard about what they have produced. By engaging them cognitively in the process of feedback we stand a greater chance of embedding it in their memory. By making students think we are also changing the feedback from looking at was has been, to what could be. It aims to move learning forward. The question we need to ask ourselves is, does the feedback we give do anything? This leads me to my second principle, based on the work from Sadler (1989).

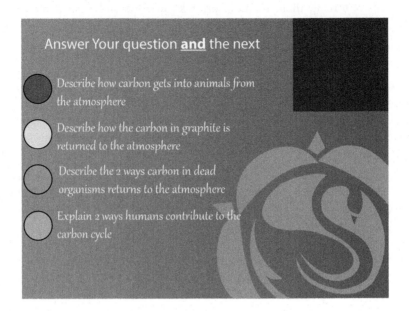

Figure 4.1 Target Feedback

> **2** Feedback aims to reduce the gap between where the student is and where he or she is meant to be

Every student we teach is unique, with a particular level of ability. When we give feedback we usually write comments or make judgements on quality based on two things: what we would expect of this student based on their ability and what we expect of this student's work compared to an exemplar. For instance, when we work with a student of low ability, although we want them to achieve as much as they can, we sometimes think something along the lines of, "Well, for Tim this is actually pretty good". On the other hand, we might say, "This is nowhere near the example that I showed the class". Either way, right or wrong, we are comparing the work of a student against something. If the work doesn't meet our expectation, a gap is formed. The role of a teacher and the feedback they give must aim to close this gap.

But how can my feedback close the gap?

As already discussed, one way is to ensure that feedback causes thinking and therefore learning. The way we structure feedback is also important. As Hattie and Timperley (2007, p. 88) advise, to close this gap teachers and students need to be thinking: Where am I going? How am I going? And Where to next? If our feedback follows this rule of thumb, and includes the previous principle as well, it stands a good chance of moving learning forward.

Another important role of feedback is to develop self-regulation. When we provide feedback that does this and students begin to develop the knowledge to do something with it, they can begin to monitor whether they are closing gaps themselves. Part of this comes from how much content knowledge students have. The more they know the better they will be at analysing how well they are doing. Driving content knowledge in lessons is therefore a fundamental principle. So what feedback strategies might help us support students in closing the gap? Well, the first has to come through your initial lesson planning.

Challenge students

Many researchers, educators and authors have stressed the fact that feedback is only beneficial when the task is challenging. If the task is too easy, feedback isn't helpful. So as teachers we need to know our classes and use our experience to pitch the challenge of our lessons accurately. We need, as accurately as possible, to design lessons that push their learning. We then need to take the advice of Damian Benney, a deputy head-teacher from Penyrheol, when he told me that

> The key is to set tasks that are worth reading/assessing/marking (delete as appropriate). Tasks have to be designed that, as far as possible, unpick how a student thinks about a topic. These are worth the time. These tasks go "fishing for gaps" and will identify where students have misconceptions, errors or omissions.

Crafting these types of task require subject knowledge and experience. Getting a student to simply shoot from close range in an unopposed goal isn't challenging for an experienced footballer. The feedback I get when they score won't tell me anything. However, make it competitive by adding defenders, a reduced playing area and some conditions, and all of a sudden I begin to find out a bit more about what the student can do. Then I can look at the feedback I give to move that performance forward. When you design your next lesson, think about what it is you want students to learn. Then begin to decide what tasks will challenge students and get them thinking hard. Only when this happen will the true gaps become apparent.

Use models, WAGOLLS and examples of excellence (bring in Berger!)

One of the most transformational books I ever read is An Ethic of Excellence by Ron Berger (2003). The book highlights that maybe we don't aspire to have our students create exceptional work as much as we could do or even think we do. In his story, Ron demonstrates how his classes produce work which is years beyond what we would expect. To get to this level Ron talks about how he uses models, or as I explain them, examples of excellence. These models act as exemplars of what exceptional work in particular fields looks like. By showing students high-quality models, students know what is expected and can "carry around pictures in their head of quality work" (p. 83).

This is extremely powerful when trying to close gaps with feedback. As Sadler (1989, p. 121) explains, "the learner has to (a) possess a concept of the standard (or goal, or reference level) being aimed for, (b) compare the actual (or current) level of performance with the standard, and (c) engage in appropriate action which leads to some closure of the gap".

Models and examples of excellence can come in many forms. Many individuals keep copies of student work which has been produced to the highest standard. Art, for example, is a subject whose walls and cupboards are a treasure chest to help inspire students. Many teachers write their own examples of excellence to demonstrate what is required. And then there are examples from the greats within our subject domain. Authors, writers and musicians whose work we can turn to in order to show students what we are aiming at. When pieces of work or drafts are completed, we can compare the students work against the example and identify the gap. What is even more powerful about using models is that this gap can be self-monitored by students. By having a clear understanding of the goal, the students can f evaluate where they are in the process. And we have the foundation of a conversation revolving around where they are, where we are aiming to get to, and what steps they need to take.

I was recently introduced to a term I had never heard of before: WAGOLL. WAGOLL stands for What A Good One Looks Like. A WAGOLL, like the models and examples of excellence discussed earlier, allow teachers to show students what high quality work looks like. Once again, these allow students the opportunity to see and understand what is required from their work. The beauty of WAGOLLs is they can be constructed in many ways, from the teacher writing one themselves to ones that are either co-constructed with students or made up of the student's own work. You can refer back to the WAGOLL in your verbal or written comments, drawing attention to areas where students have worked well or where they may need some more direction. The WAGOLL makes it transparent, accessible and directed. As physics teacher Wendy Daly explains:

> WAGOLLs can be used successfully in all types of lessons and as part of the marking and feedback process. Dylan Wiliam in his work on the importance of formative assessment is a proponent of reviewing work well before the end point so that mistakes and misconceptions can be highlighted early on and intervention put in place to "plug the gaps".

The WAGOLL can be given out three quarters of the way through a lesson and the students use it to go back over their work, refining and correcting. The teacher can circulate and make note of any key omissions or misconceptions. These can then be highlighted to the whole group, while the subject content is still fresh. If different pupils have been working on different pieces of work it will be necessary to produce different WAGOLLs.

When the books are marked, the teacher only has to check the quality of the use of the WAGOLL as the work has already been carefully marked.

Hinge questions/diagnostic questions

You can't close gaps if you aren't aware of them appearing in the first place. One way to identify them live in your lessons is through hinge/diagnostic questions.

I talk more about hinge and diagnostic questions in Chapter 3. Briefly, they are questions which allow the teacher to get a response from every student and assess whether we can move on. Readers of the work of Robert Bjork or even Rob Coe may now be screaming that what we see in lessons is performance, not learning. They may well be correct. If I tell a student that the nutrient that aids growth and repair is protein, asking them what nutrient aids growth and repair five minutes later doesn't tell me they've learnt it. However, in a lesson we need to be able to assess what gaps there may be. Well-designed hinge questions do help in this area. After teaching a difficult concept, pose a question with multiple choice answers before you move on. Answers are numbered one to five and students raise their hand, displaying the relevant number of fingers when asked. By scanning the answers you can get insight into which students might have got it and which ones might not. The question itself has to be worthwhile. For example: Who was Chelsea's Goalkeeper in the 1994 FA cup final?

1. Frode Grodas
2. Dimitri Kharine
3. Ed de Goey
4. Dave Beasant
5. I don't know

This requires some subject knowledge and is therefore challenging. The answer you give will thus provide some feedback on whether you knew it or not. However, if I asked it the following way, you would get less useful feedback:

1. Tom Hanks
2. Dimitri Kharine
3. Hampshire
4. The Coliseum
5. I don't know

These types of question don't have to be factual. They can also look at skills or processes as well – for example, where an apostrophe needs to go in a specific sentence – option a, b, c or d. If there are numerous incorrect responses, then you can go back and reteach the section again. If there are one or two incorrect responses, you can then close the gap with just those individuals.

Talk to your students

Verbal feedback should never be underestimated. We talk to our students all of the time in lessons and what we say is extremely valuable to them. My student survey showed that students liked verbal feedback and David Carless warned that our written comments can be confusing. I would urge you to go and see any PE, drama, dance, art or music teacher in your school. These teachers give verbal feedback all the time. They aim to get round to as many individuals as possible, unpicking with them how they can get better. Talking to students allows you to really identify the gaps in knowledge and have that discussion about how to move forward. You can ask them to summarise how they're doing and what are they finding difficult and explain what they've learnt. You can instantly engage with further probing or stretch questions. You can make feedback bespoke and use language that is clear. It is a powerful but undervalued part of the feedback process. For some, if it isn't evidenced, it's not important. This has led to the dreaded "verbal feedback given" stamp. My advice is to refine how you give verbal feedback: make it a priority and plan how to make it better. And bin those stamps!

Dirt

Whenever I speak to people about feedback, I show them a photo of one of my students' books. They look over my comments and say that the feedback seems really good. What they fail to see is that nothing has been done with my feedback. There is no follow up from the student at all: I might as well have not bothered. If we are to close gaps, we need to ensure that our feedback is acted upon. We need to make it so important that they can't help but interact with it.

One way of doing this is through DIRT time. This has numerous meanings but the one I stick to is Dedicated Improvement and Reflection Time. If students don't independently act upon feedback, we need to find time for them to. At its simplest, DIRT involves setting aside ten minutes at the start of any lesson that follows marking/feedback. By doing this we are telling students, "I have written something important in your book. So important that I feel it will move your learning forward a great deal. Something so important I want you to read it and act on it now".

Some teachers say: "If we spend ten minutes a lesson acting upon feedback we'll never get the content covered". I totally get this. When time is limited and pressures build upon us, lessons become very precious. However, if a student builds a misconception in topic A, then another in B, C, D and so on, they could walk into Year 11 with a number of errors that are so engrained it will take a lot of both time and effort to undo them. It's better to nip things in the bud before they root in. And ask yourself why you bother giving feedback if students don't do anything with it.

I will give a few more ideas in Principle 3, but in essence DIRT involves the following procedure. Once books are marked and a method of feedback given, hand them back to the class. Instruct students to read their feedback, answer any targets/feedback questions, or even redraft a part of their answer. This frees you up to intervene with those who need it and push on those who are ready to move on. Every student receives the same quantity of feedback, given in a way that causes thinking and closes gaps. Any feedback not answered can be returned to or set as homework. Emphasise the point that they can't leave it – feedback must be acted upon. Some teachers encourage students to use a different colour pen in DIRT so it makes it apparent, and maybe easier for you, to see who has done what was asked.

The beauty of DIRT is that it is simple – like many of these ideas. But all of them stretch and challenge as well as support and guide, and all involve student engagement. In an ideal world, they shouldn't add to our workload but aim to follow my third principle, inspired again by Dylan Wiliam.

---

3 Feedback should be more work for the recipient than the donor

---

If we aren't careful, myths, whisperers and good intentions can see our marking and feedback policies become a multi-page document with numerous appendices. If this is happening, something has gone completely wrong. The strategies we are asked to do also need to ensure our workload isn't doubled or even tripled. The key is that the people who need to do the most work in this system are not the teachers but the students. It is their education, their learning, so we need to devise methods that require them to take the action.

Before we start I need to clarify the word "work". Poor feedback practice over the years has seen teachers simply give more work as a means of feedback. But, as we know, that is an extension task, not feedback. What I mean is that the balance between teacher and student needs to be adjusted so that it is the student who is putting in more effort. And as teachers' time is precious, I will not labour the point, but instead go straight into some strategies we could all implement.

Proofread

How many of you, when you read a set of books, see numerous silly mistakes and misconceptions? Things you know students know. We can find ourselves screaming into an empty room. The errors are so obvious. Things that students would notice if they had two minutes to check.

So why not make time at the end of a lesson for students to check their writing *before* they hand it in? The proofreading can be as directed as you feel is necessary. If you've noticed a number of similar errors appearing when you were chatting to students in your lesson, ask them all to make sure they haven't done the same. If you are having a push on spelling, grammar and definitions, ask them to spend the time looking at these things in particular. Not only does this reduce your workload, it also teaches students the value of checking their work. It teaches them self-regulation. It reinforces skills. Don't make it a bolt-on. Make it a valued and important part of your lesson. See Figure 4.2.

Proof reading:

Books are going to be collected today for marking. You have 5 minutes to do the following.

1. Check that your work is presentable. If it is not, rewrite it now.
2. Check for spelling and grammar errors.
3. Check that your definitions are accurate.
4. Check that you have answered/completed the work you were set. If you haven't, complete it now.

Figure 4.2 Proofreading Protocol

Burning questions

Involving students in their own learning is extremely important. Burning questions involves students using their gut feeling and instincts. It asks them to read through their work and highlight an area that they feel least confident in and would like you to scrutinise. For instance, if a student felt that their answer to a question on a particular topic was weak or had gone off on a tangent, they would use a highlighter to indicate the section where they would like your advice. When they hand it in, you can use marking codes on the majority of their work and devote more time to the area they have suggested needs more support.

Marking codes

Marking codes are nothing new but their simplicity should make them something we embrace more than we do at present. They allow us to read pieces of work and quickly annotate, along the margin, areas where there are good elements (to reinforce as a habit) and areas needing attention. They aim to be more informative than simple flick and tick. Marking codes at their simplest just point out what is wrong. A "Gr" code indicates that there was an error in grammar. A "Dev" may indicate the student has used a developed statement that would access them higher grades. But marking codes could act more like feedback questions.

Many years ago we implemented a marking code system in our department. It was simply to help us pick out errors in student work. It was quicker than extensive comments and corrections, but ultimately students would look at it for a few seconds and then they were done. There was still more effort put in by the donor than the recipient. A few years later I began asking whether these comments could shift from pointing things out to making students think. Experienced teachers might say here that will it's what you do with the codes that counts. Follow it up with DIRT time and problem solved. Maybe. But in students' eyes, some codes aren't that important and don't require much work. A simple code to point out a spelling is wrong may require them to write the word out three times but that is it. Could codes provide a more cognitive challenge? Indeed they can. See Table 4.2.

Table 4.2

	Answer meets the required standard. You would get full marks.
	Answer is outstanding and includes additional content, terminology and structure. Answer is more than marks expected. Identify why your answer is so good.
TV	Answer is too vague. It is on the right track but is missing a key explanation, definition, key word or example. Rewrite it.
RTQ	Your answer is not what the question was asking. Please read it again and answer it.
TECH	Your answer is missing the technical terminology required in GCSE PE. Please improve your answer using specific terminology.
SPaG	Your answer includes incorrect spellings and grammar. Please identify them and correct them.
PR	Presentation is below expected standard. Rewrite your answer again using a title, clear handwriting, correct pen colour etc.
RW	You are using too many words to explain your answer. Remove any redundant words and make it more concise.

The codes here can be shared with all students, stuck inside the front of books and become the first port of call in DIRT time. A RTQ (Read The Question) directs students to the fact that they had misread the question. If they get this code they would need to scrutinise the question once more, reread their answer and compare the two. They then need to give it another go. A code of RW means they have done what is commonly known as "waffle on". They need to check their answer again, remove Redundant Words and rewrite it in a more succinct way. TECH highlights the importance of academic language and asks students to add specific terminology to their answer. Each code is designed to inform and then transform. Codes become more than a tool for marking and instead a time-efficient way of pushing students on.

Dot marking

When teachers spot an error, there is the reflex to rectify it. Then we mark their books a few weeks later and see the same error again. But if we've done the correction for them, what have they actually learnt? An easy way to overcome this is dot marking. Simply seek out errors in students work as usual. Instead of correcting it, leave a dot in the margin adjacent to the line the error is on. When you hand it back, students have to work out where the error is. Once they have spotted it, they must correct it. If they can't spot it, that is when you intervene.

Whole class marking

There is an understanding that although whole class feedback is easy to give, its effectiveness is not that great. Unless we are really specific, many students won't be aware if the feedback we give to the whole group is directed at them or not. If they don't believe it is, they probably switch off

In 2016, I visited Michaela School in London. One of the reasons for the visit was to observe the way they marked. Part of the school's innovative drive was to make workload more manageable for teachers. This included how they tackled marking and feedback.

At Michaela I spoke to English teacher Jo Facer. Jo explained a way of speeding up marking while also making more beneficial to her classes. Jo checks books regularly. Instead of annotating every single book, writing comments and questions followed up with targets and DIRT, Jo simply keeps a record of things that appear in every book. Armed with nothing more than notepaper, Jo reads each book and make notes on things that were coming up. She keeps track of excellent answers – writing down the names of students who had produced some. She makes a note of spelling errors that repeatedly crop up. She then writes down areas that as a class went well and what she needs to readdress next lesson due to misconceptions. On average it takes her around 30 minutes to mark 60 books. You may be asking what students do with a book with no comments in it. Where is the thinking? How is this closing the gap? What happens next is where the process really comes alive. See Table 4.3.

Table 4.3 An adapted version of the feedback sheet

Who has produced good work? – **House Points.**	What questions were answered well? – Who?	Who do I need to speak to personally? Why?	Poor spelling and definitions:

What were the areas of weakness? Why? How will I reteach this next lesson?

Jo dedicates a chunk of the next lesson to this feedback. Her notes have become her lesson plan. Jo uses the visualiser to go through each section and distributes a green pen to each individual. As she goes through the corrections, the students annotate them in their own work. Jo gives them time to amend any misspellings and errors. She guides them through incorrect content and uses the students work as models. After watching her class for ten minutes, the students' books are covered in improvements, all skilfully guided by Jo. By leading corrections from the front with the camera, the teacher is able to question, support, stretch and challenge as she goes through it. She can ask for opinions and advice. It ties in very closely to Doug Lemov's "show call", which was mentioned earlier. But what about those who didn't have any errors? As the teacher you will have observed that when you checked them. This whole process becomes over-learning and reinforces content so students have a stronger grasp. The teacher can also skilfully target those individuals during the process and push them on. It becomes bespoke and responsive. As geography teacher Calum Lacey explains, the technique can make a huge difference to teachers as well:

The impact has been, to say the least, dramatic. The time it takes for me to properly mark a set of GCSE books has been slashed from many, many hours (granted, I was a slow marker) to less than an hour. The best I've managed is about 35 minutes for a 26-strong class. I no longer dread needing to mark books and I'm terrified to admit there's a part of me that almost enjoys it now. It can be done easily while doing other things to relax, it increases pupil accountability, encourages a growth mindset in my classes and also allows pupils to easily show rapid and very effective, lasting progress. It's effective, sustainable and has had only positive impacts on my classes.

To recap

- Feedback should cause thinking.
- Feedback aims to reduce the gap between where the student is and where he or she is meant to be.
- Feedback should be more work for the recipient than the donor.

References

Berger, R. (2003) *An Ethic of Excellence; Building a Culture of Craftsmanship with Students.* Portsmouth, NH: Heinemann.

Butler, A. C., Karpicke, J. D., & Roediger III, H. L. (2007) The effect of type and timing of feedback on learning from multiple-choice tests. *Journal of Experimental Psychology: Applied.* 13 (4). pp. 273–281.

Butler, R. (1987) Task-involving and ego-involving properties of evaluation: Effects of different feedback conditions on motivational perceptions, interest and performance. *Journal of Educational Psychology.* 79. pp. 474–482.

Butler, R. (1988) Enhancing and undermining intrinsic motivation: The effects of task involving and ego-involving evaluation on interest and performance. *British Journal of Educational Psychology*. 58. pp. 1–14.

Carless, D. (2006) Differing perceptions in the feedback process. *Studies in Higher Education*. 31(2). pp. 219–233.

Didau, D. (2015) *What if Everything You Knew about Education Was Wrong?* Carmarthen, Wales: Crown House Publishing.

Dweck, C. (2006) *Mindset: The New Psychology of Success*. New York: Random House Publishing Group.

Education Endowment Foundation (EEF) (2018) *Feedback*. Available at: https://educationendowmentfoundation.org.uk/pdf/generate/?u=https://educationendowmentfoundation.org.uk/pdf/toolkit/?id=131&t=Teaching%20and%20Learning%20Toolkit&e=131&s=

Hattie, J. (2012) *Visible Learning for Teachers. Maximising Impact on Learning*. Abingdon: Routledge.

Hattie, J., & Timperley, H. (2007) The power of feedback. *Review of Educational Research*. 77(1). pp. 81–112.

Hattie, J., & Yates, G. (2014a) *Visible Learning and the Science of How We Learn*. Abingdon: Routledge.

Hattie, J., & Yates, G. (2014b) Using feedback to promote learning. In: Benassi, V. A., Overson, C. E., & Hakala, C. M. (Eds) *Applying Science of Learning in Education: Infusing Psychological Science into the Curriculum*. Retrieved from the Society for the Teaching of Psychology web site: http://teachpsych.org/ebooks/asle2014/index.php

Hays, M. J., Kornell, N., & Bjork, R. (2010) The costs and benefits of providing feedback during learning. *Psychonomic Bulletin & Review*. 17(6). pp. 797–801.

Lemov, D. (2015) *Teach like a Champion 2.0: 62 Techniques that Put Students on the Path to College*. San Francisco, CA: Jossey-Bass.

Lipnevich, A., & Smith, J. (2008) *Response to Assessment Feedback: The Effects of Grades, Praise, and Source of Information*. Princeton, NJ: Educational Testing Service.

Nuthall, G. (2007) *The Hidden Lives of Learners*. Wellington: NZCER Press.

Ofsted (2014) Ofsted inspections – Clarification for further education and skills providers. Available at: https://assets.publishing.service.gov.uk/government/uploads/system/uploads/attachment_data/file/457350/Ofsted_20inspections_20_E2_80_93_20clarification_20for_20further_20education_20and_20skills_20providers.pdf

Oxford Dictionary – English Oxford Living Dictionary https://en.oxforddictionaries.com/definition/feedback

Pashler, H., Cepeda, N. J., Wixted, J. T., & Rohrer, D. (2005) When does feedback facilitate learning of words? *Journal of Experimental Psychology: Learning, Memory, and Cognition*. 31. pp. 3–8.

Sadler, D. R. (1989) Formative assessment and the design of instructional systems. *Instructional Science*. 18(2). pp. 119–144.

Tomsett, J. (2015) This much I know about . . . what REALLY WORKS when preparing students for their examinations! In: *johntomsett.com*. 24th April, 2015. https://johntomsett.com/2015/04/24/this-much-i-know-about-what-really-works-when-preparing-students-for-their-examinations/

Wiliam, D. (2011) *Embedded Formative Assessment*. Bloomington, IN: Solution Tree Press.

Willingham, D. T. (2009) *Why Don't Students like School? A Cognitive Scientist Answers Questions about How the Mind Works and What It Means for the Classroom*. San Francisco, CA: Jossey-Bass.

Differentiation

Isn't that just making 30 worksheets for my 30 students?

Reflecting on how I nearly drowned in the well-intentioned idea of differentiation

I have to admit that once in a while an idea or initiative in teaching simply passes me by. Or I get told about an idea that I think can't be that complicated but actually is. Or an idea that seems so well intentioned that I need to do it however difficult it may be to implement. For me all those issues came with differentiation.

On the face of it, differentiation seems so obvious. Every student we teach is different. Every student has different learning needs. Every student has a different level of topic knowledge. Teachers need to ensure that every lesson caters for them all. So, I adopt the mantra of "No child left behind" and furiously begin designing lesson plans that help Stephen who is a low-level reader, Jasmine who is one of the school's gifted and talented students, Gavin who is a level four boy who struggles to engage in lessons. The potential number of combinations of so many variations is vast. No matter though, differentiation makes sense so I persevere.

After a while I find myself producing 30 different worksheets for the 30 different students in my class. I plan to vary the lesson due to preferred learning styles and bring in different types of questions and feedback for them all. I plan groupings that change with each activity so that students are supported where needed. And as I stand in the middle of this differentiated haven of greatness, I realise I haven't a clue what the hell is going on in my lesson (which took me hours to plan). What is wrong with me!

Before you start screaming, "Dave, you've got it all wrong – that's not what differentiation is", I have to say I eventually I asked myself, "But what is it then?"

I guess at its simplest it is about ensuring that we tailor our lessons to meet the individual's needs. We adapt our plans to help students have the best chance of learning. We amend what we do to ensure that everyone can access our lessons. And if we keep it that simple it can be manageable.

Unfortunately, I became influenced by the good intentions, the myths and the Ofsted Whisperers again. Although I was never directly told I had to differentiate lessons the way I did, it had grown and saw me trying to do the impossible: differentiate for every student, in every lesson, every day. If I didn't, I'd worry that other teachers were or that I was letting students down. You become your own worst enemy.

Unfortunately, when this happens we look around at what others are doing. Once again, we adopt ideas and magpie resources and make our lessons more and more complicated without really understanding why we're doing it. The guilt of missing out a child or having an observer question the way in which you are supporting particular groups can be stressful. I remember getting feedback from observations that said I could have done more to support student x when I felt I was doing loads already. How much more could I give? Differentiation had become completely unmanageable. Every student is different and, noble as it is to try and cater for every single difference, sometimes we just can't. It is a huge problem.

So what changed? Surely we need to try and plan for every child?

Yes, but not at the expense of everything else. I had to face up to the realisation that trying to work the way I was increasing workload. There was also the fact that I never knew if what I was doing was actually making any difference. What would have happened if I hadn't designed the resources or differentiated my objectives? Could I have spent my time better on other things?

Secondly, I realised that schools can be guilty of looking at differentiation the wrong way round. If I asked you to list the numerous ways you've differentiated (good or bad), a few of the following might well come up:

- Setting classes to help differentiate.
- Having differentiated learning objectives (Must, could, should/All, some, few).
- Differentiated worksheets – ones for more able, ones for less able.
- Easier tests for less able, harder ones for more able.
- Labelling students as less able/more able – in your planning, not to their face.
- Task selection based on difficulty where students choose what level they want to work at.
- Creating tasks relating to grades which certain students work on – this is an A* task, this is an A task, this is a B task . . .
- Having success criteria for different groups of students – this is what the high achievers need to do, this is what the middle need to do, this is what the low achievers need to do.

These are exactly things that I was taught to do during teacher training, CPD sessions and conferences in my early days. On the surface they don't look like bad things. Yet I wonder if you might see the common theme? Or what these types of strategy might do

These strategies all lower the bar of expectations. *What, huh? How is that??* The eight strategies listed in this chapter rightly identify that students are different. They also group students into categories or allow students to do that themselves. But all of them send the message that some students don't have to do some of the tasks (normally the more able have to do the most, the less able the least). The worst example of this is the dreaded "Must, should, could" or "All, some, few" objectives, which I still see being used today. Having these in lessons tells students that once they have completed the *must* or *all* they can sit back and relax. You said that this is all I need to (or must) do so there you have it.

There are newer versions of this sort of thinking, such as chilli levels, which a head of geography, Mark Esner, explains:

> When I trained to teach and started teaching we were required to provide differentiated learning objectives where we would say what all pupils would achieve, what most pupils would achieve and what some pupils would achieve. This always struck me as a way of ingraining low expectations and an admission of failure. I would always rather look for ways to support pupils to ensure that they all learnt what they need to learn.
>
> This problem reached its apotheosis with the rise of tasks given "chili levels" and pupils encouraged to choose a level of difficulty that met their perceived needs. A one chilli task was easier than a two or three chilli task. The big problem with this approach is that it ignores the source of complexity (what actually needs to be learnt) and focuses instead on the activity that pupils are completing. If the "easy" activity means that pupils learn what they need to learn then why are we suggesting some pupils do something more difficult? If the easy activity doesn't mean they learn it, then why is anyone doing it?
>
> This kind of backwards thinking arises when teachers are planning lessons to please observers rather than to help their pupils. Differentiation by task needs to be replaced by differentiation by support and this needs careful, nuanced, planning based on a teacher's knowledge of their classes rather than gimmicks.

Part of the problem here is that we label our students. Why do we believe that some students *must* whereas others *could*? We can be guilty of calling some students "More able" and others "Less able". And we then have different expectations of them. This may seem valid but it doesn't always lead to the best outcomes.

A story of Pygmalion, Matthew and the Golem

A character in a well-known Greek myth, Pygmalion was a Cypriot sculptor who fell in love with a statue he carved. Pygmalion made an offering to Aphrodite to persuade her to grant his wish to have a bride who would be the living likeness of his "ivory girl". When he returned home and kissed the statue, it felt warm and began to lose its hardness. It eventually morphed into a woman who Pygmalion married. The message behind the myth is that if we want something enough, we'll get it. But what has this got to do with schools?

Robert Rosenthal and Lenore Jacobson (1968) conducted an experiment that linked very closely to this and resulted in what in now known as the Pygmalion Effect. Rosenthal gave all the students at Jacobson's elementary school a disguised IQ test. The scores from these tests were not shared with teachers but Rosenthal gave them the names of students who, based on the tests results, could be expected to be "intellectual bloomers" in that academic year. These students made up about 20 per cent of the cohort in the school, but they weren't actually picked as a result of the test, they were picked purely at random.

Unaware that these students weren't really "intellectual bloomers", the teachers taught them throughout the year. At the end of the year, Rosenthal retested the students with the same IQ test. All the students showed a mean gain in the test, but the experimental group (the "late bloomers") in the first and second grade showed significant gains compared to their classmates (first grade improved 15.4 IQ points compared to the control group, and second grade improved 9.5 IQ points compared to the control group). As I explained earlier, these students were chosen at random, yet they improved more than their peers. Why?

The result can be seen as a self-fulfilling prophecy: if we increase our expectations of students, they will respond. Teachers may have subconsciously changed the way they behaved towards the so-called "intellectual bloomers". In the Heroic Imagination Project video (2011), Rosenthal identified four possible elements of this:

1. Classroom climate – There may have been a warmer climate towards those the teachers had higher expectations for. The students might have felt more supported and valued. The teachers may have been kinder or more supportive towards the "intellectual bloomers".

2. Input factor – The teachers may have taught more content to those who they have more favourable expectations. They've been labelled as bloomers so we stretch and challenge them more. We teach them more in our lessons.

3. Response opportunity – Those who teachers have higher expectations for have more chance to respond in lessons. Teachers call on them more often. They let them talk for longer and help shape their responses.

4. Feedback – If more is expected of a student, they are praised more. They receive more positive reinforcement. These students are given more differentiated feedback when they get an answer wrong.

It is worth noting that the biggest effects were with the lowest year groups (the fourth graders were the only other ones who showed improvements in the IQ tests for the "intellectual bloomers"; the rest were similar in both the experiment and the control group). Rosenthal suggested a number of reasons for this – for instance, that the teachers knew the students more in later year groups and the older students were less malleable. Either way, the Pygmalion Effect highlights an important factor – that if we raise our expectations of students, there's a strong chance that they will rise to meet them.

The reverse of this is the Golem Effect. Part of Jewish mythology, the Golem was a clay creature created to protect the Jews of Prague. Unfortunately, over time the Golem grew more and more corrupt and span violently out of control. In the end he had to be destroyed.

In 1982, Babad, Inbar and Rosenthal conducted an experiment with 26 trainee PE teachers. In their last year of training, each of them undertook a pre-test to secretly ascertain their level of bias. This was not shared with them but 11 came out as non-bias teachers, and 15 came out as high-bias teachers.

The teachers were told that they were part of a large scale study commissioned by the Israeli Ministry of Education to observe progress, social behaviour and peer interactions among students. The teachers did not know that it was in fact *they* who were being observed, not the students as they had been led to believe. The teachers were asked before the study began to nominate three "high expectancy" students and three "low expectancy" students in their classes.

The research team then spun another lie and informed the trainee teachers that additional students in each class had been identified as "late bloomers" in PE. They told them that this had been as a result of a complex statistical method and was backed by the government. They were in fact randomly assigned. They weren't late bloomers at all!

All of the nominated students (high, low and late bloomers) would be taught lessons as normal and then physically tested at the end of the process. So how do you think they fared?

As you might expect, the high bias teachers behaved more dogmatically towards the students perceived as low expectancy. Both types of teachers gave the low expectancy students less attention and less reinforcement than the high expectancy students. High bias teachers directed more criticism at the low expectancy students and less at the high expectancy students and late bloomers. They were also less friendly to the low expectancy students compared to the late bloomers and high expectancy students. In the tests, the low expectancy students performed less well than the others.

What the Golem effect highlights is that when we "place" lower expectations on individuals (or the individual does it themselves), it leads to lower performance. It is another form of the self-fulfilling prophecy. If we don't think they're intelligent or they say they're not bright, we inadvertently teach them differently and limit what they achieve.

Before I tie everything together, I want to look at the Matthew effect.

For whoever has will be given more, and they will have an abundance. Whoever does not have, even what they have will be taken from them.
–Matthew 25:29, New International Version

In simple terms the Mathew effect can be translated as the rich get richer and the poor get poorer. Originally coined by Robert Merton (1968), it refers to the fact that in the world of science, eminent scientists get more credit than lesser-known researchers, even if their work is similar, senior scientists seem to win all of the prizes, even if most of the work is completed by a graduate student.

In 1983, Herbert Walberg and Shiow-Ling Tsai looked at its application in education. They too found that those who were advantaged continued to be so. Keith Stanovich (1986) found that those with early success in reading continued to gain later success. Poor early readers ended up falling behind. The gap between the groups widened over the years.

In other words, those who struggle in education will continue to struggle and ultimately not do as well. Those who do well will get pushed harder, have greater expectations placed upon them, be given more challenging content and learn at a greater rate than those who do not. They will build up a greater bank of vocabulary and knowledge which they can draw upon when learning new things. Those who do not, can't.

If we only set the high achievers challenging work and have lower expectations of the low achievers, we inadvertently impose the Pygmalion and Golem Effects. We praise and stretch Robynn and Andy, who we believe can do well. David and Jess, who aren't as bright, suffer the consequences of the Golem effect. They are given easier work. They aren't expected to do as well as Robynn and Andy and ultimately fulfil this. Over time the gap gets wider.

At my first school I had a chat with a very wise colleague called Marianne Fox about differentiation and all the nonsense strategies we were expected to include in our lessons. I'm not of course talking about proper SEN or EAL support. Marianne very much clarified things when she said, "Ultimately, every child in that class will sit the exact same exam at the end of Year 11. If we're making bits easier for some students, they're not going to know anything to write in it". And that was it: my thinking was changed. It was time to throw out differentiated objectives, levelled worksheets and individualised plans. Dawn Cox, a secondary school head of RE, has a similar view:

> Differentiation by task (giving different children different tasks), particularly in a secondary key stage 4 context, is nonsense. All students are working towards the same exam. They all need to do the same thing to achieve a grade 9. The skills are the same and so is the knowledge. If you get one student to do something perceived to be a "lower" skill, for example "to describe" but another a "higher" skill, for example "to analyse", you are limiting the former in the development of their skills. This has commonly come from the perpetuated misunderstanding of Bloom's Taxonomy. In my classroom I give them all the same task which requires the same skills and the same knowledge but I may structure it more for some students. I usually start with a scaffold and then students can choose whether to use it or not. I know that not all students will get full marks but that I have given them all an equal chance to attempt to achieve them.

Sadly, this poor use of differentiation by task limits those students that need the most opportunity to access all the skills needed and creates some sort of divided classroom where a teacher spends their time separately copying and secretly distributing different worksheets. In my opinion this is one of the worst cases of low expectations in classrooms.

Change the word "differentiate"

It may be a minor point but talking about how we can *challenge* students, rather than *differentiate* for them, does make a difference. It puts me in the frame of mind where I to push students, rather than make things easier. It reminds me to aim high, rather than pitch low. It reminds me that everyone can achieve, not just the few. And tied into this comes my first principle.

---

1 Aim high and support up

So you're saying it's all about having higher expectations? Be more Pygmalion?

It's really apparent when I look back that some of the strategies I employed limited the progress some children could make. They put a ceiling on what they could achieve. Giving a C grade student a particular worksheet might seem helpful, but why can't they try an A grade one to learn what an exceptional standard requires? Why not smash through that ceiling and do better? Why should a so-called "less able" child be denied the right to get a grade beyond what a target grade set for them? I'm not talking about those with very specific support needs. Those students require proper support. What I'm talking about is those who could do better. Why plan for low expectations? Why not show students what exceptional looks like and get as many of them as possible a step closer to it.

Do what Ron does

I've mentioned Ron Berger before, and with good reason. Ron was a public school teacher in western Massachusetts for 25 years. He worked primarily with younger students. Like any teacher, he wants his students to produce great work. Except that he has a different idea of what that is. Imagine you are the teacher of a Year 6 class. What do you expect great work for them to be? What would a great piece of art or written work look like?

If you're like me, you probably think of work that is well presented with virtually no errors. If it is written it has neat handwriting, no spelling mistakes, uses good vocabulary and really communicates what it is it is trying to. It shows personality and grips the reader.

If it is a piece of art, it is beautiful and makes me think. The choice of style is well considered and the use of light, shade, tone and colour brings the child's idea to life. Ron takes this a few steps further.

In *An Ethic of Excellence* (2003), Ron describes his years of work in the classroom that has seen students surpass what many of us would expect. He talks about how, as a teacher but also a carpenter, he aims to develop excellence and craftsmanship. He wants people to see how proud he is of students whose work is beautiful, accurate and of the highest quality.

His book describes how his third graders created field guides to local amphibians that look almost professional. How his sixth grade students produced radon gas reports for the homes in his town – reports so accurate that it wasn't just used by that town, but was requested by towns all over the state. How his students created blueprints of houses drawn to standard architectural scale and incorporating the exact same components as a professional drawing. All of this from students aged 11 years or younger.

Berger doesn't work in a private school or a school for gifted. His demographic is pretty usual:

> In my classroom I have students who come from homes full of books and students whose families own almost no books at all. I have students for whom reading, writing, and math come easily and students whose brains can't follow a line of text without reversing words and letters, students who can't line up numbers correctly on a page. I have students whose lives are generally easy and students with physical disabilities, and health or family problems that make life a struggle. I want them all to be craftsmen. Some may take a little longer to produce things, some many need to use extra strategies and resources. In the end, they need to be proud of their work and their work needs to be worthy of pride.
>
> (p. 2)

And that's it. Ron has the belief that his students can do great things. He is the ultimate Pygmalion ambassador. But how does he do it? Here are a few of his strategies:

- You need to create a culture where excellence is the norm – Now this is difficult to do. If it is the norm for children to dislike school and ridicule those who try hard (known as "try-hards" in one of the schools I've worked in) then students will find it hard to do well. They meet their self-fulfilling prophecy. As a teacher we need to work hard to make our classroom the place where the culture is that it's good to do well. Doing this isn't easy but it can be done. From my experience as a PE teacher, it comes with feedback, practice, support and small successes. When a child finds it difficult to master a skill, we go in and talk about what excellence looks like and give small targets on how to slowly get there. Students practice and we support. When students see themselves improving I hone in on it. That small success becomes a conversation. That conversation builds self-esteem. That self-esteem builds confidence. That confidence leads to a new target of how to use it in a game. And now when they get into a game they feel confident to use it. More feedback, more practice, more support and more successes lead to the positive feeling we want students to experience. It's here we can then begin to challenge more and push them further, with them knowing we're there to help support them achieve these higher challenges. Classrooms can work the same. Make it supportive. Sanction those who ridicule. Celebrate successes. Make them feel valued. When we dissect work, be harsh but fair. Show them how to make it better. Believe in them and they will feel the success. It will feel like a slow ship turning but that ship will turn. It's slow but make learning the norm in your classroom.

- Build literacy through the work – Place an importance on developing strong readers and writers. Surround students with literature and great writing. Develop vocabulary and be fussy about its use, whether in writing or in spoken word.

- Model excellent work – Students need pictures in their head of what exceptional work looks like. Develop a bank of resources for this. Collect great work. Keep old essays from students. Gather examples from the real world. Expose students to the best examples possible to show what greatness looks like. With this model in mind, they can try to work towards it.

- Drafts – Many students create one draft of a piece of work and hand it in. What happens if it isn't correct or has errors/misconceptions in it? Sometimes we provide feedback but this doesn't always get acted upon. Students need to think of work as drafts and look to continually improve it. When feedback is given they need to act upon it and make the work better. If it's not perfect, it's not finished. We could settle for second best, but we'll only have to pick up the pieces later in the year.

- Critique – Ron spends a great deal of time focusing on the students work. He organises sessions where they unpick students work and look at what is great and where we could improve. He zooms in on specifics and uses it as an opportunity to teach them how to make their work better. The feedback becomes a learning opportunity. As a class they look, analyse and see the steps to improve.

- Be relentless on creating good work – If work isn't good enough, create a culture to try and improve it. If you do poorly in a test, work hard until you do well in it. Don't set limits on children. Don't categorise them into able and less able. Expect that everyone can do well and help them (through the strategies listed here) to get there.

If there's one thing Berger has taught me it's that students have the potential to do amazing things, well beyond what we might usually expect. It literally reshaped my thinking of how I approach lesson design and the tasks that I choose to do to support learning. It's not an easy task but if we have the culture, the expectations and the support, our students can amaze us. So why are we limiting them with some of our differentiation strategies?

You make it sound so simple. But what could I do to aim high?

It is difficult. We all have students in our lessons who struggle and we may revert to setting them easier work. But persist with aiming high and consider the following points.

Remember what we (think we) know about the brain

We have already referred to Daniel T. Willingham's key message, "Memory is the residue of thought" (2009, p. 54). And that's a really crucial point. If we set differentiated work that is easier, how much thinking is actually taking place? What chance is there that this will transfer into learning over time? And if it is easier, what knowledge will they be missing out by completing it? Clearly we need to be mindful that different students have different levels of prior knowledge, different students have different levels of vocabulary understanding and different students are affected by cognitive load in different ways. However, what we shouldn't do is dumb down the work. Willingham again: "Instead of making the work easier, is it possible to make the thinking easier?" (p. 13).

Many of us get differentiation the wrong way round – we give the less able less work, covering less knowledge, and have lower expectations of its quality. We all have classes where Richard can't even write in full sentences so how on earth can we expect him to write an academic essay? But we should still be setting our expectations high, then supporting students to meet them. Can we do this by making the thinking easier – carefully breaking it up in a way that allows students to access it? In a moment I'll explain how we might just do that.

There needs to be some struggle

Linking in with the last point, we need to ensure that every lesson, every task and every moment of learning has an element of struggle in it. Not so much struggle that students lose motivation and give up, but enough to make individuals think hard about what they're doing. As with sportsmen and women, an element of desirable struggle keeps students moving forward without levelling off.

But how much struggle is the right amount? John Hattie (2012, p. 109) argues that we need to ensure that "all students are working 'at or +1' from where they start". We should be aiming to push students slightly beyond where they currently are. This is a fine balance: if we get it wrong and make students struggle too much, they won't have any success and might think they never will. We need to ensure they feel knowledgeable and skilled enough to attempt the challenge. They need to feel they can push themselves and that it will benefit them in the long run. So what would adding another level (a plus one) look like in your lesson with your students? Let's have a look at a few practical ideas.

Know your students – really well

It is our number one duty to know our students. Those with special educational needs or English as an additional language will need specialist strategies and support. There are much better books than this one on the subject and better-qualified people than me, so I must apologise and recommend that if necessary you seek those out. What I can do though is talk about mainstream schools and how we might work with the majority of students in order to differentiate more effectively. Let's quickly address what I believe we *shouldn't* do!

Don't use VAK – One of my biggest pet hates if I speak to people about differentiation and when they speak about tailoring lessons to their students learning styles. As discussed in Chapter 2, superficially I am matching the needs of my learners to the planning of my lesson. Except it's not benefitting anyone. As I explained in Chapter 2, working this way a) gives students a reason to opt out, b) adds considerably to your workload, and c) has absolutely no research to back it. Vary tasks – yes. Get someone to draw out a story line if it may help them plan their writing. But expect Tim to *only* draw something, Eve to *only* act it out and Edmund to *only* write a one-page essay? Nope.

Don't give students target grades! – I expect many of you will say you wish you didn't but that schools insist on it. The problem once again is that this becomes a self-fulfilling prophecy. It affects how we as teachers, and children as learners, work in the classroom. When I had to give target grades I would instantly group students and deal with them differently. I would support those with higher grades, giving them more work and challenge. I *hoped* those with low target grades would manage to write a sentence.

Target grades also place a ceiling to what people believe they can do. One of the worst sentences that can come from a student's mouth is, "Sir, what do I need to do to get my C grade?" C grade?! Why not aim for a B? It becomes a situation where students do what they *need* to do, rather than what they *could* do. Why not help everyone try and get the best outcome possible? The biggest bone of contention is that a student may be predicted an A* or a grade 8/9 at GCSE, but this may well not be subject-specific One student reacted in disbelief when I was told to share with him his target grade of a level 7 in core PE for the end of the year. "Level 7? I may be good in maths and science but I can't even catch a ball!" How can a target generated from one set of subject data accurately transfer to another?

Don't just say you do growth mindset – In my first school I read up on the work of Carol Dweck (2012) and began to share it with staff and students. A few years later I ran an INSET session called "Don't just say you do Growth Mindset".

On the face of it, trying to promote a growth mindset with your students sounds obvious. When giving them challenging work, some students with a more fixed mindset will withdraw effort, will guess, copy, hide their struggles or simply give up. As a teacher we want to change this attitude. We want them to see mistakes as a process of learning (which we know it is. We want to avoid learned helplessness.

When approaching challenge and differentiation, we need to have this in mind and subtly chip away at attitudes and beliefs while continually nudging students forward. This is where your subject knowledge, feedback and instruction come into play. Believing in students, showing them that they can do better and having high expectations all tie in.

What doesn't work is simply doing growth mindset. Don't assume that a few inspirational quotes from famous people who have overcome difficulties will make the mark. Students need more than that.

What is required is you knowing your students really well, expecting great things and really believing in them. Cleary enough that they also believe in themselves. Sometimes Ciara will need a pep talk to get her to believe that she can do well. Sometimes we'll need to insist Chris stops comparing himself to others around him and giving himself a hard time because he's not doing as well as them. Sometimes we'll need to spend five minutes giving Ollie some feedback on his work. Not on him, but on what he produced and the way he produced it. Subtleties like this help.

Don't say you do growth mindset if you actually don't.

So if that's what to avoid while aiming high with your students, how could knowing our students really well actually help us?

We have already seen, Graham Nuthall (2007, pp. 35–36) points out that "students already know, *on average*, about 50 percent of what a teacher intends his or her students to learn through a curriculum unit or topic. But that 50 percent in not evenly distribute". For example, some students know a bit about the topic, some a lot and some almost nothing. Izzie knows lots about the sliding filament theory, but when you move onto gaseous exchange in the respiratory system, she knows almost nothing. So how can you find out what they know?

Data – a very basic starting point

I like data, but only if it has a purpose and helps teaching and learning. When you get a new class you are probably given data on them. Whether this is reading ages, KS2 assessments or data from previous exams, it can give you a heads up on where the class *might* be. If the data shows that the class on average has performed highly on assessments in the previous year, we have a slight indicator of where we might need to pitch lessons. If the data isn't as good, we know we can still aim high but we may need to tweak our planning, change our explanations or think harder about how to get students up to an A*/grade 9 answer. But I've said *might* and *may*: the data doesn't tell us everything. It doesn't tell us that Jamie knows lots on World War II but not so much on the Romans. It tells you more than you knew before, but not enough to base all your decision-making on.

Pre-tests

One of the simplest ways I have of learning what my students do or do not know is having a 10 minute multiple choice pre-test at the start of each unit/topic. Although it still doesn't give you everything, it does help build up a picture. The design is really important. Most exam boards now have online software that helps build exam papers. Use this to help you structure it. And have the option "I don't know" at the end of each one so that students avoid guessing and actually tell you if they don't know. I can't close gaps if they simply hazard a guess. Make this explicit with students before they start.

If you think that the "I don't know" option could still lead to inaccuracies, cognitive psychologist Yana Weinstein once told me to use confidence scores after each question instead. As students answer the multiple choice question, they write 1 if they were confident with their answer, all the way to 5 if they weren't. Again, it helps build up a picture.

Once we have a better (but not completely accurate) idea of what they do and don't know, we can then adapt our planning. We may find out that the so-called low achievers actually know more about this topic than the so-called high achievers. We may have to rethink who we support more intensively.

Write down everything you know

Such a simple thing – at the start of a topic, share with students what the topic entails, and then ask them on a blank piece of paper to write or draw everything they know about it. There will be things they forget which they'll remember when you prompt them, but the process of sketching it all down is less like a test, and gives them more freedom to get down anything that comes to mind. Once again it will also give you an idea of who may need your attention more.

Start lessons with a driving question, or at least a task that gives you an opportunity to see what they might know

We start each lesson with a driving question. These questions are specifically designed to contextualise the lesson and give a concrete example to tie the learning into. For example, when I talk about aerobic and anaerobic energy systems in biology, I use the question, "Who would win in a 600 m race between Usain Bolt and Mo Farah?" For the next few minutes, have a think yourself.

Usain? Mo? The answer is that the experts believe it could potentially be a draw. The reason for this is because this distance is too long for Usain and would make him reach the limits of his anaerobic system, and not long enough for Mo's aerobic system to kick into full flow to make him win. And when I pose this question to Year 9 GCSE classes, one or two students will mention aerobic or anaerobic in our follow up discussion. At this point I can ask everyone if they have heard of these two terms. If faces are blank, I know the majority of the class don't and it's off to work I go. I also know that a few students *do know* what these terms mean and I can adapt my instruction for them accordingly.

And so?

If I go into a lesson and pitch the level of challenge wrong, I could be wasting valuable learning time. Time we don't have in our crammed curriculums. As Nuthall (2007) said, different students know different amounts. How can I challenge them all if I don't have a bit of an idea who knows what? There's a chance I could teach a lesson and at the end of it, students say they already know it. Having an idea is a good starting point.

Make the thinking easier, not the task

Once you have an insight into what students *might* know, you can start to plan how to stretch and challenge your class. It may seem like I'm talking about a "once size fits all" approach, I'll explain later in the chapter how to add layers to it.

Remember what we know about novices and experts

It's important to remember what we discussed in the memory and feedback chapters. In any given topic, any student could be deemed a novice because they haven't had much exposure to the content, irrespective of what their target grade or data tells you. A student who has a target grade of an 8 could easily know nothing about tectonic plates if they've never experienced it. This is why data should be taken with a pinch of salt. However, once we begin to build our own picture of what students might or might not know, we can refer back to what we know about novices, intermediates, experts and cognitive load.

If a student is a novice, they will probably have little prior knowledge on a given topic. They might not have the information in their long term memory to be able to understand what it is you are trying to teach them. That's not to say they won't ever learn it, but it may take longer. What we shouldn't do here is misinterpret this as low ability. Instead we should realise that as a result of less prior knowledge, they may not be able to process everything at once and learning might be slower. So, all the strategies that we spoke about in Chapter 2 will now come into play for these students. The use of concrete examples, worked examples, layering terminology and so on.

From Chapter 4, which focuses on feedback, we also know that novices benefit from immediate feedback based on content and vocabulary, which can be more corrective. Experts meanwhile will benefit from less feedback and more prompts to self-regulate their own learning. Same lesson, different students, different levels of understanding.

Improve their knowledge

I'll keep this one short. For all students it's important to develop their knowledge. For novices we need to build their background knowledge and expose them to things they might not know. Teach them key terms, definitions, vocabulary and the like. Make them read in lessons with you and talk about what they've found out. For experts it's about manipulating that knowledge and using it more coherently. You're aiming high for both, but supporting them in subtly different ways.

Before they begin, expose them to examples of excellence

A student won't know what a high quality piece of work looks like unless we show them. As we discussed in the feedback chapter, keeping and showing examples of excellence allows students to build up a mental image in their head of what they are trying to achieve. It helps them to have an end point to which they can reference their current work to and make amendments as needed.

In *An Ethic of Excellence* (2003), Ron Berger uses examples and models all the time. Some suggest this is simply teaching students to copy rather than produce work of their own, but it simply isn't the case. We use models all of the time in the real world. It helps us evolve, progress and develop. When I watch TV shows like Masterchef; The Professionals, I am mesmerised by the way the chefs cook. I watch intensely how they work and pick up on the little snippets of information that have fed into producing a dish that is out of this world.

Models can be incredibly helpful for students in the classroom too. Models help me show what excellence looks like. An excellent essay shows my class how to structure essays in a sophisticated way. How to use language or technical words to improve its quality. How to support ideas by the careful selection of quotes. It gives them something to aim for. I keep work from previous students, examples I've written, or examples from experts.

Just showing them a model won't significantly improve a student's ability to write, draw or compose. That's where the skill of the teacher comes in. We need to dissect the model with the class – highlighting the important bits so that students can hone into them and understand their inclusion. Question students so that they become part of the process and begin to get an insight into how the model was crafted. Ask things like:

- Notice how the author has started the paragraph. Why is the first sentence so important?

- Why do you think that they used this quote rather than the one that we chose? Why is theirs better?

- What is the artist trying to portray by including this feature in their painting? What message is it trying to get across?

- Can you see how the writer has chosen to use technical words like x and y rather than using z like we have? What has this done to the quality of what we're reading?

If we can show (some of) the things that comprise excellent work, we can begin to show how they might achieve it themselves. A good ten minutes unpicking excellent work is never time wasted if it helps set the bar high.

Show the excellent work in the room

When I first began developing the use of excellence examples, I used a camera or iPad to snap students work as it was produced in the lesson. I would wander around, looking over shoulders to see what students had written. When a good piece of work appeared, I would take a picture of it and email it to myself quickly. I'd then open the image up on the whiteboard and as a class we would study it. A live model in a class can make things seem achievable for other students. Individuals can begin to think "If Mia wrote that, so can I".

As technology improved, I got myself a visualiser which sat on my desk. As students produced good work, I would ask if I could take their book, put it under the visualiser and ask students for their attention. With the work under the camera I would read it to the class. I would point to key vocabulary, great explanations or strong examples. As the class became more experienced, I would hold back on my critique and ask students to discuss what was so good about the work before I gave my input. The value of showing live work on screen cannot be underestimated

If the culture is right, show work that we can make better

This takes the right setting, but if showing how to make work better is the norm, we can even begin to take students work at random to be displayed under the camera. The key principle here is that we need to explain to the whole class that this isn't to humiliate individuals for poor work, but to collaboratively help make any piece of work under the camera better.

When this culture is embedded, we are able to display work which has common errors. These errors are ones that the majority of the class may have made. We can work together to change words that might have crept into students work. We can correct the incorrect use of a definition. We can remind everyone of the better example to use as our discussion point. Great work is powerful, creating it together is even more so.

As they start, help them aim high and support up – using scaffolds

I've stood in a classroom before and unpicked an excellent piece of work. I've waxed lyrical about the style, the structure and the content. I've scribbled all over it and annotated points in the margin. I've put bullet points on the board that have sum-marised what we've seen as we've gone through. And then I've done what every naïve teacher does and finishes up by saying "Now off you go!" What on earth could possibly be wrong there?

Well, for those students in your class with better prior knowledge, a better bank of vocabulary and more exposure to great writing, they can probably go off and string some eloquent paragraphs together. They will probably need some refining but they won't be too bad.

For those that struggle to get their ideas on paper, or struggle with spelling, or have no idea where to even begin, it may be daunting. The quality of their work is going to be lower. But we don't want it to be. We want them to aim high as well.

At this stage using a scaffold can be very helpful. For those who have a higher starting point, a scaffold like a writing structure or framework can be a reminder of what we saw in the model, and what they should include in their own construction. For those who need more support, these scaffolds can be vital – the prompt that starts their writing off, the inspiration for organising their paragraphs, the reminder to include quotes, technical terminology and examples. For both types of student it has something to offer.

But what scaffolds, writing frames or framework should I use?

It depends on what you're trying to achieve. And I know that's not helpful. I went through a phase when I tried every strategy I could get my hands on. Experience led me to work out that it's important to understand *why* something might work. Let me explain.

The four part process – I had a lower set group. The quality of writing that these students were producing wasn't very inspiring. People kept telling me to use things like

PEE as it was the Holy Grail. Once again, one size doesn't fit all and what my students were required to write didn't always suit this process. It also felt quite restrictive. It became very apparent that students lacked the ability to accurately define or describe concepts in their answers. They also failed to consistently incorporate academic vocabulary and explain their application.

Luckily, I stumbled across the "four part process" on teacher and blogger Lee Donaghy's (2013) blog. Originally deployed as a scaffold for EAL students, the method got close to linking everything together that I needed to with my students. Reading how Lee used it in his lessons (four blog posts on the one technique) allowed me to really understand *why* this might work. It helped students focus on how to write excellent sentences. The process seemed fluent. It pulled together all the elements of a great sentence.

Using it in lessons for me began with everyone using the method in a quite directed way. Everybody used a template until I was sure that students understood the importance of each component. As students got better, one by one, I removed the template and insisted on the structure. I would feedback to individuals, giving them specific advice and guidance. As students got better, they were allowed to write their own sentences and paragraphs. At different points I would remove a layer of the scaffold when I felt that good habits had been learnt. Each time a layer was removed, a different level of challenge (individual feedback to whole class scrutiny) was added.

Graphic organisers – This was something I stumbled upon by accident. Early on in my career I was looking at ways to help students plan work without rushing straight into it. Some of the concepts I teach, can be quite complicated. Some students find it difficult to see how concepts overlap or become a consequence of one another. When looking for ideas to support lessons like this, Lisa Pearce, a transition teacher in Hampshire, introduced me to graphic organisers. Simple things like Venn diagrams, Double Bubble maps, Cause and Effect maps and the humble spider diagram all help students get their ideas on paper and manipulate them before setting off on their task. As a teacher I can wander round the class and see who is struggling and will need more support or prompting, and who is flying and needs me to stretch them further. It's right there on paper in front of them.

For the student it allows them to get what they know into a visual form before they attempt to see the connections and interactions. For the aerobic/anaerobic energy systems, the use of a Double Bubble map helps them see the similarities and differences quite clearly. It helps join the dots.

Once this understanding is gained, students can go off with the plan and create work that is more coherent that if they hadn't used it. Again, those that need it more will use it more than those who need it less. Either way, a simple scaffold can help every student grasp difficult concepts.

At first glance – Doug Lemov is the master of all things challenge. One thing I've seen used time and time again is sentence starters. Some are really helpful. Some are very average. In a blog post in 2014, Doug took sentence starters a step further, showing how, carefully designed, they can add rigour to students' work. He described a workshop he ran with teachers where they had to write a sentence about Bruegel's painting "The Fall of Icarus". After explaining the background story and where Icarus was in the painting, delegates went off for two minutes and crafted their sentence.

The sentences they created were good. However, Doug and his team knew that they could make them better with the use of a sentence starter. He gave them the opening "At first glance". Delegates had to write their sentences again with this three-word opening.

The new sentences were more complex and of higher quality A thought-provoking opening forced the writers to approach them differently.

Armed with this strategy I began including sentence starters for all the challenging tasks I would set. The way they were designed allowed two things to happen:

1. They provided a subtle prompt for what students should include.
2. They were worded in a way that stimulated thought.

Let me give you an example. Years ago, when posing a question about the structure of the heart, I might have asked students to use sentence starters such as:

- "The heart has valves . . . "
- "Blood flows through . . . "
- "The first chamber . . . "

On the face of it, these are fine. They help students start their sentences and give a subtle prompt where to start. However, after reading Doug's post, these starters became:

- "Without these valves . . . "
- "Blood returning to . . . "
- "The chambers differ . . . "

Why might these newer sentence starters be more challenging?

The second set provokes more thought. For instance, "The heart has valves . . " might produce an answer such as, "to keep blood flowing in one direction and stop backflow". Technically it's right. However, "Without these valves . . " stretches students to come up with an answer such as "blood may not move in its designated direction and instead return to a previous chamber. This backflow causes regurgitation at the valve, meaning the heart has to work harder to pump the same amount of blood".

A simple tweak to a sentence starter can make a big difference.

I do – we do – you do

I mention this again later in Chapter 6 because techniques like this are really important. If we want to aim high, we need to ensure students know what this looks like. As we said earlier, models are excellent at showing where we would like to end up. Scaffolds can guide us there. The technique of *I do – we do – you do* accompanies us on the journey.

It's a form of explicit teaching and the token name it has been given acts as a reminder of the stages.

The initial one is the *I do* stage. Here we, as teachers, model the process of how to tackle a challenging task for the class. We show them how we would attempt to complete the task and explain our workings as we go. It involves metacognition and sharing our thinking with the students. The process can be combined with previous strategies such as using a visualiser or graphic organiser.

As we attempt a problem, we show students where we might start. What is the problem asking us to do? What things do we need to include? What topics are involved? How might I begin to solve or answer the problem? This has been a pivotal part of tackling 8 or 9 mark questions with my classes. Instead of expecting different students to get different outcomes, I show everyone how to potentially get full marks. I do this by planning the whole response aloud, and then crafting the first paragraph. As I do this I talk through the intricate details. I make a fuss about my choice of words. I make it clear why I included the example I did in the second paragraph. I verbalise my thought process so students understand why I'm writing what I'm writing. As this is happening, students are taking note or beginning to copy parts of what I have done. I am making the whole process explicit.

Like all scaffolds, we then release some of the responsibility to the students (*We do*). As a group we collaboratively create the second paragraph using my plan. Initially I write whatever the class say I should. We then stop, read it out aloud and review what it says. More often than not it makes no sense. Students try so hard to emulate my use of vocabulary and inclusion of specific examples that their paragraph becomes incoherent or confused. At this stage I ask them to work in pairs to discuss what is wrong and what would *they* do to make it clearer. After a few moments we come back together and tackle it again. This time with clearer ideas of what we want to achieve. The answer, still under my guidance, uses the students' thoughts to redraft it and improve its quality.

You do involves just that. Once I am sure that most of them are ready to have the scaffold removed, I can ask them to create the third and final paragraph themselves. At this stage, hopefully through formative assessment throughout the previous two stages, I can then go and work with students individually and help them create an answer that might have previously been weak. I can further stretch those who need it while supporting those who need extra input if they are to achieve the high standard I expect.

So aim high, show excellent models and scaffold up? Is that it?

As a starting point, yes. If you notice, many of the strategies described earlier involve your skill as a teacher to create exceptional work. There aren't a million different laminated sheets with colour co-ordinated target tasks for the different abilities. It is often just you, high expectations and the skill of your craft.

If students are finding it difficult, don't scrap it and opt for something easier. Stick with it, but alter how you teach, support or scaffold it. It may take a lesson longer, but the outcome will be much better. However, many of the reasons students find work difficult or get stuck could have been identified, planned for and avoided before the lesson started. This leads me onto my second principle.

---

2 Work out where the support may be needed

If we're aiming high, there are (understandably) going to be parts of your lesson that will be extremely challenging for students. This doesn't mean we should either omit these from our lessons or only expect a few to "get it". How will that help when a student is called to explain it later? What might they write in their exam? "Sorry, I don't know that. My teacher never taught us it".

When a concept or topic is difficult, we can take action before the lesson to ensure that the outcomes we intend are actually achieved. And by doing so we can ensure that we still enable all students to be challenged. How might we go about it?

Use what we know about the students – remember what Nuthall said

If you've managed to do an activity prior to this topic to ascertain what students might or might not know, you can use this information to help plan for challenge. If you've conducted a pre-test or "write down everything you know about ...." task at the end of the previous lesson, you have some information to help plan the new topic.

We're essentially looking for what level of expertise students *might* have. Who knows what? What have the majority of the class not got? Who are the potential novices, proficients and experts? A good pre-task can provide great insight into where we might need to plan challenge. It allows us to have a better idea about who we might need to support up to meet our high expectations and helps us think how to do it.

Work out where the roadblocks may be

Every challenging topic has a difficult concept. Every challenging lesson has a moment where students get stuck. As we become more experienced, we begin to notice when these sticking points (or road blocks) may be. We begin to know how to respond to them better in lessons as we've encountered them a number of times before. Experience is important.

But experience takes time. And even now, after more than a decade in the classroom, I still have limited experience with some topics, and it shows. For instance, our new GCSE has a topic that focuses on the various volumes of the lungs. It took a couple of days planning the lesson and chatting it through with colleagues to get my head around what terms such as "inspiratory reserve volume" and "expiratory lung volume" meant. Harder still was thinking about how on earth I would explain that to my students. Here was the first roadblock in my lesson, primarily because it was one for me. Knowing this meant I knew it would be one for my students. Sure enough, as the lesson progressed, the various terms did confuse them. However, knowing it was a difficult area meant I had strategies in place to deal with it.

When experienced teachers work with trainees, the mentors quickly spot where a lesson may face some difficulty. They know where students may get confused or stuck. To the experienced teacher it is almost like it's signposted with flashing lights. For a trainee it isn't as glaringly obvious. With new topics this may also happen to us so called experienced teachers with new topics. It's therefore important to get a colleague to cast their eyes over our plans. This collaborative approach helps us to ensure lessons sticking points are identified. Once we know where they are, we can begin to tackle them. *So, what things should I be looking for?* Here are a few ideas:

- Any complex concepts which have layers of content attached to them may need to be highlighted. For instance, teaching "Global atmospheric circulation" in Geography is difficult as you can't see it happening (just the effects) and the language is tough. Reconstruction after the American Civil War in History requires students to understand American politics and know the various layers of policies. With these topics we know they have complex layers. This should therefore highlight that this may be a sticking point that needs attention before the lesson.

- Any topics that have lots of complex terminology and new vocabulary. According to Beck, McKeown and Kucan (2013) there are three tiers of vocabulary. Tier 1 are the common everyday words. Tier 2 are words that are used across various subjects and are important to know. Words such as analyse, evaluate or justify fall into this category. Tier 3 are content specific vocabulary and are usually only found in that subject. For example, words such as isotope or vasodilation don't appear very often in conversation and usually require explanation about their meaning and use. If your lesson has a high number of tier 3 vocabulary, you may need to be aware some students may find this a roadblock. How will you get this vocabulary shared, understand and used?

- Abstract topics. Sometimes things we encounter are one way or another, right or wrong, or either a or b. Sometimes, some of the topics we teach aren't as simple as that. Sometimes the idea behind them are quite abstract. With this, students may struggle to grasp the meaning because they've never encountered this before. If something isn't as clear as a or b, be prepared to plan how to unstick students when they become stuck.

- And simply, if a topic confuses us, it's probably going to confuse students. It's as simple as that.

Remember what we said about cognitive load, working memory and prior knowledge

If you go back to Chapter 2, you'll remember that with any given topic there will be novices, those who are proficient and those who could be deemed expert. Each of these require us to tweak the way we teach. For instance, novices can do with information broken down into chunks, supported with scaffold and with worked examples to explain processes. Experts need less input as they have more prior knowledge. They can draw upon previous information to make sense of new concepts. These students need less support and are able to manipulate information more easily in their working memory and make sense of it more effectively. A scaffold only adds to extraneous cognitive load and hinders their learning. Experts need more open questions or problems to solve in order to challenge them. Worth remembering when planning who to support with what strategies.

It's also worth remembering that novices, due to their low prior knowledge, might not know what to focus on or pay attention to. All this information may be completely new to them and, as they have nothing concrete to attach it to, we may need to signpost important points: make it clear what is important, what steps should be taken next, what examples to refer to.

A final point to remember is the impact of Mayer's Multi-media Principle (2014): "People learn more deeply from words and graphics than from words alone" (p. 59). The idea is that as we present instruction on content, there is a greater chance it will be learnt if it combines words and images than words alone. Explaining gaseous exchange for example can be a complicated process, talking about alveoli, oxygen, diffusion, haemoglobin and so on. Combining this with an image of an alveoli cross section can make it easier for the working memory to process the information and make sense of it. However, there are some warnings. Mayer (2014) suggests:

- Delete an extraneous material – Don't clutter instruction with unnecessary images or text. It causes distractions and overloads working memory.

- Signal/highlight important material – As said earlier, use cues to highlight important material. Underline key words, add arrows to point to key parts of an image. All to help draw attention to difficult material.

- Redundancy effect – "People learn more deeply from graphics and narration than from graphics, narration, and on-screen text". So, don't have an image, then text, and then read the text out to the class. Students might focus on things like reading the text when they don't need to (because of your narration) and therefore not pay attention to the image.

- Place text near the graphic – Like the benefit of worked examples, having words far apart split a student's attention. Keep them close and students can process the information easier.

- Segment what you present – Students find it easier to process information when it is presented in segments rather than in a whole unit. So, if you have a process such as the water cycle, present each stage one at a time rather than as a whole.

- Introduce key words first – Before introducing complicated concepts, share the key terminology first. That way it becomes easier to process when they are presented.
- Narrate rather than use text – By removing text and simply narrating the information, students free up space in their visual channel, allowing them to focus more on the instruction.

Plan your explanations – what will you say?

Early on in my career, I didn't think too deeply about how my explanations could be improved. In fact, my only focus initially was reducing the length of them because I had been told- and fully accepted- that teachers should never talk for more than 10 minutes. However, the primary concern of an explanation should not be brevity, but clarity, and the notion that the expert in the room should be effectively silenced is one that is thankfully becoming outdated. When I focussed more fully on explanations, I realised that they were much more complex than I first imagined.

One area that I looked at first was the notion of expertise. Great explanations do need to start with the teacher having a strong understanding of the subject. I realised my subject knowledge was strong enough to "wing it" in explanations, but taking time to go deeper into my subject was crucial for me in ensuring that my explanations stuck. The next stage for me in crafting a solid explanation was to appreciate that novices don't think about things in the same way as experts, and that meant trying to pre-empt the common misconceptions in any explanation and filling in the gaps in knowledge that would add meaning. My explanations now have the built-in question: where might it go wrong?

One mistake I found myself making was asking if everyone understood or saying something like "thumbs up or thumbs down if you understand". This kind of self-reporting told me something but probably not whether my explanation was actually effective. Often, it would lead to the revelation 10 minutes down the line that they didn't understand at all or me stopping and re-teaching for the one student who claimed they didn't get it. Instead, I changed my approach and now tend to ask a multiple choice hinge question with several possible correct answers or use mini whiteboards- anything that will tell me who understands what. Then reteach everyone, reteach some or move on as appropriate.

(Mark Miller, English teacher and Head of Research School in Bradford)

I recently read *Harry Potter and the Prisoner of Azkaban* with my five-year-old daughter. I have to say that she was gripped by the story and loved every moment. On a Saturday in January, we realised we had 80 pages left to go so decided to have a day where we would finish it. As with the previous two books in the series, when we get to the final moments of the story, the excitement is brimming on my daughter's face.

All was going well until the part where Hermione unveiled how she used a Time Turner to attend all of her classes. In the final few chapters, they used the Time Turner to save the day. It was here that my daughter got incredibly confused. I knew that this (the process of going back in time) would be a very abstract concept for a five-year-old and sure enough it was. Even though I had been laying the foundations in the pages leading up to it, my little one clearly didn't get what was going on. And that's when I had to try and explain it to her. It took about ten different versions, using concrete examples, images from the book and even drawing a diagram of the incident at the lake near the end of the book, but we almost got there. My daughter had a "sort of" grip on what had happened.

What I learnt from this is that I had assumed that I would be able to explain it to her. I knew that time travel would be new to her, simply because she's five. However, what was clear was that my off the cuff explanations weren't good enough and it took a long time to finally get some of the point across.

This happens in lessons as well. We know a topic that we're teaching has something complex in it. We know that students may be exposed to something very unfamiliar. But how often do we plan what we're going to say? If a pre-test indicates that students don't know much about this topic we need to use a fantastic explanation to make it easier for them to understand. For a long time, I used to simply "wing it". It is no surprise that the outcome was hit and miss. Sometimes I managed to explain it well. Other times I just added to the confusion.

If we know where a sticking point is and an explanation will be called upon, take time to practice what you will say. And what do you say to help them provide clarity? Here are a few starting points:

Use of stories – In Chapter 2, Daniel T. Willingham (2009, p. 66) explains that using stories in your lessons can help working memory ("the human mind seems exquisitely tuned to understand and remember stories – so much that psychologists sometimes refer to stories as 'psychologically privileged'").

It could be extremely beneficial to tie our explanation into a story. Dan Brooks, maths and economics teacher in Columbia, explained that he used the story of washing cars with students on a Saturday morning when introducing dividing ratio into given amounts. The story is concrete for most of us and can help make sense of the new material about to come up. Students who usually struggle to engage end up involving themselves. Attaching your content to a story can make a big difference.

Use terminology or phrases that makes it memorable – A long time ago I was asked to teach netball for the first time. One lesson I doubled up with a colleague who was also new to the sport. We had the job of trying to explain to a group of Year 8 boys the various positions on court. As novices, this became quite complicated. That was until my colleague said, "If you haven't got a G, you can't go in the D". For those who are not familiar, out of the seven positions, only those with a G on their bib (for example, GK – Goal Keeper, GA – Goal Attack) are allowed into the D. Anyone else in there is offside. Those new to the game can be quite frustrated as they keep wondering out of position. However, this simple phrase made it memorable and quickly clarified the sticking point.

Conflict – Again, advice from Willingham (2009 p. 67): conflict can also help make teaching (in this case our explanations) memorable. For example, every year I teach gender in sport as a topic. Some find it quite difficult to see the inequalities and how they have become entrenched. Each year I use stories, but also allow conflict to take place to highlight the stereotypes, discrimination and indifference that characterise male and female sport and sport coverage. Every year I lay the trap (as such) and every year the conflict causes debate. The understanding that comes from this is better for it and also makes breaking down these entrenched views much easier. The outcomes of those lessons still come up in exam answers to this day.

Use images – As I pointed out in relation to the work of Mayer (2014), visuals with text/words can be really helpful. Especially so with explanations. You can do it in two ways. When you know you're going to deliver your explanation, supporting images on screen can help you make the complex simple. The other way involves you picking up your whiteboard pen and annotating what you say as you say it. Many a time my scribbles of the lungs, the ribs, the diaphragm, intercostal muscles and the various arrows showing the mechanics of breathing make what I'm saying a bit easier to understand. It doesn't have to be a work of art, but the visual summary as you talk makes a lot of difference.

Practise, practise and practise – You may feel silly but don't underestimate the importance of practising your explanations. Do they sound right? Do you get stuck at certain points? Could you make them better? Without practising, you'll never know until it happens – and that may be too late.

Plan questions to help unstick

If I go back to the story of reading Harry Potter to my daughter, at intervals I would pause and ask her questions to check that it was making sense. There would be no point ploughing through it if she didn't have a clue what was going on. New parts of the story would be unclear as she hadn't grasped the last part. The questions helped.

With a class of thirty students, you might not be able to always operate as I did with my daughter on a one to one basis. When there's a tricky topic, therefore, it would make sense to plan questions for those moments. What could you ask to check students understand? What questions might help break the topic down into more digestible parts?

I know it's the marmite of taxonomies, but SOLO taxonomy helps me to do just this. If I need to I can ask questions about the main principle (uni-structural), the components of it (multi-structural), how they link together (relational) or how other topics are involved (extended abstract). I can have some of these pre-planned before the lesson and use them when needed. I could build them in directly after the sticking point to force students to unpick what they've just been taught. Questions shouldn't be left to chance when potential misconceptions are identified before a lesson.

Make sure your subject knowledge is high

One of the biggest problems in my teaching is when I don't know enough, or don't have enough depth to my knowledge, to even begin to unpick a complex topic. If I don't know how x fits with y, how am I supposed to explain it to my students. When working out where the support may be needed, I need to ensure that I have the subject knowledge in place to provide a better explanation or have a clearer example ready to share. Reading up on a topic and knowing it better may take time, but it is a sure-fire way to help you be ready for those complex concepts. I'll pick up on this more in the next principle.

Poor planning leads to . . . well you know

Build up a picture of what your students do or don't know before a lesson. Work out where the tricky parts may be. Think about your explanations, your questions and the stories you might use. Attend to your own knowledge and ensure that your prior planning helps make your lesson more accessible and successful. What happens in the lesson comes next.

---

3 Differentiation is teaching, and very responsive

For many years, I held a guilty secret, one that I kept very close to my chest. Nobody suspected, nobody at all. Granted, I might have nodded when it was mentioned in meetings. I might have extolled its virtues to every conscientious trainee teacher to cross my path. I even might have showcased it in my lessons – but only when someone else was watching. Yet when my classroom door was closed, I avoided it.

Because differentiation was not for me.

During the bad-old-days of Ofsted checklists and graded lesson observations, I had to hunker down. I felt like a sinner. From time to time I would throw a sumptuous banquet – three separate sets of resources; all/most/some learning objectives; intricately organised in-class ability groupings, etc., etc. The truth was, however, that these infrequent flourishes served more to expiate my nagging guilt than to provide any decent learning for my students. I was in a moral quandary: differentiation seemed the epitome of virtue – yet also a pointless waste of time.

So instead I got on with teaching: working out my students' strengths and weaknesses; researching my lessons; explaining things as clearly as I could; asking questions; giving feedback; making mistakes; trying to rectify them later. The usual stuff. I would teach everybody the same thing in the same way, always trying, and often failing, to teach everyone as equals. I would ignore the target grades, my default position being that, given time, everybody can learn everything. Over time, my students started to do well ...

But still that nagging doubt. One-size-fits-all is evil and, sooner or later, I will be punished for it.

One day, sometime in 2013, the epiphany came. I realised that differentiation is teaching. I realised that differentiation lies in the skilfulness of our responses to the anticipated and unanticipated difficulties our students encounter. In other words, all that planning and thinking; that was differentiation. All those tailored chats with students; those were differentiation. All those equal expectations; they too were differentiation.

Differentiation, I learnt, lies at the heart of teaching. It is about high-expectations, challenge and the belief that, given time, any child can get there. While many children have complex needs and seemingly insurmountable learning gaps, they will never catch up if we give them a second-rate education. These children do not need our sympathy; they need our help.

(Andy Tharby, English teacher from West Sussex)

Like Andy, one day I realised that differentiation is just bloody good teaching and being responsive. We can plan how to tackle the sticking points with good questions, fantastic explanations and a number of. However, when that lesson starts, it's the skilfulness of a teacher that provides the most challenge and differentiation.

It's us, in that moment, working with the students

Not having differentiation can make us feel a little nervy. What if somebody comes into my lesson and I haven't got anything to show how I'm helping the various students? What if they want to see what worksheet I'm using? What if they want to see the scaffold for this student and the challenge task for that one? When these are our thoughts, we need to consider who differentiation and challenge is actually for.

Since I mustered up the courage to teach the way I feel benefits my students more than anyone else, I began to realise that the craft of teaching is real differentiation. We deal with hundreds of questions a day. We have students ask for help every lesson. We have those who get it quicker than others. In these instances, we chat to the individual. We unpick what might be causing confusion. We question them to check their understanding. We ask more questions to push them on. Each conversation is different, because each child is different. And when we've had these conversations, we leave a student with a plan of what they need to do to move forward. This for me is real challenge and differentiation.

So just teach them? It's that simple?

Not entirely. For the experienced teacher who has taught a curriculum a million times and worked with numerous students, it is easier. For the novice teacher it's much harder to be responsive – primarily because you've never encountered some of these challenges yet. What I'm getting to is that we need to be in the lesson and constantly on top of things. Constantly talking, assessing, answering questions. Building up a picture of who knows what and what we might do to support our students there and then. This is a real skill. A lot to take on at first but something that gets easier the more experience we develop.

Know the topic so well you can break it down a million different ways

This has to be our number one priority. No amount of worksheets, of differentiated tasks, of differentiated objectives can substitute for the skill you need to answer a curve ball question that a student throws at you. They happen all of the time and unless we know our subject unbelievably well, how can we respond to it? And it's not just questions. Sometimes students find a solution or an answer that isn't quite correct but is quite ingenious. We have to correct it, but we've never thought about that ever possibly being an answer. Students surprise us.

I remember my colleague Jessica (an NQT) tell me how in her rugby lesson with a Year 8 class she explained the rule about passing backwards. Jessica is a rugby player herself and has coached as well as taught rugby for many years. However, a *more able* girl kept turning her back to the opponents try line and passed behind her. Technically she is passing backwards, or in her mind she is passing behind her and they mean the same thing. However, if you know rugby you know that when we say pass backwards, we mean the ball has to be passed back towards your own try line or back down the pitch. You're not allowed the pass the ball forwards, or up the pitch or towards your opponents try line – even if you yourself turned around. Jessica said that she had never ever seen a student do that before. She had never even considered a student would do it, especially one of the *more* able. In her planning, how could she prepare to differentiate for a student misinterpreting that rule that way? And that's where her experience, expertise and knowledge of the sport came in, allowing her to respond to the situation and correct it. That is the art of differentiation.

Ask yourself how well do you know the topic you're teaching next week, the week after, next month? If you could rank order topics in terms of how confident you are at teaching them, which ones would be near the bottom. What bits of them don't you know much about? What do you find difficult when explaining it? Make it a priority to know these as much as the ones near the top of the list. And don't do this just because that topic is about to come up. Do it now, as it takes time to get a deep understanding and will also mean that you can interleave the knowledge into current topics – which, as we know, benefit students' understanding and long-term retention.

And when you are learning more about these topics, know the finer details. Do you know enough about the intricate details of the topic to deal with random questions? We should also step away from the phrase, "But that's all students need to know for the exam", and instead go beyond the curriculum and look to help our students learn things that are amazing. What is the DNA of the topic? What are the fundamentals? What are its various components? How do they link together? How do they relate? What other topics link in? How do these topics influence other topics? How are these topics used within its real life domain? What is the next level of this topic beyond GCSE? I am still conscious that it's the marmite of educational taxonomies, but SOLO taxonomy in a purely planning process is incredibly helpful for this.

One final thought. Ask yourself again how much of school directed CPD is built on developing your subject knowledge. This year our school is allowing us a day to use an INSET day for our own development. A history teacher could try and arrange a bespoke visit to the National History Museum and chat to the curators. An art teacher could do something similar at a gallery or even spend the day meeting a professional artist. Something that pushes your subject knowledge and hence benefits your teaching.

Get among the students

When I first started teaching, one or two bad habits would always seem to creep in. As I've described, I would give students a task and then within a moment of setting them off, I would go over and ask them how they were getting on. They hadn't even had a chance to comprehend the task let alone put pen on paper.

Other times I would set them off and then let them go on indefinitely. I'd not go over and check on them. Maybe because of lack of confidence, I would let them just work, blissfully unaware of how they were getting on.

As my craft as a teacher developed, I realised that I had to get in more often. I was once told (in practical PE) that I needed to speak to at least half of the class every lesson. I needed to get into the mix and find out what was going on. Since then I have made that my mantra, every lesson.

To be responsive you need to get among the students. You need to look over shoulders and check work. You need to see what they're writing down and get a picture of their working. It's ridiculously simple but vitally important. You need to chat to students and find out what they know, what they understand and what they're thinking. You could ask questions such as:

- How are you getting on?
- How are you tackling this task?
- Tell me what you think the question is asking you to do?
- Explain to me what you're planning to do.
- Chat through with me what you need to do to answer this question.
- Is there anything that's causing you confusion?
- Anything that doesn't make sense?
- Read me your answer so far.

Little questions like this begin to give you an insight into what's going on. A while ago when I was trying to do this in a more structured way, I would keep a to ensure that over a two-week period I spoke in some depth to every student in the class. It allowed me to find out what students knew. It allowed me to understand their thinking. It meant I knew my students. I began to realise how each individual worked and what I could do to support them. I found out more that year than I had in the previous six. It's now become a habit. You may call it formative assessment. You may call it assessment for learning. I call it teaching.

Make it live

Once you've worked the class and seen what they are doing, you need to act, there and then. If a student is struggling you need to support them. If a student is flying you need to stretch them. Every student in that class can be pushed further, and we need to do it during the lesson.

Now this sounds stupidly obvious, and it is. But it is so important that I need to make a point of it and show you how you can do it purely with the skill of your own teaching, not with reliance on time consuming resources.

As I've mentioned, one of the biggest game-changers in my career was the purchase of an IPEVO visualiser. These are basically the new age version of an OHP. A camera you plug into your USB port which you can display work on so the whole class can see. It has literally changed my teaching for the better.

With a visualiser to hand, you can use what you've found out from getting amongst students to respond to what is going on. For example:

Model work – When a student gets stuck it may be because they don't know how to construct their sentence, paragraph or essay. When a student produces good work, do they know how to make it better? Do they even know what *better* looks like? Modelling work at that moment in your lesson is priceless.

As I scan the room and look over as many shoulders as I can I begin to notice what's going on. I begin to get an understanding of where people may be flourishing, and where people may be getting stuck. I become very aware that my teaching led to these various outcomes. If I see an excellent piece of work that others aren't quite achieving, I'll pick it up and take it to the visualiser. Under the camera I read out sections of it, complimenting it with numerous questions about the content, style and structure. I'll ask students what they think and what evidence there is for excellence. I discuss it with the whole class because I want everyone engaged. Everyone will benefit if I go through it another time. As we're unpicking it, I'm annotating the "good bits" on the board so that we have a sort of criteria which other students can go away and include.

After we have modelled, dissected, questioned and annotated, I allow time there and then for students to make those amendments to their own work. What is the point of showing brilliance if nobody betters their own work?

But we don't stop there. At that moment the whole class has benefitted except for the student whose work it is. We've praised their working but what have they learnt? Maybe I've reinforced that they should continue to develop good habits and use this structure, example or terminology again, but have I stretched them?

After the class has made their improvements, we turn back to the model. We begin to talk about what we can do to make it better, as there always is something. Like the critique work of Ron Berger (2003), we focus on one thing at a time. Is it terminology? Is it the example? Is it the explanation? We repay the modelled work by stretching it and making it better. We ensure everyone, including the student whose work it is, gets support.

Common mistakes – Good challenge and differentiation involves responding to common errors. When I see the same mistakes coming up time and time again, I stop the class and head to the camera. Under it I begin scribbling down an example of sentences I've seen. I ask the class to see the similarities. They think. I question. They respond. We work out that there has been an overuse of a particular word or an inaccurate reference to a key word. I tweak it. We learn, we improve, we correct.

Moving work up – This takes confidence and also a certain classroom culture. At times we only focus on good pieces of work. What about those who feel they are stuck and can't get to that level? This is where their trust in you allows you to pick up a piece of work from an individual who isn't quite there. Displaying it under the camera allows the class as a collaborative entity to help improve it. The approach is that we're not criticising but instead helping a peer to improve something they are invested their time into. We're showing that we can help support them make their work better. And by doing it as a class, I am helping them be able to respond to it in the future if it crops up again. Once again, we display, we question, we amend and allow time for improvements.

Feedback

After I stepped away from following the so called "Ofsted tick boxes", I stopped looking at the glitzy differentiation people were shoe-horning into lessons and began to listen to the skilful conversations that teachers had with students. The feedback that Mr Ainsworth gave when a student couldn't see how to develop their self-portrait painting anymore. The feedback that Mrs Egerton gave to a Year 10 student who thought they had finished their essay, when a few words of wisdom opened up a new chain of thought. The feedback that Miss Darby gave the struggling Year 7 who couldn't understand tectonic plates. How she adapted her explanation to make it clearer and highlight the stages one step at a time. These things aren't on lessons plans or highlighted on PowerPoint. What they are is individualised bespoke feedback that responds to the work taking place in the lesson. It's responsive teaching. It's a skill. It needs subject knowledge and experience. It is one of the most beautiful parts of a teacher's craft and is the essence of differentiation.

Questioning

Your skill at questioning needs to be high if responsive differentiation is to be effective. It goes hand in hand with the feedback you give. Spend time developing your questioning. Always think "How can I stretch this further" or help to make it better? Use techniques from the questioning chapter such as Doug Lemov's (2015) Right is Right or Stretch it. Ask why, how, when, what, where and how a lot. Be patient and allow students to articulate their thought process, solutions and ideas. Questioning is a powerful tool for differentiation. What you ask one student could be completely different to what you ask another. That's why spending time improving how we ask questions is so important.

Level up

What happens if somebody's work is really good? What do we say to make it better? We might not know what the next level is.

An ex-colleague's little tip is having a bank of exam questions up your sleeve. Go GCSE. Go A-level. Know what gets asked at the next level. Once we're familiar with what the next academic level looks like, we can stretch Key Stage 3 students with real exam questions. We can filter parts of A-level into GCSE. Students will be pushed, stretched and challenged. When you feedback that that was an A-level question they've just nailed, the confidence and reward is clear to see.

So you're saying scrap all the fireworks tasks and just teach. That's easy. But what if I get observed?

What I'm saying is ditch the things that increase workload, reduce content knowledge and don't benefit students. Don't shoe-horn strategies into your lesson for the sake of it. Differentiation comes from fantastic teaching. If an observer says they can't see how you've differentiated, they're plainly looking for countless resources and objectives. I suggest you ask to get observed by somebody else. If they can't see your skilful teaching, I'm not sure they're the right person to observe you.

---

4 Differentiation doesn't need to be visible or just for observers

---

This isn't an excuse for not doing preparation or planning. You should 100 per cent prepare for challenge and differentiation. If not, your lesson will falter. And getting good at challenge and differentiation takes time. Selecting what to do, how you'll do it, how you'll respond takes practice. Developing subject knowledge and various skills takes time. However, ask yourself these following questions.

1. Will this strategy benefit my students? Will it support those who struggle, those who are coasting and push those who are working well? *If so, do it.*

2. Is this strategy for differentiation/challenge for my students, or just to show someone that I'm differentiating in my lesson? *If it's for your students, do it. If it's for an observer, observation or someone else, don't bother.*

So, make differentiation purely for your students and no one else.

To recap

- Aim high and support up.
- Work out where the support may be needed.
- Differentiation is teaching, and very responsive.
- Differentiation doesn't need to be visible or just for observers.

References

Babad, E. Y., Inbar, J., & Rosenthal, R. (1982) Pygmalion, Galatea, and the Golem: Investigations of biased and unbiased teachers. *Journal of Educational Psychology*. 74. pp. 459–474.

Beck, I., McKeown, M., & Kucan, L. (2013) *Bringing Words to Life* (Second Edition). New York: Guildford Press.

Berger, R. (2003) *An Ethic of Excellence; Building a Culture of Craftsmanship with Students*. Portsmouth, NH: Heinemann.

Donaghy, L. (2013) Red scare unit – Lessons 1 to 3. In: *What's Language Doing Here?* 10th November, 2013. Available at: https://whatslanguagedoinghere.wordpress.com/2013/11/10/red-scare-unit-lessons-1-to-3/

Dweck, C. (2012) *Mindset: How You Can Fulfil Your Potential*. London: Robinson.

Hattie, J. (2012) *Visible Learning for Teachers. Maximizing Impact on Learning*. Abingdon: Routledge.

Heroic Imagination TV. (2011) *The Pygmalion Effect and the Power of Positive Expectations*. Available at: www.youtube.com/watch?v=hTghEXKNj7g

Lemov, D. (2014) At first glance: A sentence starter adds unexpected rigor to writing. In: *Teach Like a CHAMPION*. 13th January 2015. Available at: http://teachlikeachampion.com/blog/first-glance-sentence-starter-adds-unexpected-rigor-writing/

Lemov, D. (2015) *Teach like a Champion 2.0: 62 Techniques that Put Students on the Path to College*. San Francisco, CA: Jossey-Bass.

Mayer, R. (2014) Research-based principles for designing multimedia instruction. In: Benassi, V. A., Overson, C. E., & Hakala, C. M. (Eds) *Applying Science of Learning in Education: Infusing Psychological Science into the Curriculum*. pp. 59–70. Available at the Society for the Teaching of Psychology web site: http://teachpsych.org/ebooks/asle2014/index.php

Merton, R. (1968) The Matthew effect in science: The reward and communication systems of science are considered. *Science*. 159. pp. 56–63.

Nuthall, G. (2007) *The Hidden Lives of Learners*. Wellington: NZCER Press.

Rosenthal, R., & Jacobson, L. (1968) Pygmalion in the classroom. *The Urban Revue*. 3(1). pp. 16–20.

Stanovich, K. (1986) Matthew effects in reading: Some consequences of individual differences in the acquisition of literacy. *Reading Research Quarterly*. 22. pp. 360–407.

Walberg, H. J., & Tsai, S. (1983) Matthew effects in education. *American Educational Research Journal*. 20(3). pp. 359–373.

Willingham, D. T. (2009) *Why Don't Students like School? A Cognitive Scientist Answers Questions about How the Mind Works and What It Means for the Classroom*. San Francisco, CA: Jossey-Bass.

Isn't teaching English just for English teachers?

> How literacy shouldn't be a bolt-on in our lessons

There are times during your career as a teacher when an initiative, full of goodwill, ends up feeling like an "add on", something that only seems to be done because we've been told to. These initiatives often highlight an area where as an education system we are probably lagging behind. And as with any area that needs addressing, the decision is to focus on it.

"Literacy" became a buzzword midway during my teaching career. For me it was that "add on". That thing I had to force into my lessons because it appeared on lesson plans and observation proformas. Like many new initiatives, literacy was rolled out during whole school training. Its importance was highlighted and strategies to tackle illiteracy were shared. Literacy co-ordinators appeared. Literacy boxes appeared. Literacy tips of the week appeared.

Literacy is important. It really is. Around this point in my career a report came out that caught my attention. In the Department for Business, Innovation and Skills' Survey of Adult Skills (2012), England's teenagers had one of the worst levels of literacy, coming in among the lowest of all of the countries in the survey. Out of the 24 nations in that survey, England ranked 22nd in terms of levels of literacy for 16–24-year-olds (p. 32). These are individuals who have just finished schooling. The National Literacy Trust (2018) reported on its website that around 15 per cent of adults in England can be described as "functionally illiterate". Headlines of this sort look alarming and encourage critics to attack the education system.

The issue for me though was how the problem was highlighted. It is key that new areas for development don't feel forced or become a tick box exercise. For years I had bulldozed my way through lessons throwing out facts and information. I had set exam questions, homework and essays which students completed. I had marked them and made comments on how accurate the information being communicated was. What I had never done was really consider the way they were communicating it. When the term literacy was propelled to the top of school agendas, it still didn't fully feel like my job. Having dictionaries on the table, doing spelling tests and implementing SPaG marking policies didn't seem to have much substance: they were simply papering the cracks. Something this significant needs to be rolled out better. I believe that three things are necessary:

1. I need to be told, and shown, that literacy is an issue. I needed the facts to open my eyes and hammer home the message that I needed to play my part.

2. I need to be told what this meant for me in my subject. Sometimes whole school strategies don't feel personal. Teachers sometimes can't connect with them or feel that they are a priority. To develop literacy in my subject, I needed help to see how to do it in my subject.

3. We need to be wary about what we call it. The great Geoff Barton insists we don't call it literacy at all. We should understand that good teaching develops literacy and literacy is part of good teaching. He is right. Literacy is a vast component of teaching yet it's bunched up into one term. If we're going to go whole school, by all means use the term but unpick it so every teacher knows what is required. As George Sampson said back in 1921, "Every teacher in English is necessarily a teacher of English, every teacher, without exception" (p. 63). At that time, knowledge of my subject was my priority. Getting students to remember definitions and make meaning of information was my primary focus. How the students constructed sentences and used accurate grammar was an afterthought. I probably thought that was the role of the English teachers in our school. I couldn't fully see how the two things overlapped. It came about from many years of not recognising that every teacher has a duty to improve literacy levels. It was following Twitter English teachers like Chris Curtis, Kenny Pieper, David Didau, Anne Williams, David Bunker, Jo Facer, Kerry Pullyen, Matt Pinkett, Caroline Spalding, Lisa-Jane Ashes and many other amazing teachers that showed me the error of this thinking. Yes, there is still work to do and yes I still need support, but developing our students' communication through my teaching is now top of my agenda.

Addressing the problem

I'm writing this bit of the chapter as I sit in a conference about PE teaching. We had a fantastic opening keynote by an ex-elite sportsman talk about mindset and grit and about how he was influenced by his PE teachers, and how this took him to be British number 1 and eventually go on to do a lot of media and journalism. His message was that we need to inspire the next generation, not only in practical PE but also in PE physiology and psychology. At that point I was sold. Such good sense. Doing well in GCSE PE opens up a number of scientific jobs, a number of media jobs, a number of commercialism areas. The list goes on.

However, the series of "sub keynotes" that followed completely deflated me and in fact made me very angry. Speakers began nearly every section with "The students found the reading and writing element of it too tough so we chose to put them onto an easier course . . . " Now I am realistic. I have a family. I want my two daughters to leave school with good grades. But the underlying message was if students find the writing element, the rigour of the higher assessment objectives, the length of written work a struggle – switch them.

The teacher in me was furious. It felt like presenter after presenter was saying that instead of tackling the difficulties in literacy and writing that come with the new specification, we should side step them. It felt as though results had become the primary concern and that improving levels of reading, writing and subject knowledge should be sacrificed. If I didn't mishear them, this is part of the problem that I spoke about earlier. Messages like this carry the danger of having some teachers feel they don't need to worry about reading, writing and communication if they can get higher grades on courses where they're less necessary.

Why this bothered me was the fact that along with good grades, I would like my daughters to be able to write well. I want them to understand language. I want their vocabulary to continue to grow – for them to understand what these new words mean in context. Be confident to use them in conversation. And that for me is what teaching is about. I may get a grilling because I didn't go for an easier course to boost my grades. But I want my students to be better writers, readers and communicators. I want them to know a lot about a lot of things. It may sound like I'm chasing a dream, but it's what I want.

It's therefore important that we as teachers know how to support those who struggle with reading and writing. It's important we don't just leave it to the English teachers. I need to ensure I am skilled enough to help students but humble enough to seek further support myself. That's what this chapter is about. Not grades, not results (although they are incredibly important), but helping to set students up for life.

That's noble, David, but is it realistic?

We need to be realistic. I struggle myself with some of the ways the English language directs us to write. I know I can't fix every problem. However, I can do my bit.

The demographic of students I have worked with during my career has mainly been students whose first language is English. I have very little experience of EAL students so don't feel I have the specialist knowledge to support the challenges of this particular. However, I have boys who read very little and struggle with it. I have girls who write so much that their writing becomes too complex to make sense. I have those who write only a few words and those who write beautifully. I have those who write how they speak. I have those who have no idea how to start a sentence. Those who struggle with spelling and those who pull out fascinating facts supported by well-reasoned argument.

Even in the classrooms I work in, there's so much I can do to help support students' reading and writing. My teaching of this may not build a skyscraper, but I can help lay the foundations and construct a few of the floors. I know some may need to access "softer" courses, but why not aim high and help those who struggle with reading and writing rather than taking the easy option?

So how much do I need to know about English, literacy, grammar, spelling . . . ?

Ask yourself this question (unless you're an English teacher!):

> Have you ever written something and then reworded it because you were not confident about the grammar or structure of the sentence?

I have, a lot! There have been numerous times where I couldn't remember whether to use a semi-colon or whether to use an apostrophe before or after an s. And this is probably true for many of our students. Things like grammar can cause huge issues and is the number one thing that causes me worry when writing. But if we let it become our demon and never truly tackle it, how can we tackle it with our students? For a teacher of any kind, it is important to know the rules around key language components such as grammar and spelling. A conversation with Caroline Spalding, an English teacher and assistant headteacher in Derby, made me realise my first key principle.

---

1 Be relentless in your demand for "the basics"

As a PE teacher I have been particularly inspired watching, and reflecting on, the way people coach students in physical skills. There are stories from the world of sport of great coaches like Sir Clive Woodward, Pep Guardiola and Sir David Brailsford. Could the same principles and approaches be applied to all learning? Every time we teach a child a brand new sport, it feels as though we go back to square one. We finish the unit on rugby just as the students became more fluent at passing, their movement gets better and their positioning improves. When we move on to handball, the first lesson is like going right back to the beginning again with a class full of novices.

When this happens we go back to basics. We work on the fundamental movements again, linking them into some of the other sports we have covered. We practise and practise, increasing challenge and content and giving timely feedback. We focus on students getting the basics right. If they aren't, we intervene. We make sure it's done right every time and then practise it perfectly until it becomes habit.

In the classroom I never did this. Or if I did, I did it too late. My philosophy as a practical teacher didn't transfer into my theory lessons. I didn't intervene like I did on the playing field. I lowered expectations for poor answers. Not in the terms of the content; that I picked up on in an instant. What I lowered was my standard for how they wrote. I would tell students that their grammar wasn't accurate but didn't really correct it. I would let them know their spelling was wrong but never followed it up. I would scribble over sentences that waffled on, but did I ever show them how it should be, as I would in a practical lesson? Nope!

Be relentless

As Caroline Spalding, an English teacher and assistant headteacher from Derby told me, "Rare is the Year 11 student who truly doesn't 'know' when to use capital letters and full stops or how to spell homophones correctly – does classwork in every subject reflect this?" That's a good question.

When we are faced with a piece of work that is littered with spelling mistakes, we probably don't pick up every single one because we (rightly) worry that we'll decrease students' confidence and self-esteem. Telling them we can't read their work at all can be quite demoralising. However, we need to tackle it. We need to have a culture where students see that we're trying to help them. We want their efforts to be read.

Be relentless on . . . handwriting

One of the things that frustrates me most is students' handwriting. It used to be because I couldn't read it and that really bugged me. "If they can't write clearly, why am I bothering trying to decipher it?" Now it bothers me because I see individuals working really hard on getting their thoughts down on paper, and nobody can read it. That's such a shame and a waste of their efforts. Handwriting is a gateway to a student's thoughts. If we can't read it we don't know what they actually know.

Handwriting has its issues. We might assume that the intelligent students write well, and the not so bright students write poorly. We unconsciously stereotype. This isn't always the case, though. Some of the most intelligent students I've worked with have very weak presentation skills. There are also the students who write too quickly and the speed of the process makes work difficult to read. There are students who have never had good handwriting. Then there are the ones who are simply lazy and aren't bothered about what their work looks like. The worry is that poor handwriting builds a self-fulfilling prophecy whereby students whose handwriting is poor avoid writing.

I remember a teacher who had become frustrated about the presentation of one of her student's work chatting to an English teacher in their school, only for that teacher to show them the work that student produced in their lesson. The work in the English book was neat and legible – nothing like it was in the other teacher's lesson. Why? You might suggest that it's because it's from an English lesson and part and parcel of the subject. But handwriting is handwriting. Some might say that students care more in certain lessons. If that's the case then we need to work out how to harness that care in all our lessons. Others might say the demands of a subject differ. Some lessons allow slower thought formation and more time to get ideas down. Other subjects are crammed full of facts, definitions and meaning. There's not much time to get through all the content.

Whichever way it is, we need ways to help students improve their handwriting, otherwise they may put effort into a well-crafted answer only to get no marks because it can't be deciphered. Losing a few marks here and there might not sound like a big deal, but if it means missing a grade boundary then it means quite a lot. So how can we help?

Insist on a culture where presentation matters

The third slide on every one of my lesson PowerPoints is a recap of the rules in my classroom. Ninety-nine per cent of the time I quickly skip on, but I know it's there for reference if students don't follow them. One of them is that if work is poorly presented, the student must redo that work. This may seem harsh but it was put in place at the very beginning of the GCSE course because I don't want students losing marks because we can't read the work. I also want my students to take pride in their work. At some point they're going to be working in the real world where communication and presentation matter. When I introduced the rule I made it very clear why it was in place. I told them how it benefits them. The number of students who have had to rewrite their work is very low. It's low because I made a point and explained the importance.

However . . .

If we become too obsessed with presentation and get too critical, we will lower students' self-esteem and have a negative effect on handwriting. It's a slow process so give it time. But you knew that already.

Make their work feel like it matters

If a child writes in their exercise book every lesson, but it never ever gets read, there is a chance that after a while they will worry less about the presentation of their work. It may seem simple but acknowledging student work could help improve the care that students take. It doesn't mean marking every book. It could be as simple as walking the classroom and looking over shoulders. Praising good work when you see it and mentioning presentation in the conversation. Make a point of it and it becomes a prominent part of your classroom. Keep referring to it and it becomes a good habit. Don't mention it and don't be surprised if presentation is poor.

Make them write a lot

If I wanted to get better at a particular skill, let's say a free kick in football, I would probably dedicate a lot of (distributed) practice to it. If I wanted to get more cardiovascular endurance for my running, I would probably run a lot. A while ago an ex-colleague of mine said that students could easily go to a lesson without the need to write anything. They don't need to write to learn. I didn't say anything at the time, but I didn't agree. If we want students to develop their handwriting they need opportunities to practise it. And when they do, we need to check how it's going – intervening when necessary.

If we want them to develop writing stamina, especially with the new curricula demands, we need to take on John Tomsett's advice from #TLT17 and get students to write until their hand hurts. Why? Because without dedicating time for them to practise their writing, it can't possibly improve. Steve Graham (2009, p. 27) estimates that in early years education, students need 50–100 minutes dedicated handwriting practise a week to master it. If that hasn't happened we may need to build in time in our lessons. Do you have periods of extended writing in most lessons? If you don't it might not be a bad idea to add some in.

Make them slow down

When I try and get my ideas on paper quickly, it usually ends up a massive page of scrawl. Students are the same. When speed increases, so – with some – does the quality.

Automaticity and fluency in writing is really important. In the context of answering exam questions, writing at speed is equally important. Take too long and you run out of time and inevitably rush towards the end. However, if writing too quickly and poor handwriting is an issue, insist on students slowing down. Get them to focus on one sentence at a time. Give them slightly more time than they need to construct it. Build it up to multiple sentences, paragraphs and whole essays. Each time give them slightly longer than they need and insist that they slow down what they write. When handwriting improves we can begin to increase speed.

Slowing down also helps relieve one of the biggest issues with handwriting. Those with poor handwriting spend more time than others concentrating on the process. They dedicate so much attention to it that they add to working memory load, which leaves less space in the mind to consider what they're writing *about*. When they try to write quicker this only adds to the problem.

Cursive or non-cursive

Writing cursively (joined-up) seems to be the end goal of all handwriting. It's where we naturally end up as adults. Sometimes I feel frowned upon by colleagues if I write non-cursively. However, my non-cursive handwriting is much more legible than my joined-up writing. So why do we turn our noses up at it? Maybe it's perceived as being a slower form of writing. Maybe we fear it looks childish. Whatever the reason, Steve Graham (2009) suggests that to improve handwriting with some students, writing non-cursively might be beneficial for four reasons:

1. Many children come into early education knowing the formation of individual letters. When trying to join up these students might have to relearn the formation to allow them to be joined up. This may be a struggle. Add to that the fact that nearly all of the text they read in books, articles and sources is written non-cursive, it might help them to revert back to it.

2. There is some (dated) evidence that non-cursive writing is easier to learn than cursive writing.

3. Non-cursive writing, when mastered, can be as quick as cursive. So speed of writing needn't be a worry.

4. Use of non-cursive (traditional manuscript) might actually facilitate reading development due to the fact (as I mentioned earlier) that most text is not cursive.

So might stepping away from non-cursive writing be the answer? Alison Sefton, a deputy head and head of science from Shropshire, has thought about this:

> The skill of joined up writing is apparently no longer a requirement in American schools, and several countries have dropped cursive writing from the curriculum or made it optional. Maybe it's time we think about doing the same in this country?
>
> For many years I have wondered why we continue to teach cursive writing in primary schools. Once, almost an artform, it appears to me that the skill of joined up writing has become a real stumbling block for many pupils and can hamper their ability to succeed in formal examinations once they reach secondary school. Whilst I get used to the handwriting of those I teach, for an examiner looking at the inky trail of a dying spider, I worry that they will not be able to interpret what is in front of them and my pupils will miss out on vital marks. I have regularly discussed with pupils how to improve their handwriting "so that the examiner can read your answer" and more often than not, this has led to my suggesting they print instead of joining up. Initially, pupils are sceptical; joined up writing has been ingrained in them for so long; but once they try it they rarely go back. Taking away the need to join up their writing seems to lead to a sense of relief in pupils – taking the focus away from that and allowing more time to focus on the answer. Why do I think this works? All teachers know the impact of modelling as a method of instruction. Look around your classroom . . . where is joined up writing modelled? In the books you ask the pupils to read? In the worksheets you ask them to complete? On the slides you use to teach them a new topic? On the displays around your classroom walls? I cannot remember ever observing a lesson where joined up writing is modelled. So why do we continue to insist on pupils using it?

Highlighted paper

One reason why writing is difficult to read is that students don't vary the height of the letters. Tall letters (l, h, b, f . . .) sometimes end up the same size as small letters (a, e, c . . .). One way to tackle this is by using highlighted paper – paper which has the lower half of each line shaded out (normally in yellow). What this makes students do is keep small letters inside the shaded section, with tall letters expected to break out of that and reach the top of the line. It's wonderfully simple.

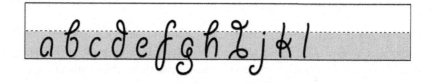

You can download highlighted paper for free from numerous websites. If you want to keep work in books, ask students to use a ruler to draw a line halfway between each line in yellow, and encourage them to keep small letters below it, and tall letters rising above it.

Spacing

Sometimes words are spaced so close together that they merge into one. My five-year-old constantly tells me how to spell words in a sentence, saying "finger space" as she moves onto the next word. When she writes, she physically puts her finger between words. I know that she is simply practising writing, with little thought about understanding what she has written. Her working memory is focused on spelling a word and working out how to get the letters on paper. Lots of teachers in secondary still insist on methods like this. Some use the basic "Place your finger between words". Others use a ball of blue tack. Some even have a small circular sticker that they put between words to get students into good habits. Whatever method, the spacing of words can be an area to focus on to improve legibility.

Write the key words in capitals

Ed Allchorne, a biology teacher in Bath, told me once how he insists students write the keywords in a sentence in capitals. This isn't tackling the larger handwriting problem, but it's a small step that any teacher can implement to alert the reader to the fact that the student knows what the keywords are and has sequenced them correctly. Ed now does the same when modelling his own work with students, underlining them to add even more impact.

Write bigger

Nancy Gedge, consultant teacher at the Driver Youth Trust, said that for her 14-year-olds, getting them to write slightly bigger was a revelation. She said that sometimes habits might be too embedded to change and some students might get tired of being told they are too messy, but simply increasing the size of each word makes it easier for the reader to interpret. Simples.

Be relentless on . . . spelling

This will be a quick point as SPaG is a big thing in schools and you don't need any extra bombardment from me. However, there are a number of times when students repeatedly misspell words, and if we teachers let it go, the problem won't disappear. So how can we tackle spelling?

Introduce new tricky words before a topic

If you have a topic with "tricky" words (anaerobic, respiration, gaseous, oxygenated, haemoglobin?), it might make sense to share these words with students before they use them. Spend a few minutes getting students to familiarise themselves with them, copy them out if needed or add them to a resource such as a knowledge organiser so they can call upon them when they need them. Teach them how to spell them right from the start and there'll be a chance they'll learn it correctly, and use it correctly, from then on.

Hit the commonly misspelled words hard!

The most frustrating words I read are *loose* rather than *lose*. *Alot* rather than *a lot*. *Everytime* rather than *every time*. Breaking these habits can be difficult but they haven't developed on purpose and we need to emphasise that they're not right. I spend lesson after lesson tackling these errors as they crop up. I may get students going "Here he goes again!" but after a while the bad habits slowly disappear.

Rules

Reminding certain students of rules such as "i before e except after c" helps them spell some of the commonly misspelled words we come across. Sorry if that's obvious, but in the fast paced nature of a lesson we might forget that they either don't know that, or forget it as they put pen to paper. Look for them and highlight them where needed.

Note down commonly misspelt words

Every time I mark books or tests, I record things like misconceptions, good bits . . . and spellings on a little sheet of paper. At the start of the next lesson, we have a spelling test using those words. Ninety-nine per cent of the time, the fact I focus on them means that students spell them right. However, afterwards I go through their spelling them on the board, explaining why they are written this way. Learning the subtle differences is important.

Spelling tests

Why not. Not only do they help with spelling the complex words which are so important in our subjects, they also act as a retriever of knowledge. If I ask you to spell a word, there's a high chance you will think of the meaning of that word or maybe even elaborate on it further in your mind. As we saw in previous chapters, that can only help.

Wait, you haven't mentioned we need to be relentless on . . . grammar and punctuation

I know I know. But if I go into all the various rules around grammar, this book will evolve into something it's not. Grammar is difficult and its correct use can be a stumbling block for both student and teacher. Learn the basics which you can reinforce in every lesson (when to use capitals, when to add a comma, when to split a sentence into two with a full stop).

When marking, use things like SPaG marking codes to highlight areas and then explain common errors to the class.

Grammar is important and there are numerous resources and books available which I urge you to read up on to ensure that we know our stuff so we can help students know their stuff.

The basics? That's hardly revolutionary

I get that. But it's the small parts that contribute to the bigger picture. If we let the basics slip, there'll be more that we need to tackle later on. If we can chip away slowly at some of the things which students should be able to do but can't/forget/didn't know, we develop better habits. We work to the ethos that *perfect practice makes perfect.* However, there is another area that need developing and that teachers like you and I can help with: reading.

---

2 Encourage students to read a lot

Initially this principle was worded "Make your students read a lot" but the very wise Kenny Pieper, an English teacher and author from Scotland, advised that the word *make* was a bit harsh and might put children off reading. He is right. I have students in my class who I know avoid reading at all costs, and making them do it will not inspire a love of reading in them.

For many years I simply assumed reading was done in English lessons and the most I had to do in a PE theory lesson was get students to refer to the textbook. However, reading books isn't simply the job of English teachers and getting students to read a short paragraph from a textbook isn't enough.

This section isn't exactly about ways to get students to read more. It isn't filled with a million whizzy ways to get students to run to the library and borrow armfuls of novels and stories. There are many amazing strategies in schools and in public libraries that do that. Instead what it intends to do is explain why we should be adding reading (which is subject relevant) to our lessons. It looks at some of the benefits of doing so and how to support it. It also looks at why some students don't engage in reading, explaining the barriers they face, and what we can do in our classrooms to help build up their confidence in this area.

So why is reading so important?

I really didn't take reading seriously in my classroom. I knew reading was important but had never made the explicit link to other areas of writing, subject knowledge and simple communication. I naively assumed that all I needed to do as a teacher was give students information, get them to read an exam question and then write a beautiful answer. The reading bit seemed the smallest part of the sequence. I waltzed through, blissfully unaware.

So what's changed?

I have referred to the OECD Survey of Adult Skills (2012), which ranked the literacy levels of our 16–24-year-olds pretty low. With that knowledge we could have made a knee jerk reaction and got silly with our policies. However, well thought out and carefully implemented strategies are bringing about improvements in key areas – such as reading.

In the National Literacy Trust's 2017 publication "Celebrating Reading for Enjoyment: Findings from our Annual Literacy Survey 2016", reading seems to be on the up. One of the most promising headlines was that the "Reading for enjoyment levels" have gone up since 2013, with 6 children in 10 (58.6%) saying that they enjoy reading either very much or quite a lot.

Like all reports it also indicated areas to focus on. For instance, 64.9 per cent of girls enjoy reading compared to 52.4 per cent of boys. This deficit with boys continues to be an issue as students get older, with 72.4 per cent of 8–11-year-old boys enjoying reading compared to 43.8 per cent for 14–16-year-old boys. For girls the respective figures are 82.8 per cent, and 53.3 per cent. So there is clearly a gender issue with reading, especially as boys get older.

The report also highlighted something else, which might seem unexpected. There was no difference in reading enjoyment between Free School Meal children (FSM) and non-Free School Meal children. Both had a reading enjoyment of 58.3%.

So why am I looking at reading for enjoyment levels rather than national reading ages? Well, many strategies that improve reading ages are very specific and generally run as separate programmes outside of my lessons. I have less control over them. Reading for enjoyment is something I know I can help with.

Reading has numerous benefits. The National Literacy Trust (2017) lists them as follows:

- Reading for enjoyment supports wider learning
- Children who enjoy reading are:
  - More likely to read daily (47.5 percent v 9.9%).
  - More confident readers.
  - Read more books in free time per month (6.26 v 2.38).
  - Spend more minutes reading books (44.23 v 19.4).
  - Have higher reading scores (105.53 v 94.01).
  - Have better reading ages with age (10 year old – 10.8yrs v 9.5 yrs. 14 year old – 15.3 yrs v 12 yrs).

(pp. 1–3)

The problem is that I haven't got the opportunity or time in lessons to really dedicate parts of them to reading novels and stories. I wish I did. Nothing would make me happier than saying, "Right class, let's get your reading book out for the next 20 minutes". Unfortunately, the new curriculums mean there's more content to cover than ever before. But what I can do in lessons is try to break down the barriers to reading. I can try to introduce more texts in lessons and help students feel more confident about reading them. And not just reading them, but actually understanding them. When I speak to students they say, "I'm not good at it, I don't like it, and as a result I don't do it". That's a culture and belief I need to change. Why aren't they good at it? Why does reading worry them?

Okay, go on . . .

I need to introduce you to the work of Anne Cunningham, Keith E. Stanovich, David Kilpatrick and E. D. Hirsch, Jr.

As I mentioned in the chapter on differentiation and challenge, Keith E. Stanovich borrowed a term used by Robert K. Merton (1968) called the Matthew effect. It's based on the biblical notion that the rich get richer and the poor get poorer. Stanovich (1986) used it to explain that good early readers end up with a better vocabulary and a greater enjoyment of reading. He states,

> The very children who are reading well and who have good vocabularies will read more, learn more word meanings, and hence read even better. Children with inadequate vocabularies-who read slowly and without enjoyment-read less, and as a result have slower development of vocabulary knowledge, which inhibits further growth in reading ability .
>
> (p. 381)

People like me were blissfully unaware that this was an issue in the classroom. But it makes so much sense. If students vocabularies and word knowledge is poor, of course they won't enjoy reading.

A study by Betty Hart and Todd R. Riley (2003) followed 42 families for over two and a half years, observing and recording the various factors affecting the vocabulary growth of the children (starting age of 7–9 months). It looked at how the socio-economic status of the various families affected how rich a vocabulary these children developed. Although all of the various families were similarly engaged in the funda-mental tasks of raising their children (discipline, good manners, clean themselves, etc.), the depth of vocabulary varied vastly across the children.

The researchers found a number of things, including how vocabulary use at age three was a good predictor of reading comprehension and language skills at age nine or ten. What they also found out is that different socioeconomic groups had exposure to different numbers of words. For example, low SES (socioeconomic status) children heard on average 616 words an hour. Middle class or average SES heard on average 1,251 words per hour. Professional families of high SES heard on average 2,153 words per hour. Hart and Risley predicted that in a four-year period, the high SES child would have experienced 45 million words, the middle SES would have experienced 26 million words, while the low SES would have experienced only 13 million words. That's a difference of over 30 million words!

But wait a minute David, this study includes words spoken to the child by the parents, not just reading

I know, I know. There is a link between words that children know through dialogue and reading, which I'll expand on later. But for now what I'm highlighting is that some children are exposed to far more words and word meanings than others. And that's a problem. And how does this link to reading? Well, reading is another way to develop or enrich vocabulary depth. According to Cunningham and Stanovich (2001), "reading volume made a significant contribution to multiple measures of vocabulary, general knowledge, spelling, and verbal fluency" (p. 143).

There was quite a lot of research published in the 1980s on the acquisition of vocabulary and its effects. A number of studies showed that reading helped develop vocabulary better than some instructional programmes. For instance, Daniel T. Willingham (2014) and E. D. Hirsch, Jr (2003) concluded that in a classroom setting, things such as reading comprehension and vocabulary are best supported by extended time reading and listening to texts and then discussing the facts and ideas with the students.

Why? Nagy et al. (1985) conducted a study with 57 eighth grade students to see if they learned words through incidental learning from written texts. After reading a 100 word text, the students were tested on word knowledge and meaning. The study concluded that a large proportion of children's vocabulary learnt over a year was a result of reading. This is only one study, but it links with others that place a similar emphasis on reading.

So what sort of number of words are we talking about?

Nagy and Anderson (1984) estimated that, as regards in-school reading,

> the least motivated children in the middle grades might read 100,000 words a year while the average children at this level might read 1,000,000. The figure for the voracious middle grade reader might be 10,000,000 or even as high as 50,000,000. If these guesses are anywhere near the mark, there are staggering individual differences in the volume of language experience, and therefore, opportunity to learn new words
>
> (p. 328)

What! Those differences are huge. But ask yourself how much reading do you do in your classroom to contribute to this? Nagy and Anderson's study quoted here focused on the amount of reading *in school*. Up to a few years ago the reading in my lessons consisted of the words on my PowerPoint slides or a few paragraphs from a textbook. That's not a lot. So how does this differ from out of school?

In 1988, Richard Anderson, Paul Wilson and Linda Fielding studied 155 fifth grade students to see how much reading they did out of school and how it affected reading achievement. The students came from a city school and a village school and logged their out of school activities over a space of six months. Students undertook three reading tests during the study. Anderson, Wilson and Fielding then gathered the data and estimated how many words a student might read per year based on how much time they read per day, combined with their reading rate (speed). These estimates, if correct, are astonishing.

For example, a low reader in the 10th percentile, averaging 0.2 minutes of reading outside of the classroom per day, would only read 8,000 words a year. 8,000 outside of the classroom is not much compared to Anderson's previous estimation of a low reader reading

100,000 words inside the classroom. So that would mean that in total (in class plus out of class), a low reading student would be exposed to around 108,000 words a year.

By contrast, the avid reader in the top 98th percentile averages 90.7 additional minutes of reading a day outside of the classroom. According to the estimate, this means that, over a year, they read an extra 4,733,000 words. Combine this with the potential 50,000,000 words they read inside the classroom and it's nearly 55 million. Wow! And compared to the 108,000 words of the lowest readers . . . well, what can I say.

So, I'm guessing this exposure to words is really important

Indeed it is. If Hart and Riley's estimates of 45 million spoken words heard over four years, and Anderson et al.'s estimates of 50 million words read per year are anything to go by, some students will clearly develop a wider vocabulary than others. And that has its benefits. For example, Nagy and Anderson (1984) estimated that for every word learnt, there could be an additional one to three words that an individual will be able to interpret. Learning the word *responsible* might help a child understand the word *responsibility*. Knowing the word *lead* might help understand the words *leader, leadership* or *leading*. When students have a wider vocabulary they can make better and quicker associations with new words or possibly "old" words in different contexts. And that's really important for teachers to know. Some students might not have a clue what we're talking about, not because they're "dumb" (as I've heard many students label themselves), but because they've never heard many of the words we use. Similarly, students might not use a variety of words in their work because they have had so little exposure to them and are unsure how to use them correctly.

So what are the barriers? What is causing this deficit?

There are numerous reasons, some of which I don't feel confident I can influence so will leave to more experienced educators. However, there are a few interesting things that I think we all need to be aware of.

In David Kilpatrick's 2016 Reading League session, he explained that reading fluency is in large impacted by the size of an individual's *sight* vocabulary. These sight words are effortless and pre-cognitive words that "pop" out when we read. With a large sight vocabulary, most (or all) words "pop out". This means that reading is fast and accurate. With this, a student can turn their attention to text comprehension. David then goes on to say that if you have limited sight vocabulary, reading is effortful and often inaccurate because too many unfamiliar words require strategic decoding.

I had never considered sight words before, but it makes so much sense. Take the words that my five-year-old daughter is working on at the moment. Some words like *the, of, and, mum,* and *all* take her a split second to recognise. Other words she has to sound out and then blend. Because she has limited sight words, reading is slow and difficult. Most of her working memory is spent decoding letters, sounds and what the word is. Often we have to recap the sentence just to make sure she has understood what she read.

David explains that the key to developing sight words is a person's orthographic mapping: the ability to quickly add words to your sight vocabulary. If you are good at orthographic mapping, reading is fantastic as you pick up these new words. But what about those with poor orthographic mapping? You might think that simply getting them to read will help. It won't, because you're trying to get someone who struggles to read, to struggle to read. They need a bit more support than that. David likens this to getting some students to write on normal writing paper and some to write on laminated paper. Good orthographic mappers (those with the normal paper) will be fine as they put pen to paper. Those with poor orthographic mapping (writing on the laminated paper) will struggle. They may make some marks or have a bit of the ink latch onto the laminated surface, but it won't be like using normal paper. That's how it is for poor orthographic mappers. Words just don't "stick" as well. So how do we combat this?

David explains that students need to be explicitly exposed to new vocabulary. He suggests that we are probably only directly taught a tiny fraction of the 40,000 to the 90,000 words in our sight vocabulary. David suggests that it takes 1–4 of these explicit exposures for the word to become part of your sight vocabulary. Poor readers may need 15, 20 or even 30 exposures. But once it is stored, it can't be unstored. You can't unsee sight words. And as this bank of words increases, so does reading fluency. And once reading fluency improves, students can spend more time on comprehension. That's where learning our subject can really be supported.

You mentioned fluency leads to comprehension

I did. As E.D Hirsch Jr (2003) describes, the more fluent students are at reading, the less they have to dedicate conscious attention to work out the words, rather than work out what they mean (comprehension). The converse of this is that poor readers face numerous struggles with reading. According to Cunningham and Stanovich (2001), the fact that they have lower decoding skills, a lot less practice, and difficult materials (for them) to read, makes reading an unrewarding experience. They also go on to point out that the lack of exposure to text and reading for a less skilled reader

> delays the development of automaticity and speed at the word recognition level. Slow, capacity-draining word recognition processes require cognitive resources that should be allocated to comprehension. Thus, reading for meaning is hindered; unrewarding reading experiences multiply; and practice is avoided or merely tolerated without real cognitive involvement.
>
> (p. 137)

Because the process is slow and difficult, most of a poor reader's working memory is dedicated to working out what each word *is*, rather than what each word *means*. When this difficulty persists, individuals begin to avoid reading, which leads to the gap getting bigger. Since, as Cunningham and Stanovich claim, most researchers are convinced that vocabulary development comes from reading and language exposure, avoiding the process is something we as teacher need to tackle.

Similarly, if we're dedicating more of our working memory to decoding words, these words can be forgotten before we get a chance to understand them. This is why we find some students have to re-read a text a number of times. Not because they weren't concentrating but because they might have forgotten what it was they have just read. If an individual's reading fluency improves, the space in working memory is freed up and students can actually spend more time understanding the text.

But that's not all. If we can engage our students with reading, and reading because they want to, their vocabulary will increase. And this increase will also help comprehension in the following ways.

Knowing more words helps us make inferences

Writers omit a good deal of what they mean. They don't explain every single little detail. If they did it would be an incredibly long book and quite boring. So when we read a book or an article we need to make inferences, using our knowledge to join the dots. An understanding of the meaning of words helps things make sense.

Knowing more helps reading – it might be more important than some literacy programmes

Willingham (2017) argues that the overemphasis on literacy instruction has a detrimental effect later on. The time spent focusing on it means that there is less time for acquiring subject knowledge. Further down the line these students won't have the background knowledge to understand a text so it may not make sense. The following exercise helps explain this.

Spend the next few moments reading this extract from an article on thermodynamics by Abrams and Prausnitz (1975, p 116).

> To obtain a semi-theoretical equation for the excess Gibbs energy of a liquid mixture, Guggenheim's quasi-chemical analysis is generalized through introduction of the local area fraction as the primary concentration variable. The resulting universal quasi-chemical (UNIQUAC) equation uses only two adjustable parameters per binary.

What I'd like you to do is try and explain what the extract is talking about.

If you're like me, you probably had to read the text a few times. Most of its words are in my bank of vocabulary, I know what they mean. Individually I can recognise them and make sense of them. Combined together, they are more difficult to interpret. Now, I know this is a really obscure example – students in secondary schools don't need to know much about thermodynamics. But the extract is for *you*. You're like a child learning about anaerobic respiration for the first time: it doesn't necessarily make immediate sense. So Willingham's suggestion is to spend more time on subject knowledge. That way, students have not only the vocabulary awareness but also the subject understanding to comprehend the text. I had never thought about the direct link between the two before but it's now become critical in my planning.

E. D Hirsch, Jr (2003) also makes reference to how knowledge benefits readers. When students have larger domain knowledge, the fluency of their reading increases. When this happens readers make connections between new and previously learned topics much more quickly. He argues that it both eases *and* deepens comprehension (p. 13).

When you know more about specific topics, things make even more sense – prior knowledge is important!

Reading that extract, I (and possibly you) had no idea what was really being discussed. However, if you happened to know about thermodynamics, it would have made complete sense. I know that's ridiculously obvious. But when we give an article or text for students to read in our lesson, they may not have a clue what they're reading. And when that happens, students use up a lot of their working memory trying to decipher what they're reading and have less of this space to make sense of it. For instance, if during one of my lessons I gave out an article explaining how elite cyclists have used technology to improve their performance and it talked about pelotons, cadence, carbon fibre, analytics, Pinarello, threaded bottom brackets and crank arms, unless students had experience of cycling it could be really confusing.

On the other hand, if you have good prior knowledge/domain knowledge of a topic, you can read the text quickly. You are more fluent. You can probably chunk information as Hirsch (2003, p. 13) suggests, as one item so you still have working memory free for other things.

As teachers we therefore need to be wary about what we're about to teach our classes. If students don't have sufficient prior knowledge of a topic, we might need to build this up first before giving them certain new materials. We need to help them build a picture so that when they read a text they can pull it all together and make sense of it.

You've hammered home the point. I get it. But how do I do it?

That's the tricky part. We've got to be realistic. I made a point at the start of this principle acknowledging that some of the reading interventions in schools (secondary for me) are done outside the classroom. We also need to stay away from gimmicks. Short-term fixes don't do anything except fix things in the short term. I also know that we can't give up large chunks of our lessons to reading (as much as I wish I could) because that would eat into curriculum time and also, as any of you have silent reading in tutor time know, it is doubtful how many students would actually engage in it. And anyway, does simply adding more reading help reading? Well as I said earlier, this principle is about encouraging students to read more. Knowing the importance of this and the barriers that students face, what small steps could I employ?

Change the culture: introduce texts into your classroom

How often do you look at the topic you're about to cover and then actively seek out an article to go with it, something to explain or support what it is you are teaching? If you do, that's amazing.

Articles can be extremely helpful. Searching for relevant ones and sharing them in your lessons creates the culture that reading will help us learn more in this subject. After a while it becomes the norm. Print enough copies for every student to have one and have a format that will enable them to store them safely so they can refer to them in their own time. And why? Because if we know reading is important, we need to help students make that link as well. Just as we ask them to write, answer questions and discuss, we can get them to see reading articles and texts as part and parcel of our lessons.

Choosing these texts is really important. Pitching it right takes skill. You will want to choose a text that suits the class or different ones for the various levels of reading ability in the class. There are numerous websites and apps that can sort text by level of difficulty. There are also websites like the BBC's that have articles carefully written for a wide audience.

Once you have found a relevant text, it need to be introduced in a way that tells students that it is important yet does not put pressure on students by exposing their flaws. Use the article wisely so students interact with it in a variety of ways. Mix silent reading with teacher led narration. Combine reading an extract with reading full pieces. Alternate between texts full of facts and texts which do something else, like provide summaries. All the time make the text important, but not something to trip students up on.

If you recall, in the chapter on memory I mentioned the work of Daniel T. Willingham (2009) and how stories make a useful tool. Stories may be trickier to find in a search engine, yet they could provide so much. Consider business studies. If we were explaining business growth, we could either find a text which provided facts, definitions and examples or find something similar but telling the story of Richard Branson and how his Virgin empire grew to incorporate media, banking, travel and more. Same topic but two distinctly different articles. A story may provide context and help students make sense of the topic more easily. Not easy to come across, but stories as a text can be powerful.

And once we have text in our classrooms, we need to reward interaction with them. When a student finishes reading a text, praise them. When they refer to it in an answer, praise them. When they use it to form an argument in a class discussion, praise them. When this is reinforced, reading texts and referring to them becomes the norm.

Talk passionately about reading

We are role models. Believe it or not, some students actually take notice of us! In lessons, talk about reading. Talk about books that are relevant to what you are covering. Talk about websites, magazines or other resources that could support their studies. Talk passionately about the benefits of reading. Hopefully one or two in your class will be inspired by your energy and read one of your recommendations.

It could also be talking passionately about the text you are about to read with the class. Katie Ashford (2015), a deputy headteacher and director of inclusion from London, described in a blog post how she gives a "story version" before she reads. It's an outline of what will come up. She explains how this "*enables and deepens comprehension because, whilst reading the story, pupils have something to 'hook' the new text onto*". Talk about books with the love they deserve and it may break down some of the barriers students have.

Read with students

When I visited Michaela School in London in 2017, one thing I saw in a number of classes was the teacher and student reading together. As the students sat quietly, the teacher would read the text aloud, with the students hooked on their every word. It was beautiful to watch. There was more to it though. After a few sentences the teacher would pose questions to the class to see if they understood what the text was about. When a new word appeared the teacher would use their craft to explain its meaning in a way that meant everyone grasped it. When a key point came up the teacher would take time to discuss its importance.

If we just give a text out and leave it for students to read, we can't be surprised if they don't. If we read to students we need to ensure they are part of the process. Reading out loud exposes the students to texts in a different way. How a teacher uses various words in context, varying pitch and tone, subtly changing their emphasis on different parts, all helps student's comprehension. Hearing tricky words for the first time used in a sentence can help individuals understand how to use them themselves. Questioning them throughout the process helps make meaning. Read the opening section and then set them off. Let them read it and then choose a section to read to them. Either way, the process can be a helpful tool.

There is a debate. Should students follow the text as we're reading? Should they read as we read? It's tricky. On the one hand, it ensures everyone follows along. At any point I can stop and refer to a part of it and everyone should know where we are. But if a student has poor reading fluency with few sight words, will they be distracted by reading along? Would they be focused on decoding words rather than listening to you? Remember, their working memory is occupied with multiple things. Then there are the able readers. Would they prefer just to charge on and read the rest of the text? Are we holding them back? Whatever you decide, reading with your class can be one step in the development of reading with your students.

Teach them key vocabulary (and what it means) first!

This is a very complex topic area and one that I will need to expand on later in the chapter. As mentioned, I was impressed at Michaela School by how the teacher explained the meaning of potential new words. Every English teacher is probably screaming, "But that's what you're supposed to do! We do that ALL OF THE TIME!" However, I didn't. Of course if there was a tricky word I would explain its meaning. Difficult word – meaning given – move on – job done. What I learnt that day was that I needed to do this more skilfully.

Isabel Beck, Margaret McKeown and Linda Kucan's (2013) book *Bring Words to Life* is a fantastic introduction to vocabulary instruction. Right from the start, the authors highlight how an individual's reading comprehension is linked directly to vocabulary and word knowledge.

Their whole approach is to explicitly, and robustly, teach vocabulary. But it's not as simple as just throwing key words at students. Far from it. The study by Nagy et al. (1985) showed that of 100 unfamiliar words met in reading, roughly 5–15 will be learned. So throwing new words and more texts at students doesn't work. We need to go a bit further.

One consideration is which words do we choose to teach? Which ones should we explicitly take time to develop? We have to be selective. How many you choose to introduce each lesson may depend on your subject or topic. To help, Beck (2013) and her co-authors split words into tiers:

Tier 1 words – The everyday words that we learn in everyday conversation. They are very basic. They have high exposure and are very familiar. These words rarely require specific instruction. Examples include run, happy, hungry and hot.

Tier 2 words – These have high utility for language users across a variety of domains. They are found in text and less so in conversation. They are less likely to be learned independently. However, knowing these words has a powerful impact on verbal functioning. They include words such as sequence, parallel, conduct and correspond. Knowing these words can help in many different domains.

Tier 3 words – These are low frequency yet high domain specific words. For instance, words like cytoplasm, ectomorph, glycolysis and hydraulic. As they are rarely used outside of a particular domain, they are best taught when encountered in a specific topic.

Beck et al. (2013) suggest that it's best to focus on Tier 2 words because knowing these will have the biggest impact across subjects and curriculums. This was unexpected. I would have spent most of my time developing a Tier 3 word vocabulary – words like *glycogen* when we did respiration or *intercostal* when doing the mechanics of breathing. I thought students would know Tier 2 words from conversation and reading.

Many teachers on hearing this will begin to make vocab lists. That is a good start. However, just giving Tier 2 lists to students doesn't solve the problem. It requires teaching. That is the bit I never knew. Beck (2013, p. 10) and her co-authors suggest teaching students around 400 of these important words a year. Clearly we don't do that all in one go, and not all of them through your subject. That's where joined-up thinking across departments comes into play. Why not meet as teachers, subject leads or SLT at the start of the year and select the words which have the highest utility and make a whole school concerted effort to get as many students as possible knowing these (and their meanings). Just think of the impact it could have!

Create a list for your subject or topic

Start small. What will be the Tier 2 and 3 words in the next topic you teach? What subject/domain-specific words do students have to know that they have probably never come across in conversation or reading? For Tier 3, this could be words like *electro-magnetic* or *isosceles*. For Tier 2, it might be *distribute, proportion, contrast* or *capacity*. Look to see what words come up in textbooks or articles related to the topic. Pick the ten words that you will spend time explaining when they arise.

There is a discussion about when you teach these words. Some say teach them at the start so when they pop up, students recognise the words, know their meaning and a text makes sense. Others think these words should be highlighted as they crop up so they are taught in context and grasping the meaning easier. As always, it's for you to make the choice.

Either way, knowing the words you want to cover is a sensible first step. It ensures that things aren't left to chance and vocabulary is developed. The lists can be printed and shared with students so they can make reference to them.

When they appear, make them known

Whenever you are asking students to read a text or are reading a text aloud, home in on complex words (tiers 2 and 3) when they arise. But there's a skill to doing it. Take these two scenarios:

Teacher: Ok class, follow along as I read the text. *As you move you produce heat, as you respire you produce waste, when you digest food you take millions of molecules into your body*. Right class, who can tell me what the word **digest** means? Can anybody explain it?

Compare that with this . . .

Teacher: OK class, follow along as I read the text. *As you move you produce heat, as you respire you produce waste, when you digest food you take millions of molecules into your body*. Right class, I'm going to focus on the word **digest**. Digest means when a substance is broken down in our intestines with the various nutrients, such as carbohydrates, absorbed into your body

Can you spot the difference? Can you see why one of the scenarios is better than the other?

You might notice the simple mistake I used to make. Years ago I would have asked the class what *digest* meant. Beck et al. (2013, p. 42) suggest that tempting though this is, it leads to guesses and misconceptions that can be hard to change. In the second example I don't ask about meaning, I give it to them straightaway. Some of you may be saying that asking them the meaning provokes thinking and telling them doesn't. I used to be the same. However, years of students getting meanings wrong began to get a bit infuriating. When an incorrect explanation was given, some students used the term in that sense further down the line. I know telling them seems didactic, but tell them correctly and you'll have fewer errors to correct later on.

When one of your identified words appears in a text it's important you pick up on it. Don't be scared to pause reading and home in on a word. If the word *impose* appears with a Year 7 group, tell them what that word means. Apply it to a story or situation so they get that word in another context. Ask yourself whether they could now use that word accurately in a conversation with a friend or teacher. If not, have they learnt it well enough?

We learnt earlier that we need multiple exposures to a word before it becomes a sight word, so ensure the process begins to happen.

Offer alternatives

You could also use another technique and talk about alternatives. For example, when you pick up on a particular word, ask the class if they know any other word that could replace it. Here's one possible scenario:

Teacher: So as we've just seen, the writer used the word *produce* in this sentence. We now know what that means. So who can give me another word we could replace *produce* with? Is there a better word?

What is happened here is that we are investigating synonyms. We are looking for similar vocabulary. We do this for two reasons. Firstly, this allows students to attach the new word to one that may already exist in their vocabulary bank, which means they can hold it in their memory more easily. Secondly, it means that students are associating it with a familiar word and are more likely to understand its meaning the next time they come across it. Again, this aids comprehension and fluency.

Summarise the words that have appeared

After reading a passage, article or excerpt, summarise the key vocabulary that came up. Focus on them one final time. Ask students to remind you of the definition you gave when you first talked about a term a few moments earlier. Ask them to give a new example of the word in use. Get them to finish a sentence for you with that word in it. The more they get comfortable with these words, the more confident they will be when meeting them again.

Thinking about how we develop student's vocabulary shouldn't be an afterthought. Lindsay Maughan, assistant principal and English teacher from East Durham, says:

Recognising that I needed to deliver lessons that incorporated explicit vocabulary teaching became a defining moment in my teaching career. In fact, I had had (up until this point) little awareness that I was leaving my students' vocabulary development purely to chance. I'd stop and check that students understood words in the text as we were reading, but was any of it actively planned prior to the lesson? No, I guess not. It was when I was teaching a more able class that this realisation became more apparent. It became crystal clear to me that whilst indeed they were more able, their limited vocabulary was a barrier to their progress and was inadvertently capping their achievement. The problem lay in their inability to articulate themselves with greater precision and subsequently their writing and discourse always lacked that refinement attributed to A*/grade 9 students.

As my skills in developing this particular class' vocabulary grew, so too did my understanding that we needed to ensure all our classrooms are vocabulary rich ones. For many students, the classroom is the only place where they can be taken out of the world of everyday conversational discourse – mostly simplistic – and into one that uses discourse to challenge and promote higher order thinking. And since my appointment as Assistant Principal with responsibility for Teaching and Learning, I've been able to lead on a wider scale whole school training and initiates designed to close the vocabulary gap.

Now, each unit of work (for all subjects in school and across both key stages) has a knowledge organiser that outlines a range of sophisticated vocabulary that students need to know in order to make successful responses. This is a one size fits all or "teaching to the top" as we refer to it. I regularly test their recognition, understanding and memorisation of these words through short tests that begin each and every lesson. It is the exposure and familiarisation process that is key to the success of this.

To begin, I'll introduce them to the new words, giving definitions, example sentences, and synonyms and antonyms for each. In the lesson that follows, I make sure to use the words in my own discourse so that the class can hear the word itself in action, checking intermittently that they are following and can recall what the word meant. I set challenges for the class to use the words in dialogic exchange (both in peer discussion and during whole class feedback), using the oral rehearsal strategy to ensure that they can first verbalise these words before I expect to see them using in writing. And then finally I ask them to write short paragraphs using the words that I can later check to gauge their understanding. And so the process repeats. The key to all of this is exposure, familiarisation, memorisation and repetition. I've introduced other strategies to make the topic specific vocabulary "stick" by hooking new words into mnemonics such as the title of the topic (e.g. An Inspector Calls – Apathy, Neoteric, Indifference . . .). I find this increases the speed at which classes can recall all words for a topic. They use this bank of words when planning responses in an exam, drawing on more sophisticated vocabulary to piece together and form an argument.

Before my appointment as Assistant Principal, I have held various roles including Head of Literacy Development and Whole School Intervention Lead and it's still something that I hold very close to my heart. I'm currently in the process of designing a whole school vocabulary intervention programme focusing specifically on tier 2 vocabulary which will replace part of our "traditional-style" reading intervention programme. It is hoped that if we catch students early in Year 7, using a system of spacing, interleaving and retrieval practice, we can create a programme of study that can have lasting impact on learners. Vocabulary, too often, is treated as the poor sister to reading and writing when schools should instead be investing greater time and effort in ensuring that we close the vocabulary gulf that exists between the "word rich" and "word poor".

Teach them more knowledge!

Writing this book has involved reading absolutely everything I can lay my hands on, and most of this was research papers. The thing is, most of these papers take an absolute age to read. Some were so complicated that I had to spend time researching what on earth the research was saying.

Cast your mind back to the chapter on memory. In that chapter I introduced you to the term palaeomagnetism. Earlier in this section I gave you an excerpt from a paper of thermodynamics. In each case, I'm guessing the average person has limited knowledge of the topic. Consider the following:

> When demagnetizing rocks in palaeomagnetism, an unterminated great circle path is sometimes obtained instead of a direct observation or endpoint determined from the linear segment near the origin of a Zijderveld plot. Such a situation cannot successfully be analysed using packages such as LINEFIND or Linearity Spectrum Analysis (LSA).
> (McFadden & McElhinny, 1987)

As with the thermodynamic excerpt, this made no sense to me. My brain is trying to comprehend all the new words while also trying to make meaning of the whole piece. By the time I get to the end of the text, I have forgotten a large chunk of what I've just read.

E. D. Hirsch, Jr (2003, p. 13) describes how reading fluency is increased by prior knowledge:

> Prior knowledge about the topic speeds up basic comprehension and leaves working memory free to make connections between the new material and previously learned information, to draw inferences, and to ponder implications. A big difference between an expert and a novice reader – indeed between an expert and a novice in any field – is the ability to take in basic features very fast, thereby leaving the mind free to concentrate on important features.

In other words, domain knowledge means that some readers can chunk whole sentences together as the context is more familiar, freeing up working memory to deal with other information. It also means that they can draw on schema related to words. If you read the word Australia and your brain instantly pulls forward information, memories and knowledge about it, you will understand the text more easily. Having little prior knowledge makes this a struggle.

Daniel T. Willingham (2017) found that those with higher prior or domain knowledge can do well with reading comprehension regardless of their reading ability:

> In one experiment, third graders – some identified by a reading test as good readers, some as poor – were asked to read a passage about soccer. The poor readers who knew a lot about soccer were three times as likely to make accurate inferences about the passage as the good readers who didn't know much about the game.

As we've already discussed, students starting a new topic are likely to have different levels of prior knowledge. For some, reading an article on the topic may be like my efforts reading up on palaeomagnetism or thermodynamics. They haven't a clue about the context or what all the new words mean. As a result, reading is effortful and slow and those students may be put off.

So, before getting them to read, share the knowledge that they need. Build up a foundation that will help them access the text. As outlined earlier, this could be as simple as learning new vocabulary prior to reading. It could be Katie Ashford's idea of providing a "story version" or summary about the text before you read it. It could simply be going through the main principles of the topic before we give out the articles.

What is the palaeomagnetism and thermodynamics in your subject?

Support the text and help them engage with it

If domain and vocabulary knowledge is low, students may struggle with reading fluency and comprehension. How can we support students through a piece of text? Here are some possible strategies.

Knowledge organisers

A knowledge organiser is a one page document which has all of the key information about the topic to be learnt on it. Being on one page, and organised in a very clear fashion, it makes it very accessible to a student. When reading through a text, if something unfamiliar comes up, the student can refer to it.

The best example I have seen of this comes from a biomechanics lesson where a struggling student used one to make sense of the text she was reading. Every time she came across the words sagittal and transverse, she referred to the knowledge organiser to remind herself of their meaning. She could then go back to the text and continue to read.

Summarising

To check that students have understood a text, you can ask them to summarise it. I used to set questions before looking at a text, but this meant students were searching for answers rather than reading and making meaning. Asking them to summarise afterwards, students have to have made sense of the text. They may need to read the text again or ask for more clarification.

Some teachers also ask students to write topic sentences after reading. That is, summarise the article into one sentence in order to provide a brief but concise overview.

Questioning

The bread and butter strategy either during or after reading. Discussing a text and posing questions can help ensure a piece of text is understood. It can allow you to connect the dots for those who may be struggling with context. It can give you the opportunity to quiz them about key words, the style of writing or the overall theme of the piece.

Pulling it all together either during or after reading will help students feel more confident about what they read. It means that if they read a similar piece of writing they have a sound foundation of understanding that they can transfer.

Further reading

And don't simply finish there. There is a wealth of literature on numerous topics that students should read. When you've finished reading one piece with the class, point them in the direction of another they should pick up in their own time. Supply copies of it. Share a link. Rave about it. As Kenny Pieper once told me, "Show that you care that their reading is important and show it's important to you". Get students wanting to read beyond the classroom.

We can't solve the problem but we can help

I often talk to people about how some students hate PE. They hate it because it's not *their thing*, because they're not very good at it, because it's difficult. I also talk about how simplifying a game, highlighting the important techniques, praising the good bits, and practice all help. I show that these little things increase enjoyment of PE and after a while, the barriers are broken down. With enjoyment comes more motivation. With more motivation comes hard work. With hard work comes success. I show them that PE is important and stress how I want to help them get better.

Reading is similar. Many of the students I work with avoid it. But if we make reading a priority and understand what the barriers might be, we can help students enjoy the process. The strategies discussed here won't necessarily make students fall in love with books, but they might result in the small wins that grow confidence.

---

3 Demonstrate great writing

All too often, teachers hear how a strategy is used in a classroom and then deploy it into theirs. One example of this is the use of examples and models. In the chapter on differentiation I talk about how we should share models with students to show them what excellent work looks like. Kenny Pieper once warned me, though, that there's a right and a wrong way to do this. Before I explore this, let me explain the benefits of modelling.

Models are helpful, right?

As a PE teacher, modelling happens every single lesson, regardless of the skill, technique or tactic being taught. If we didn't show students exactly what we want them to replicate, acquiring the skills would take a lot longer and the results would be a lot worse. How would they know where to plant their foot? How would they know what the full version of the movement even looks like?

In *Practice Perfect* (2012, pp. 83–104), Doug Lemov, Erica Woolway and Katie Yezzi talk about the importance of models in getting better at getting better. They use the analogy of baking a loaf of bread. You might have the recipe in front of you, but when you come to steps such as "Knead the dough to perfection" or "Let the dough sit and rise, then punch down", what does it actually mean? At first sight it looks simple, but when you get into it, it actually isn't. The authors argue that cookery shows bridge the gap. Seeing the best bakers at work on TV shows you what a dough should look like and gives you a clear visual idea of what punching it actually is.

Ron Berger, in his book *An Ethic of Excellence* (2003), describes how over the years he has collected banks and banks of models. Examples of excellence he can share with his class at any moment to show them what they are working towards, what their work should aspire to be.

So throw in more models when I'm teaching?

Yes, and no. I mentioned how Kenny Pieper had a word of warning about models. He went on to explain:

> I once had a great conversation with Pedagoo buddy Fearghal Kelly about sharing best practice. It's often never that: the analogy he used was that we wouldn't watch the Wimbledon final if we wanted to get better at tennis. We would get into practice sessions with Andy Murray and watch what he does on a daily basis. A real eye-opener for me.

And that right there is the key. What Kenny and Fearghal are saying is that simply showing a model won't cut it. It shows them what brilliance is, yes, but we should be focusing on the little things that go into making a great piece of work.

Kelly Gallagher (2011) says, "I think if we're going to be effective teachers of writing, it all starts with modelling". He asks whether we assign writing or teach writing. For a long time, I simply assigned writing. I would set students a long mark question, then sit back and see what they created. I didn't really teach anything. I didn't really intervene. Not as I would if I saw a student tackle incorrectly in rugby or perform a cartwheel with errors in gymnastics. Luckily, people like Kelly Gallagher opened my eyes.

Kelly describes how he shows his students what he does when tackling a big question. He models the process. He might even write his own example, which he shares with the class, and then show a model from an expert writer. What he's doing is unpicking that model with the students. He's not simply saying, "Hey class. Here's what a perfect answer looks like. Off you go".

So why are models helpful for things like writing?

The key work here is Kirschner, Sweller and Clark's (2006) paper on cognitive load.

As we have already discussed, when students are novices in a new area, their working memory can become overcrowded with information and they can experience cognitive overload. They don't have relevant prior knowledge or schema stored in their long-term memory to make this easier and struggle to complete the task. It's all new to them.

Both Rosenshine (2012) and Kirschner et al. (2006) point out how models can reduce this cognitive overload. Having the teacher model and think out loud while answering the question helps support the cognitive processes. It helps direct attention to the important points, which eases the burden on working memory. Using Kirschner et al.'s worked examples can help break the model down into small steps which students can follow to achieve mastery. The teacher goes through each stage of the model, explaining exactly why they are working this way so that the class fully understand both reasoning and process.

And that's key. We can't simply *show* what a good answer looks like. We need to guide students through the process.

So talk them through how the excellent example (or model) got to be so good?

Yep. As Kelly Gallagher (2011) says, "The teacher in the room is the strongest writer in the room", so share your expertise. You know why the great answer is great, so tell them.

Graham and Perin (2007, p. 15) list the most effective methods for supporting writing. One approach linked together models and writing strategies.

The writing strategy they describe is called Self-Regulated Strategy Development (SRSD). The method helps to explicitly teach an approach to writing. They split it into six sections:

1. Develop background knowledge – The knowledge that is needed to use the strategy you have selected to write successfully.

2. Describe it – Describe the strategy, its purpose and the benefits. Help students understand why you want them to write in a particular way.

3. Model it – Model how to use the strategy.

4. Memorise the strategy – So that when you set them off, they can remember it and include it in their answer structure.

5. Support it – Scaffold and offer support as they're working. Help them achieve mastery.

6. Independent use – Students then use your writing strategy with little or no support.

At the heart of this is the use of a model and the discussion of why you are asking them to use a particular writing strategy/structure – as well as how to use it. The SRSD method alone has an effect size of $d=1.14$ so it has a huge impact on writing. As you can see, it involves you teaching writing rather than just assigning writing. It involves your explicit instruction.

Wait, wait, wait! This sounds a lot like direct instruction

As with all things, there needs to be a transfer from teacher-led to independent practice when they're ready. But spending that five minutes, ten minutes, half a lesson working through how to create a perfect answer, with a model and your thoughts guiding them along, can make all the difference.

Go on then. How do I do it?

There's no one way to do it. But understanding why it's important, and why it works, might lead you to try one of the following ideas.

Have a bank of examples

Gathering examples beforehand means you can select the right example to use as a model at the right time. If you can't find a suitable one, at least you know that and can search for one from colleagues or past students.

This bank means that you can plan prior to the lesson. Sometimes the increasingly popular live modelling (which I'll get to in a bit) requires you to really know your stuff. It involves you reacting to the class as you're writing the model live, and things can change course. When this happens there's room for things to go wrong. So when starting out for the first time, get your models ready in advance.

Create your own examples

> Teachers need to write their own model answers in timed conditions to get a real sense of the difficulties students face when writing. For some this may mean confronting their own difficulties with writing. Writing and sharing what we have written can be an emotionally wrought experience! It's good practice to remind ourselves of that sometimes!
>
> (Caroline Spalding, an assistant head and English teacher from Derby)

Nothing puts you in the shoes of a student more than answering an exam question on your own. Do it without any materials, resources or mark schemes – just like your class. I wonder how you would get on. Would you include all the relevant information? Would your structure be clear? Would you get full marks?

The exercise might identify areas which your class may struggle with. Spotting pitfalls *before* a lesson means you can plan support or avoid them all together.

Writing answers yourself also allows you to monitor your own thought process. When trying to explain someone else's work, say the work of a poet or scientist, we don't know exactly what they were thinking when they constructed their piece. I remember the popular meme shared a few years back, involving the statement:

The curtains were blue.

As the meme goes, an English teacher thinks, "The curtains represent his immense depression and his lack of will to carry on", when in fact the author simply meant that the curtains were blue. Just a bit of fun, but it highlights how sometimes a teacher can always overthink things.

By writing your own examples you know why you wrote what you did. And knowing that, you can talk through the entire process with your class. And it's here that they can get the most valuable insight.

Exam papers

In a blog post, John Tomsett (2015) explained how he had annotated a mock paper that students had sat. Instead of simply writing out the answers, John wrote down his thought process. As he put it, he was writing down what his brain was thinking for each question. This brings in metacognition.

If you're not familiar with the term, metacognition refers to helping learners think about their own learning; being able to use strategies effectively and monitor how they're working. In his post, John used the mock exam paper to model his thoughts. He showed how he, the expert, would tackle each question. It was almost as if you were in his head.

With this in hand, John would project the paper onto the board and then talk the class through the process. As he did, he modelled his thinking aloud. Students, with a blank mock and pen in hand, would then annotate their own paper. They would write down what they had learnt about the process of answering a mock paper. They homed in on key command words. They gained insight into how and why he structured his responses. They were learning from years of experience. This account was a game changer for me

I followed John's example and prepared a paper beforehand. I even got my department to do the same. In the classroom we would project the paper, one question at a time, and talk through it. And over time, students began to understand how to answer particular question types. They had gained greater clarity through the modelling. And as it became more familiar, they began to develop good habits. As good habits developed, the quality of their writing improved.

I began to do this in more of a live setting. Blank mock paper in hand, I would talk through it there and then. I would write my notes as I went along. The secret is to know the exam paper inside and out, as well as the errors from student papers. This enables you to discuss misconceptions and/or poor habits question by question and show students step by step what they might do. It takes a little longer than having pre-written papers but gives a better indication of time management when tackling an exam.

Once the paper is annotated and modelled, students then have a guide, an instruction manual of sorts, which they can refer to when working through that paper. And as a teacher you can upload it to your online platform or VLA so students can refer to it over and over again.

Use a visualiser

I've mentioned visualisers throughout this book. I tend to stay away from technology in my teaching. Not because I'm a technophobe, but because I'm yet to find something that replaces good old-fashioned teaching (and that's coming from someone who is only 36 years old!). Fancy random name generator apps used to select students to answer a question? Simply point or just call a name out of your head at random. Just remember who you asked and (randomly) ask someone different next time.

However, visualisers do what the old overhead projector (OHP) did in classrooms in the 1980s. They allow me to share my thoughts there and then and project them up onto a screen. However, unlike an OHP, a visualiser enables me to show actual work.

The beauty of a visualiser is its simplicity. It's a camera with numerous uses. For me, the biggest gain was the ability to show things live. It sped up lessons as I didn't need to awkwardly write things on a whiteboard. I could have a text already printed which I simply positioned under the camera. That saves a lot of time.

With a visualiser you can really begin to build a learning culture in your classroom, which you might not have done so easily before.

Display the model

If I used a model years ago, I'd probably have to either print enough copies to share around the class or try and embed a photo of it in my PowerPoint. Both of these would work but take time to organise. Time I could spend doing better things. And if I use PowerPoint I can't scribble on the model as I would like to. Printouts mean people have to listen and follow the text themselves. With a visualiser I just put the model under the camera and scribble all over it. The live image is on the board for all to see.

Show a worked example

Under the camera I can go step by step through a model with ease. I can guide students through the process and pose questions at key points. I can chunk key processes and highlight key areas. All the time being conscious of working memory limitations.

Write live

As I stated earlier, if you write live you need to know your stuff. It also takes a bit of practice. But it can be amazing. Students can get an idea of your thought process. They get an insight into your choice of language and examples. You can explain things as you go. You can make mistakes, question your own writing, and make amendments there and then. These all add to the experience and show students what it takes to write well.

Show students' work

This is what I had in mind when referring to building a learning culture in your classroom: an environment where you can pick any piece of student work and display it under the visualiser. And I mean any piece of work. When I first started using the camera I would (like many) go straight to the best writers in my class and display their work. This was good to start out with. It allowed me to demonstrate good work by their peers and we could unpick it together. When I got more comfortable with it, I began picking any piece of work. It didn't matter what the quality was. Getting to this stage takes trust and time. But after a while we could use any piece of work and collaboratively talk about what was good with it and what needed changing. We could offer suggestions on how to rearrange and rework a sentence to have it make more sense. We could speak as a class about using a better quote or example. We could analyse the work and pick out good habits and reinforce them. And the student whose work it was? Well, at first they thought it was a criticism. But this changed really quickly when I showed them how as a class we could work together to make their work better. I made it feel like a community and we were in it together. When this becomes the norm it becomes powerful.

Visualisers are now the cornerstone of my modelling and that of my colleagues. They are a game changer.

I do, we do, you do

In a Teachers Channel video (2015), Lindsay Young, a high school teacher from California, describes a process called I do, We do, You do. She explains that every time that she introduces a new concept, she models it first. Not everyone in the class will need that scaffold, but there may be a good number who do. In these instances she runs through the process in three stages.

In the *I do* section, the teacher explicitly guides the students through the process. By using a model, they show what the class what the end product needs to look like. They go through it at each stage, giving very detailed instructions on how to get to the final outcome. It is very teacher led. As Lindsay explains, this section is about her modelling her thinking; she's thinking aloud. At this stage Lindsay isn't looking for student participation. Doing so may lead her to believe incorrectly that they get it. For example, during the teacher-led modelling, you may get a student calling out a correct part of the process. At this point you may think "They get it" when in fact only one student does. This could lead you to think "They don't need me to model anymore", where actually many of them may need more explanation.

In the *We do* section, the teacher uses carefully crafted questions to involve the class in creating a second paragraph or alternative answer. The whole process is collaborative, with the teacher taking suggestions, but skilfully directing the outcome to be one that is of a high standard. At this stage, the teacher needs to gather enough evidence that students are ready to be released and work independently in the final section. If not, more teacher support is needed, so the *We do* element continues.

In the *You do* section, full responsibility is handed over to the student. They complete the final part of a question or work on similar problems on their own. The teacher works the room looking at how they are progressing, but the modelling that preceded this should allow them to get on and create work of a good standard (hopefully!). This is where we can look for student work to display on the board and look to model how individuals are getting on. These techniques simply overlap.

Live writing

Dave, you've just written about live writing. I know. But I wanted to share a quick tip from my colleague Robynn Alner. Our current PGCE student wants to get better at modelling. He's keen to do what we do. When we spoke as a department meeting about using models, we talked about the value of doing it live in front of the class. However, we recognised that for a novice teacher, modelling an answer off the cuff could be difficult. Robynn explained how (even as an experienced teacher) she still writes out her model answer before the lesson. She then places it on her desk but out of view of the camera and students. When she then models, or does the *I do* part of modelling, she pretends she's making it up as she goes, but taking occasional glances at her pre-planned model and basically copying it as she goes. Some over-dramatic acting and saying things like "Right, what should I write now?" hook the students in. Robynn plans for excellence and doesn't leave it to chance. She does this before the lesson and ultimately leaves students with an example that showcases what they should be endeavouring to achieve.

Remember, when you live write, you don't need to write a whole essay. Some of the best live modelling I have seen has focused on just one sentence, one paragraph or one problem.

Model the changes

Once students have been shown what to do, allow them a good chunk of time to create something of worth. Then, once you have scanned students' work, model what you've seen.

Show them common errors and model what you would do differently. This is key. Modelling can be organic. If I see that students have missed the point, probably as a result of my teaching, I take action. I stop the class and highlight what I have seen. I might display a few pieces of student work. I might write an incorrect answer myself and ask them to analyse it. Either way I make the misconception visible. I bring it to the attention of the class, then take corrective steps to improve the work. I show them what I do to make it better. I model the changes.

I'm not a fan of having a million different pens for various school policies (green pen for peer assessment, red pen for marking, blah blah blah!!) but I do insist that after I have modelled corrections, students use a purple pen to add those corrections to their work if needed. I don't do this to make it visible for book looks or the big O, but so students can see their own changes. It makes it clear what was incorrect, and what a better answer looks like. Purple means "this is a better bit" and hammers home the process of redrafting, amending and improving work.

Multiple models, examples and non-examples

When we're accustomed to working with just one model, it's time to look at using multiple models, including non-examples. *Non what?* I'll explain.

Modelling with one example is good when working with novices as it allows them to clearly see what it is we are trying to work towards. However, once we have explained a concept, there may be a need to incorporate other models. As I mentioned earlier, teacher Kelly Gallagher (2011) describes how at the end of modelling his own writing, he then draws upon a model from an author. He wants the models side by side or one after another, so that students can see the subtleties and differences. Seeing the same ideas you've unpicked but in a slightly different context helps students form a better understanding. It highlights how they can manipulate that *thing* in a different way. Great examples of this come from maths where, after modelling how to use a formula in one particular way, teachers introduce numerous other models showing the formula or process being used in a slightly different way. Multiple models help student select the correct way to answer a question further on down the line. They've seen it before so they can tackle variations of it when this type of problem/question pops up again.

Using non-examples is another approach. Very simply, this involves showing a model of an answer that isn't quite correct. For instance, a teacher could model how to use a particular formula in science correctly. They explain it clearly and walk students through the stages. They question in an effort to check for understanding. Once they have modelled the process, they then work through a number of other examples of it in action. When they are confident that students have a good grasp of what is expected of them, they then introduce examples and non-examples. They can display two examples side by side. One of these, the example, has the correct process. The other one, the non-example, has an incorrect element. Students have to work out which is the correct one and why. The two examples need to be minimally different so that students have to pay really close attention.

Non-examples need to be followed up and explained thoroughly so no misconceptions creep into students' memories. The incorrect elements should be homed in on and corrected by the teacher so the mistakes don't reoccur. Non-examples can be a great tool if the teacher models them correctly afterwards.

Right, I'm starting modelling tomorrow

Modelling long answers was alien to me; I had never experienced or observed this particular process. By the time pupils reach GCSE level it is assumed they can construct longer answers, therefore the facts and knowledge take priority. However, this is not the case and implementing modelling into my practice has shown significant improvements in the structure of the pupils' answers.

Models of good writing are important, so pupils can visually see me constructing an answer. Additionally, live modelling is even more powerful; demonstrating to the pupils my thinking process to construct an answer lets the pupils understand where I am bringing facts and knowledge into the answer.

Initially, when modelling answers for 8 mark questions I would read through the answer explaining to the class where I would give marks, and celebrating the use of keywords related to the topic. More so, the process of listening to the praise I was giving and trying to make amendments to their own answer proved difficult for the majority of pupils. On reflection, I now unpick the answer by gathering the thoughts of the pupils; questioning the pupils on how to make good sentences to even better, and challenging the sporting example used. By working through the answer point by point, pupils are able to amend their answers. Additionally after discussing a point or sentence, the pupils are challenged to improve that point further. By structuring the process this way pupils can identify mistakes in their work and make amendments accordingly. Furthermore, exam questions using command words such as; "evaluate" and "discuss" which pupils do not understand. Unpicking answers allows me to explain where the answer has demonstrated "evaluation", and the pupils can see it first-hand.

(Matthew Wagstaff, a trainee teacher from Essex)

If you're going to start modelling, please make sure you understand why. Most of the time I do it when working on extended answers. I do it when students need to write a lot. I do it when I'm showing them the difference in responses between a *justify* question and a *describe* question. I do it to highlight excellence, model structure or show corrections. Modelling helps reinforce good habits, reduce cognitive overload and really hone in on the best bit of a lesson; teaching students how to do stuff.

Don't be scared of making mistakes while modelling. As Kenny Pieper says, "*When they see me struggle it is massively powerful. Writing is hard and only improves through doing lots of it. Seeing the teacher make mistakes, edit, rewrite is one of the best lessons we can give them*".

Be specific about what it is that you're modelling, as well. You can't have a splatter gun approach. Focus on the key things, whether it's structure or use of a concept. Knowing exactly what you will say to ensure your explanation is flawless really helps here.

Be aware of the following, though. In the "Why do students forget?" chapter, I discussed expertise reversal effect. Models are great for novice and intermediate learners. Those who need parts of their process guided or refined. For them modelling is priceless. However, as a student becomes more capable, modelling can itself become a distraction and cause them cognitive overload. They don't need as much explicit guidance so we are inadvertently adding to the load. At this stage we need to set them off, just monitoring their work. If things aren't going well, we can draw upon a model to correct them.

And one last point: when we model, we are usually using a scaffold, framework or structure. But which one do we use? This leads me to my final principle.

> 4 Build up confidence in structure

There was a time when, for some strange reason, I would set students an exam question and simply set them off. I would then get the work in and bang my head against the wall. "How come, after I've just explained the concept to them, they still write poor answers? This is a GCSE lesson yet some of them write like a Year 7!?!?"

If I moan to a colleague, they then innocently ask the obvious question, "Oh, I don't know. How did you scaffold it for them?" At this point this colleague isn't my friend anymore.

After I realise that I'm an idiot, I think about what my colleague said. I realise that they're actually bang on the money with asking how I scaffolded the task for them. How did I? Usually I didn't. At least, not until they were well into the task and I realised they were going off on a complete tangent. At that point I would stop the class and put some token bullet points on the board which I hoped would correct every mistake and make the subsequent writing a thing of beauty. Unfortunately, that is neither modelling, scaffolding, nor teaching.

So what on earth is a scaffold?

A scaffold, in its simplest sense, is something that helps student get from where they are to where we want them to be. It's providing a structure or framework that will help support the task they've been set. As Wood, Bruner and Ross (1976, p. 90) explain, it's the process "that enables a child or novice to solve a task or achieve a goal that would be beyond his unassisted efforts". As they go on to say, a *scaffold* consists of an adult controlling the parts of a task that may be beyond the capabilities of the learner. This allows the learner to focus on and complete the parts they can manage.

In their study they worked with three-, four- and five-year-olds to solve a wooden geometric puzzle. The tutor who worked with the children scaffolded when the children needed help. They would things like reducing the possible choices for the next part of the puzzle. This support was required more by the younger children and less by the older. This links to a point I will raise later.

Learning to ride a bike is a real-life example. Using stabilisers on the back wheels is a scaffold. It aims to make the complex part, balancing, easier for the child so that they can focus on mastering the other elements.

In the classroom we need to ensure that we use scaffolding with students when a task may be too complicated for them to complete independently. Clearly we can't sit with every student, supporting them at every step, but a well-deployed scaffold is a good substitute.

Go on then. What things can be a scaffold?

At the simplest, anything that:

1. Acts as a tool which a student can use on their own.

2. Helps guide a student through a process.

3. Helps get the student to a well-produced end point.

It could be a writing frame used in history, designed to help pull out a point and support it with evidence. It could also be a graphic organiser to help plan out how to complete a task before we do it. It could even be the support of a teacher. For instance, the support a teacher gives in the *We do* section of the strategy *I do, We do, You do*.

So why is scaffolding helpful?

It may be obvious, but a scaffold helps a student through a process on their own, offering support in the absence of a teacher. The key is that they don't give so much information that the task becomes worthless to learning. Remember what we said in Chapter 2? If learning is to take place, thinking is required.

So a great scaffold will prompt an individual but still require them to engage in a lot of thought. Good scaffolds help limit the amount of cognitive overload placed on working memory. They allow a student to gather their thoughts and place them in a way that will help provide clarity. That's why things like process worksheets are a helpful scaffold. After the teacher has set a class off on a task, the process worksheet can direct students through the stages without their input.

Go on, there's always a word of warning

Scaffolds are great, but we need to be wary of a few things. Some scaffolds are simply glorified worksheets. Filling in blanks, no thinking required, nothing in terms of structure or content learned. That's where the process worksheets I mentioned earlier differ. As Kirschner, Sweller and Clark (2006, p. 80) explain, these worksheets provide a descriptive guide of what learners (as they put it)

> should go through when solving the problem as well as hints or rules of thumb that may help to successfully complete each phase. Students can consult the process worksheet while they are working on the learning tasks and they may use it to note intermediate results of the problem-solving process.

A process worksheet thus provides prompts rather than pointless gap filling. Kirschner et al. suggest incorporating the instructions into the example on the process worksheet rather than below it, so that a student doesn't have to constantly look up at the framework, and then down at the prompts.

Wood et al. (1976) argue that a good scaffold can only be successful if the learner understands the task, the content and the scaffold to use. If they don't, the scaffold will be ineffective. Take this as an example.

Let's say I set a nine-mark question for my students to complete. The topic is how methods of training, principles of training and training thresholds all work together to help an athlete reach their maximum performance levels for a competition. Already that's a tough question as it requires students to link three separate topics together. I ask them to use a scaffold like PEED (which I will mention in more depth later) to write their answer. Unless they know what the question is asking, how the topics interlink, or how the scaffold might help structure their answer, they won't write any better than if I let them write freely.

We come back again to the expertise reversal effect (Lee & Kalyuga, 2014). Many researchers refer to what is known as *fading*. That is, when a learner is sufficiently skilled at tackling a concept/question/problem, they don't need the scaffold anymore. In fact, as we've seen, the scaffold can be a hindrance for the expert, adding load to the working memory because they want to work independently. So as your learners get better, gradually remove the support.

Unfortunately, some teachers don't release the scaffold. This is a problem in some schools with writing frames like PEED (or PEEL or PELD or whatever). In the mid-2000s, this was the first real scaffold I was introduced to. It was a whole school literacy approach because it was noted that students struggled to write long answers. I got the point. It's a problem across the school so let's roll out a scaffold across the school. Things became consistent but then problems crept in.

For some, PEED became the ONLY WAY I WANT YOU TO WRITE IN MY LESSONS! Sorry for shouting but that's what it felt like. Students were locked into a robotic way of writing. It was even expected in Year 11. Being the rogue I was, I didn't stick with it for long. There were two reasons for this.

Firstly, PEED didn't fit into the requirements of my subject. Things were a little more complex. We didn't need to find a Point, that then needed Evidence, which we would then Explain and finally Develop. PEED didn't fit. And the types of questions we encountered ranged from justify to explain to describe to analyse. Again, it didn't fit.

Secondly, writing frames like PEED limit students freedom. When students are struggling with writing a structured response, PEED gives them a simple framework to use. But once they've got this, remove it. Understand what it does but then teach them how to move beyond it. Show them that PEED is the basis, but my good teaching and guidance can help you write even better that that! Be a teacher. You'll see writing get better as a result.

Finally, as Rosenshine and Meister (1992) point out, scaffolds are best for highly challenging tasks, but ones within reach. The ones where "the students cannot proceed alone, but can proceed when guided by a teacher using scaffolds" (p. 26). If the class is full of novices, more direct teaching will yield better results. Novices don't have the sufficient knowledge levels to use a scaffold independently. They need more explicit instruction and modelling. However, if the knowledge base is sound, a scaffold will help. So intermediates would benefit from a scaffold, before removing it when they become expert.

So how would you use a scaffold in a lesson?

- I would pick a scaffold that would really help a particular aspect – whether this is simply helping choose better vocabulary, or structuring a whole essay. Ask yourself the question

"Do I actually know what structure is required for writing a really good response?" If not, find out. That question should help you in deciding what scaffold to select.

- I would explain the scaffold/framework – maybe showing one stage at a time, or simply just one stage.

- I would show them (model) – talking about the process as I did so. I'd usually start with a simple example of its use, but then move onto more complex ones.

- I would use multiple models of the framework in action – showing have to be flexible with it.

- I would use a strategy like I do, We do, You do to release my control.

- I would monitor and assess how the students were getting on with the scaffold – providing feedback to as many students as possible.

- I would share examples of the model being used well/not so well with students – and work together to correct it or move it on.

- I would set another question which has a variance – so students have to adapt how to use the model with a different question type.

- I would release and remove the scaffold for those who needed it so they could write with more freedom.

- I would then have more practice – answering even more questions of a similar type.

What are the scaffolds you use?

None of the scaffolds I'll go into are my own. They've been acquired from a variety of sources over the years. The thing is, though, knowing how a scaffold works means I've chosen ones that do what I need them to. In the first few years of being a teacher I would have literally used any framework I was told to – irrespective of whether it would make my students better writers or not. That's what this book is trying to tackle. Choose a method that works for you, for the reasons you need it to. If it doesn't, bin it.

Scaffolds to pre-plan writing

I love graphic organisers!

Here comes my second shout out for graphic organisers. I love them as a scaffold because there are so many of them and they can often be used in multiple domains and topics. As I've said, graphic organisers are exactly what they say they are. They help organise thoughts in a visual/graphic.

These come in a range of formats: Venn diagrams, cause and effect map, double bubble diagrams, persuasion maps, the humble T-chart. What makes graphic organisers stand out for me is how they help collate thoughts in a particular structure, for a particular reason, which can then be used in a particular situation. They really help my students get their thoughts on paper before they tackle a difficult piece of writing.

Imagine a student trying to grapple with planning a complex exam question just in their head. I know that they'll have to do that in a real exam or when trying to solve a problem in real life, but when they're novices, or when we want to help support them to get a better outcome, a graphic organiser can help. It means they don't have to juggle numerous pieces of information in their working memory while trying to formulate an answer. They can get information down first and then make sense of it. It can help them think in a methodical way if they're not used to it. Most importantly of all, a good graphic organiser forces students to think, and think hard!

The following three are my personal favourites:

1 – Thinking square: A while back I had an issue where students couldn't seem to link a fact to a topic, and then expand on it. They never went into enough depth. No amount of PEED helped. For example, I could ask students to explain how various components of fitness (speed, agility, power, flexibility, etc.) link to a particular sport, like netball. I would get wishy washy answers which touched upon a point with no detail. "A netballer needs agility to move away from a player". Right … okay. So instead of giving a scaffold for the process of writing, I took a step back and gave a scaffold for the process of thinking. Maybe students didn't know what sort of detail they needed to include before they put pen to paper. I needed a plan (for their plan).

I decided to put an image of a netball game in the middle of an A3 page (see Figure 6.1). To get a better quality answer, students need to not only identify the component of fitness but also define it, explain its importance and then make a specific reference to when in that sport they would use it to gain an advantage. Around this image I placed various squares, each one increasing in size. In each section that these squares created, students needed to write their thoughts, increasing in detail as they worked their way out from the middle. So, in the first square they might identify that a netballer needs flexibility. In the next level they write the definition, that it is the range of movement at a joint. In the next square they write what that means in the context of netball, maybe how they need to lunge for a low ball, or stretch up high at an angle to intercept a pass. In the final layer they write why having good flexibility would make their performance better. Here they might write that this increase in flexibility allows an individual to be able to outreach an opponent for a pass, therefore maintaining possession. It might mean that they can have a greater stride length if they have good flexibility around the leg joints, so they can run quicker than an opponent to break free for a pass. This scaffold helps students map their thinking much easier than some other ways of planning.

Once the various strands are completed, each one can be pulled together to make a paragraph which makes a lot more sense, and is a lot more academic than "A netballer needs flexibility to stretch for a ball".

2 – Double Bubble: There are numerous times when students are required to under-stand the similarities and differences of two concepts. Take for instance the aerobic and anaerobic energy systems. Both have similarities (they both create energy) but they also have their specific differences (aerobic is usually for sustained medium to low intensity exercise, whereas anaerobic is for short high intensity exercise). Unfortunately, even

Explain and Apply

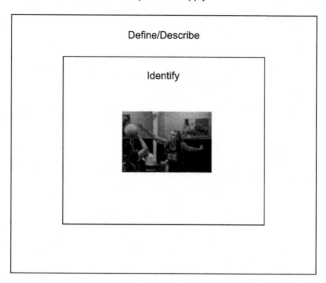

Figure 6.1 Writing Square

though these factors are very clear to us as teachers, students struggle to see them. I therefore need to scaffold this if they are to write something in any sort of depth.

A great way to get students to pay particular attention to them is through a double bubble map (see Figure 6.2). It works very similarly to a Venn diagram. In fact, you could use a Venn diagram if you're more comfortable with them. However, I try to stay away from them purely because without nudges and prompts, students can get away with writing only one or two things before we intervene. Such freedom can be a student's worst enemy. A double bubble is very different. On the outer rings there are predetermined spaces that students have to fill with information. These gaps need to be completed so help scaffold deeper thought. For instance, having these gaps means student have to think of "another two differences between mitosis and meiosis". They have to fill those spaces – they're there on the page looking up at you.

Once completed, an individual can then use it to structure their actual written comparison. They can draw upon the various pieces of information they have jotted down and plan out, in some sort of coherent order, explanations of how the two things in question share similarities and differences. And the beauty with a double bubble is every time I have used it in class, students comment on how much thinking was required to fill it out. They really had to think about what to include in the limited number of boxes. For the more able, it meant they had to exclude possible points – "There're only two boxes left but I have three possible points. Which one do I leave out?"

For the less able, it meant they had to commit to thinking about what to include. They needed to search for more answers – "I've got one box left to fill. Let's check back through

Respiratory System

Complete the double bubble diagram below to define the similarities and differences between
Aerobic and **Anaerobic** Respiration.I

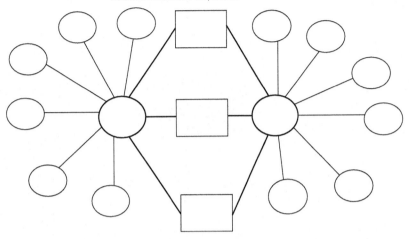

Figure 6.2 Double Bubble

the text book again to see if I've missed anything". As we've learnt from previous chapters, when thinking is high, there's a better chance it will get committed to memory over time.

3 – Cause and effect maps. There could have been other maps in this slot. I could have talked about how when students struggle to see logical sequences clearly, a sequence map is helpful. Take, for instance, moments in history that led to an event. A sequence map could help lay out the timeline.

I could have mentioned that some individuals (to my frustration) can't write persuasively. They can't give reasons for an argument and support each with a fact or example. Here, a persuasion map would help.

However, for students I've worked with, many find linking how x caused y, or how a led to b, quite a tricky task. A cause and effect map can organise this (see Figure 6.3).

In the centre section, students write the event, trend or focus. What are they zooming in on? What are they trying to understand? In the boxes to the left, they write down the things which led to that event/trend/focus. What was in the build up? What caused it to happen? What examples, facts, dates, figures and evidence can you find to pinpoint that moment?

In the boxes to the right, students write down the effects of this event/trend/focus. What happened as a result? What was the short term impact? What was the long term impact? What were the consequences? What were the positive or negative outcomes from this event/trend/focus?

Over the years I've seen this used brilliantly in history when focusing on what led to the Industrial Revolution and what its impact was. I've seen it in science when looking at an experiment. Why did y happen? What caused it? What does the results of this experiment do in the long run? I've also seen it used well in English when looking at an event in a story such as "Why did Lennie die in *Of Mice and Men*?" What led to the decision by George? What effect did it have? What might have happened if Lennie's death hadn't taken place? Using this type of map allows students to delve slightly deeper and explore more potential avenues. It allows them to map these thoughts out before thinking hard about which to include in an essay.

And what about other things?

Pre-essay – Less scaffolded than a graphic organiser, a pre-essay is a short outline or summary of what your actual essay will be about. The process involves students producing a short synopsis of what the content, order and structure of the essay will entail. Usually kept to a minimum number of words, it allows the individual an opportunity to create some form of plan before tackling the work.

A pre-essay, once completed, can be checked over by the teacher who can offer feedback and further guidance. They can have that conversation and discuss what the work could look like, and pose questions that may encourage the individual to make revisions to their draft. As it's only a very short outline, any amendments can be quickly bullet pointed in, with further elaborations annotated around the pre-essay. When the student feels confident and ready to go, they can use the pre-essay to map out their writing.

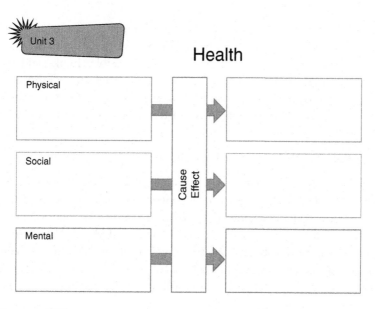

Figure 6.3 Cause and Effect

Wait. I've done this before and students still get their work jumbled up. there's too much to think about

I know what you mean. A pre-essay is a good overview. But you're right – some students may still find this too much.

Judith Hochman and Natalie Wexler (2017, pp. 83–110) tackle this very problem. Picking up on the issue that even a pre-essay may involve too many things to think about, they devised a less complex and much easier format, the Single-Paragraph Outline or SPO.

The Single-Paragraph Outline is exactly what it says it is, and that's what makes it so effective It provides a road map for a paragraph, including the start, middle and the end. Simply with the topic sentence at the top, students then list 4 possible points that they might elaborate on in their paragraph. At the end there is a space for a concluding sentence to round the paragraph off. The book goes into a lot more detail about how to ensure every element is well thought out, but the underlying principle of the method is that it allows students the opportunity to first think about a paragraph outline and then use that outline to write a complete one out properly. The fact that the topic sentence and concluding statement are written in full, with the possible 4 points only in bullet point, mixes the need for sophisticated writing with quick summarising to make it more effective *and* efficient. As their chapter explains, this can't be done by chance. To get it right, the teacher needs to model, guide, feedback and instruct students how to write each part to a very high standard. That's down to good teaching. Something I definitely didn't do in the past when I simply searched the internet for a writing frame and simply got students to fill it in.

Scaffolds to summarise

Baumann and Taylor prompts

Here we go again! Early in my career I would encourage students to use our textbooks. Now, there's nothing wrong at all with textbooks. Some textbooks are extremely well written, have all the relevant information laid out in accessible chunks, and are supported with diagrams, examples and questions. They're an underused source in some quarters.

However, I would simply say, "Right class, turn to page 43. Can you read it and summarise the main points of the text in your exercise books. Four minutes, off you go".

Ok, but isn't that what you're supposed to do?

I thought so. That was until I realised that all students seemed to do would be copy notes without actually reading the text. For some, copying things word for word from the page was sufficient. But as you and I know, that has limited impact on long term learning.

So if I wanted students to read a piece of text and then summarise its content, I needed something more robust. Something which meant the students had to actually read, comprehend and develop their writing. No pressure then. However, Rosenshine and Meister (1992, p. 27) refer to a scaffold from Baumann (1984) and Taylor (1985). Their scaffold for summarising was as follows:

1. Identify the topic.

2. Write two or three words that reflect the topic.

3. Use these words as a prompt to help figure out the main idea of the paragraph.

4. Select two details that elaborate on the main idea and are important to remember.

5. Write two or three sentences that best incorporate these important ideas.

Now this does all of the things I want it to. It forces students to actually read the text, understand it and then skilfully choose words which they need to elaborate on. The best part of it is the fact that students also have to write sentences to summarise what they have read. Limiting it down to two or three only means that students have to consider what points to hone in on and how best to communicate them in so few words.

Once you realise what this scaffold does and how it works, it can be adapted.

Kipling's questions – for a quick summary

> I keep six honest serving-men
> (They taught me all I knew);
> Their names are What and Why and When
> And How and Where and Who

A classic poem written by Rudyard Kipling (1900) and referred to countless times. Using the five Ws and How can be an effective scaffold for summarising, whether it be summarising a text or summarising an outline for a paragraph or essay. Ask students something along the lines of:

What – What is the text about?
Who – Who does the text refer to?
When – When does this "thing" take place?
Where – Where does it take place?
Why – Why does this "thing" occur?
How – How did it occur?

These questions can be tweaked as necessary. Some may not be applicable. But as a basic scaffold to begin the summarising process, it's a good starting point.

Scaffolds to start sentences

Sentence starters

One of the first strategies that was ever shared with me for a literacy focus came in the form of sentence starters. Back in the day the idea was to give students some prompts which students could use to begin. And the reason it resonated was because that was one of the persistent students concerns. "Sir, I don't know how to start?" or "Sir, I know what I want to say. I just don't know how to begin". So, what can you do about it?

My first step was to give sentence starters. I would write the question that I wanted students to answer, and then I would put together some simple prompts or opening statements that my students could refer to. So did they work? Well, not entirely, and I bet you can guess why.

First, the sentence starters were an afterthought. They didn't really do anything. Many of them were just something like "One reason could be", which didn't provoke much thought and didn't challenge anyone at all. I wonder if my sentence starters actually made any writing better.

Second, I never insisted that they were used. Maybe I liked the idea that they *could* be used, but subconsciously I wanted them to write with some freedom. However, some students aren't ready to be given such an open task. Instead of producing something of beauty, they struggled.

So, three things happened. Thing number one – whenever I set a question, I began to think about what answer I would give. If time was an issue, I would look at the mark scheme and try and unpick what they wanted (the issue with this is they give examples which feel a bit robotic). By actually thinking about *my* response, I knew what would make a perfect answer. I had experienced it so knew what might be a better way to write my response. From this I could give a stem from one of my actual sentences and see if this might prompt students or move them on. Next time you give sentence starters, make sure you try to answer the question yourself first.

Thing number two – I insisted that they were used, and actually modelled their use myself. If students don't see how your sentence starter might make their work sound more academic, why would they bother? By spending time showing them how your first sentence starter could kick off their opening paragraph, students have a mental model of why it works. They understand the reasons behind it being a better way to begin because they've heard you talk it through. It makes it more convincing. You then need to insist that they use the scaffolds. Once their writing starts to develops, fade them out. But if the quality diminishes further on down the line, bring them back.

Finally, my prompts got more challenging, rigorous and academic. This came from our friend Doug Lemov.

As already mentioned, in January 2014 Doug shared a blog post titled, "At first glance: A sentence starter adds unexpected rigor to writing". In the post he talked about how he used sentence starters to craft better sentences. He tackled the fact that some may think that we're helping students too much by demonstrating that a well thought out prompt can be a very powerful scaffold. In his example he used the Bruegel painting "The Fall of Icarus". Individuals had to write a sentence that summarised the picture. They first had a go on their own. Their sentences were fine but not spectacular. Then Doug asked them to begin their sentence with "At first glance . . ." These three words changed the entire direction of the individuals' writing. It forced them to look at the painting with different eyes. It made them think hard and ask, "What might a person miss from just one glance?". This was another game changer. It made me think really hard about sentence starters. Instead of lazy, "One reason could be", I begin limiting them to three words, and words that would make students think. Think about things they might not have done initially. In came scaffolds such as:

- Without this nutrient . . .
- The combination of . . .
- In order for . . .
- The limitations of . . .

These still aren't great, but what they do is make my students ask themselves questions like, "Yeah, what would happen if that nutrient was missing in an athlete's diet?" or "Oh, of course. The limitations of the anaerobic system mean that Usain Bolt . . .". They make students think. And that's the cognitive challenge that's needed.

Include this! Using vocabulary

There are numerous ways in which you can try and support students to include more academic vocabulary in their work. Without a scaffold, there is a chance that students simply won't. For a while I would *hope* that students used words that I had trickled down into the lesson. However, whether they did depended on which way the wind was blowing. Most frustrating of all, students sometimes shoehorned a keyword into a sentence and it made no sense whatsoever.

We want our students to include the right vocabulary in the right context. I also want my students to write more academically. This can't happen by accident. We need to pick out the words that are crucial in a particular context to move their writing forward. Words that enhance the level that a normal sentence may be at. When we have these words, probably about two or three a lesson, we need to get students to use them correctly.

One way of doing this is, as with sentence starters, to share them with students. Similar to the previous scaffold, we need to ensure that these key words are modelled in a well-crafted sentence – ideally live. As you are working this new word into your writing, questioning students as you go, you can also move this a stage further. When that word is embedded, ask them to do a literacy upgrade. This was a term I learnt in 2012 when working with local journalists on a student project. Ask students what other word could be used instead of the one we have just chosen. Is there a synonym? Are there other words we could look at making more academic? For example, ask students, "Right, we've used the word *produce*. Are there any better words we could use instead of *produce*?" Are there opposites? For instance, when you introduce a term like pessimist, explain to them what optimist means. When you speak about introverts, explain what extroverts are.

Again, insist that these key words are included in their answers. Make a list of those "that must be included in your writing!" And once again, when they are ready to fly solo, remove the scaffold.

Fragments

This was a first for me and probably will have the English teachers screaming at the page again. Hochman and Wexler (2017) introduced me to the idea of using "fragments" as scaffolds with students. A fragment, in their words, "is a group of words that is not a grammatically complete sentence. Usually a fragment lacks a subject, verb, or both, or it is a dependent clause that is not connected to an independent clause" (pp. 27–33). They give some examples:

- Settled near rivers.

- Developed a set of principles.

- Control of the empire.

They don't have capitals or full stops or commas. They can be used to start sentences, fill the middle or follow up at the end. They require students to add missing information to make them complete. But what exactly is down to the student. Hochman and Wexler demonstrate how they teach these, ranging from "speaking" them in oral activities, all the way to finding them in text and completing the sentences for the ones they've found. Fragments are fantastic scaffolds to get sentences up and running for my students. I simply share one and ask students to turn it into a proper sentence. They provide the nudge they need while bringing in subject knowledge and grammatical practice.

Scaffolds to improve sentence structure

The four-part formula

In 2013 I was in need of help with developing the quality of sentences that my students were writing. PE theory has some very heavy definitions for students to grapple with, show understanding of and then use effectively in context. When reading their work, students either use the definition in the wrong context, get the definition itself wrong, or fail to show how it is applied in a real situation. It's really frustrating but entirely my fault.

I came across a three-part sensation in a blog by history teacher Lee Donaghy. The post was titled "Red Scare unit – lessons 1 to 3" (2013). It described Lee's work with Helen Handford, a language consultant and genre-pedagogy expert, which brought about a way of developing students writing. In particular it introduced me to joint construction and a scaffold called "The four-part formula".

The formula scaffolds students to write definitions in the following framework:

Thing being defined	Verb or process	Group to which the thing belonged	Information that gives the thing its meaning

In the blog, Lee showed how he went from modelling, to joint construction, to independent construction of sentences. It was a huge eye opener and showed me how I should be teaching writing.

As with any scaffold, I needed to adjust it for my own context. So:

Thing being defined	Conjunction or connective	Definition	Meaning

Now when we need to learn a new definition, we do so using the four-part *process*. In the initial phases it is heavily scaffolded. Each student would have a template like the one here. I would be armed with a whiteboard pen and would direct students through completing the scaffold step by step. Following that came the co-construction where we would draft and draft a sentence until it was as close to perfection as possible. The whole experience, as mentioned earlier, allowed students to see the scaffold in action. As time progressed, students moved away from the framework but used different colour pens for each section. After this they moved to completing their sentences independently. But why this scaffold?

The deal sealer was the fact it encompassed everything. It had the *thing*, the *definition*, but it also forced students to add *meaning* to it – something my students always failed to do. They had to use it in context. They had to show understanding. This is what many of exam questions required yet we struggled to make it a good habit. This changed everything. Of course, you can't just throw this at a class and expect miracles. Lee's post opened my eyes to that. It may take 20 minutes of a lesson to co-construct a sentence together – 20 minutes of pure focus, modelling and redrafting. However, that could be the 20 minutes that starts the process of beginning to understand what a real sentence should look like.

Conjunctions and connectives

My final shout out to Hochman and Wexler (2017, pp. 13–14) comes with their use of the three conjunctions, "because, but, so". Conjunction and connectives are nothing new. They are such an important, yet simple, part of scaffolding sentences at a time when a lot of students in my class write very limited responses.

What I mean by that is there are times when I read a piece of work and a number of sentences lack any depth. They go so far but don't feel finished. They're missing something. For instance, a student might write:

A tennis player may be an introvert.
Calcium can be an important mineral.
Winston Churchill was a determined leader.

All these are statements I have read time and time again. There's nothing massively wrong with them. However, they lack depth. That's where conjunctions and connectives come in.

Very simply, conjunctions are words that link clauses *within* a sentence. For instance:

Winston Churchill was a determined leader because he continued to believe in victory when the odds seemed against him.

"Because" in that sentence is the conjunction. It links the two parts (or clauses) of the sentence together; that he was determined and how the odds seemed against him back in 1940–41. With that subtle use of a conjunction, the sentence has more depth and contains more information. Conjunctions come in two forms; co-ordinating conjunctions (but, or, and, so) and subordinating conjunctions (when, because, although, that).

Connectives are words or phrases that can be used to link clauses or sentences. Connectives can be connective adverbs like *however* or *therefore*. They can also be conjunctions. Commas are usually used with a connective adverb. For instance, I have just used a comma in this sentence after writing "for instance". That connective adverb linked the rest of the sentence. They can be used to compare, reinforce, explain, embellish or cross reference. Let me give you some examples:

Comparison: Similar to this, Unlike, Alternatively
Embellishment: In addition, Furthermore, Another way
Cross reference: This can be found, Another example
Adverbs: Essentially, Ultimately, To summarise

Connectives can also be used to connect two separate sentences (*Paul was in a particularly bad mood. However, he still found time to say good morning to all of his staff*). Conjunctions are usually found in single sentences (*Paul was in a particularly bad mood* but *made time to say good morning to his staff*).

As I said, none of this is new but I needed to go over the basics so that the rest makes sense. Here comes another shocking truth. I knew about conjunctions/connectives and had seen people banging on about them a lot, yet I never did anything about it. I knew my students' writing was poor but never explicitly did anything to teach my students to use conjunctions or connectives in any meaningful way. Once again, wishful thinking came into play.

One of the most basic ways to scaffold their use is providing lists of connectives/conjunctions, categorised earlier. Modelling from the teacher, co-construction and finally independent practice ensure their use is understood. Insisting that students use them to develop their sentences is a great start.

Class, I want you to pick one sentence from your partner's work which you feel would benefit from a more extended response. Once you have done that, take your work back and use the connectives/conjunction bookmark to add more detail to it. I'll come and check how you're getting on in one minute.

Hochman and Wexler (2017) describe numerous ways to explicitly teach writing to your classes. They opened my eyes to what I should have been doing all along. As with previous approaches, the key is using a scaffold and modelling it. Providing explicit instruction on how, and why, to use what it is. Talking, demonstrating, questioning as we show the process in action.

When trying to get students to write extended responses, Hochman and Wexler provide students with the opening part of a sentence. This stem is followed by "because, but and so". Students have to finish that sentence three times, three different ways. For example:

> Fractions are like decimals because
> Fractions are like decimals, but
> Fractions are like decimals, so
>
> (p. 13)

Each conjunction requires students to think hard about the subtle differences in their response. "Fraction are like decimals because" will have a completely different outcome to "Fraction are like decimals, so". As a teacher you can create stems of similar cognitive challenge and then ask students to complete them. It not only develops the skill of using conjunctions but it also demonstrates comprehension and allows students to think deeply about the content. That is a winner for me! So much so that I replace open-ended questions with activities like this to have more an impact.

The same can be done with subordinating conjunctions. Once again, providing scaffolds with a sentence stem and conjunction such as *although* or *when* or *because* can be used. Similar to the last strategy, it encourages students to write extended sentences. Give them a sentence stem such as:

> When renewable energy
> Before renewable energy
> Although renewable energy

As before, each one requires a different ending. *When* may require the process of renewable energy (how it works, what it does). *Before* may require an overview of what happened prior to advancements in its technology (fossil fuels, impact on environment). *Although* may look at some of the consequences (cost of renewable energy, limited availability, amount of energy it actually produces compared to other forms). This scaffold also similarly helps show students how different conjunctions can make the outcome of a sentence take a very different course.

Scaffolds for longer writing

IDEA

I've already talked about writing frames and using ideas such as PEED (Point, Evidence, Explain, Develop). As Caroline Spalding once told me, some people see them as the scourge of modern writing, but they do have a place.

For many of my students, the idea of writing nine- mark answers in a GCSE PE exam comes as a complete shock. "This is PE, Sir. Why have I got to write an essay?" But some students struggle to produce extended writing in any subject. Without an idea of what good writing looks like or how it's formed, a response can take many twists and turns and end up all over the show. Strategies like Pre-essays and Paragraph Outlines are good starting points, but we need to bring it all together. That's where an essay scaffold like PEED has a place.

The one that you might not heard of before and ties best into my particular subject is IDEA; Identify, Describe, Explain and Apply. The framework is exactly what it says it is (see Figure 6.4).Students would need to ensure that they worked step by step through the process, sometimes two or three times, to ensure that they

Guide to Answering Long Answer Questions/Scenario Questions	
Step 1 – Identify (To begin with, identify the topic or point from the GCSE theory course that you think links to the question)	
Topic or point 1	
Step 2 – Describe (Now, select the best one or two points and describe them in more detail. Give the **definition** if possible)	
Describe point 1	
Step 3 – Explain (Explain the definition/point **in your own words**. What does it mean? Show you fully understand the topic)	
Explain point 1	
Final step – Analyse/Apply (Link the points you have made to specific sporting examples, technique and the impact. What are positive and negative effects of the things you have identified in relation to the exam question? How will your **scenario** person use this point/topic?)	
Link point 1	

Figure 6.4 Guide to Answering Long Answer Questions/Scenario Questions

created paragraphs that went in a logical order accessed the higher parts of a mark scheme.

Initially they *Identify* what it is they are going to talk about. What is that thing?

Next they *Describe* it. This could come in the form of a definition or a well-structured explanation. It needs to share the specific content knowledge of the topic in hand.

After this they *Explain* the thing. We've had the facts, now what does that mean? For a long time I've had answers where students simply throw in a definition but have no idea of what they're talking about. They've seen a key word and "dumped" some information on the page in the hope of gaining marks. This section goes that step further and requires students to make meaning of this thing. Put it in their own words. Show they know their stuff.

The final stage is to *Apply*. It's here that I want to see that thing in action. Give me an example or scenario. What is its impact? What are the advantages or disadvantages? What difference does this thing make? How does it affect the question being asked?

When I launched this it was because that's what fitted our answers more effectively. We sidestepped PEED as that didn't. We spent time breaking down the scaffold, showing it in use with example after example. We co-constructed and redrafted. I gave a blank framework with prompt questions under each stage to support student writing. After a while I removed the scaffold to allow students a bit more freedom within the structure. It began to engrain clarity into answers. It made them more coherent. It made them more academic.

But here's an idea. Look at the requirements of your subject. What do students need to do to get higher marks? What are they missing in their own writing? Could a scaffold bridge that gap? If so, create your own subject-specific scaffold. But don't make it the be all and end all. Yes, frameworks have a place, but they won't make students' work instantly academic. They won't on their own develop vocabulary or sentences or connectives. You have to do that in combination with other strategies. And that's teaching. Understanding the what, how, why and when. Knowing when to use a scaffold and how to use it to make work better. It goes hand in hand with great feedback, good knowledge, excellent questioning and some bloody good planning. It ties in all the principles of aiming work high for all but supporting up. But when you use scaffolds:

- Choose the right one for the right area at the right time.
- Model it with the students – Show them why they should use it.
- Co-construct work with the students using the scaffold – Guide them, question them and correct them. Let them experience how to use it.
- Deliberate practise – Off they go. Monitor and feedback. Redraft and challenge.
- Remove it – When they have developed good habits, it's time to remove it.

To recap

- Be relentless in your demand for "the basics"
- Encourage students to read a lot
- Demonstrate great writing
- Build up confidence in structure

References

Abrams, D., & Prausnitz, J. (1975) Statistical thermodynamics of liquid mixtures: A new expression for the excess Gibbs energy of partly or completely miscible systems. *AIChE Journal*. 21(1). pp. 116–128.

Anderson, R. C., Wilson, P. T., & Fielding, L. G. (1988) Growth in reading and how children spend their time outside of school. *Reading Research Quarterly*. 23. pp. 285–303.

Ashford, K. (2015) How should we read texts in lessons? In: *Michaela's Blog*. 21 March, 2015. Available at: http://mcsbrent.co.uk/english-how-should-we-read-texts-in-lessons/

Beck, I., McKeown, M., & Kucan, L. (2013) *Bringing Words to Life*. Second Edition. New York: The Guildford Press.

Berger, R. (2003) *An Ethic of Excellence; Building a Culture of Craftsmanship with Students*. Portsmouth, NH: Heinemann.

Clark, C., & Teravainen, A. (2017) *Celebrating Reading for Enjoyment: Findings from Our Annual Literacy Survey 2016*. London: National Literacy Trust. pp. 1–17.

Cunningham, A., & Stanovich, K. (2001) What reading does for the mind. *Journal of Direct Instruction*. 1(2). pp. 137–149.

Department for Business, Innovation and Skills (2014) *Comparative analysis of young adults in England in the International Survey of Adult Skills 2012*. Research paper number 181. pp. 12–32. Available at: https://assets.publishing.service.gov.uk/government/uploads/system/uploads/attachment_data/file/623441/bis-14-1033-comparative-analysis-of-young-adults-in-england-in-international-survey-of-adult-skills-2012.pdf

Donaghy, L. (2013) Red scare unit – Lessons 1 to 3. In: *What's language doing here?* 10 November, 2013. Available at: https://whatslanguagedoinghere.wordpress.com/2013/11/10/red-scare-unit-lessons-1-to-3/

Graham, S. (2009) Want to improve children's writing? Don't neglect their handwriting. *American Educator*. Winter 2009–2010. pp. 20–40.

Graham, S., & Perin, D. (2007) *Writing Next: Effective Strategies to Improve Writing of Adolescents in Middle and High Schools – A Report to Carnegie Corporation of New York*. Washington, DC: Alliance for Excellent Education.

Hart, B., & Risley, T. (2003) The early catasrophe: The 30 million word gap by age 3. *American Educator*. Spring 2003. pp. 4–9.

Hirsch, E. D. Jr. (2003) Reading comprehension requires knowledge — Of words and the world. *American Educator*. Spring 2003. pp. 10–45.

Hochman, J., & Wexler, N. (2017) *The Writing Revolution. A Guide to Advancing Thinking through Writing in All Subjects and Grades*. San Francisco, CA: Jossey-Bass.

Kipling, R. (1900) *Six Honest Serving Men*. Anon.

Kirschner, P., Sweller, J., & Clark, E. (2006) Why minimal guidance during instruction does not work: An analysis of the failure of constructivist, discovery, problem-based, experiential, and inquiry-based teaching. *Educational Psychologist.* 41(2). pp. 75–86.

Lee, C. H., & Kalyuga, S. (2014) Expertise reversal effect and its instructional implications. In: Benassi, V. A., Overson, C. E., & Hakala, C. M. (Eds) *Applying Science of Learning in Education: Infusing Psychological Science into the Curriculum.* Retrieved from the Society for the Teaching of Psychology web site http://teachpsych.org/ebooks/asle2014/index.php. pp. 31–44.

Lemov, D. (2014) At first glance: A sentence starter adds unexpected rigor to writing. In: *Teach like a CHAMPION.* 13th January, 2015. Available at: http://teachlikeachampion.com/blog/first-glance-sentence-starter-adds-unexpected-rigor-writing/

Lemov, D., Woolway, E., & Yezzi, K. (2012) *Practice Perfect: 42 Rules for Getting Better at Getting Better.* San Francisco, CA: Jossey-Bass.

McFadden, P. L., & McElhinny, M. W. (1987) The combined analysis of remagnetization circles and direct observations in palaeomagnetism. *Earth and Planetary Science Letters.* 87(1–2), January 1988. pp. 161–172.

Merton, R. (1968) The Matthew effect in science: The reward and communication systems of science are considered. *Science.* 159. pp. 56–63.

Nagy, W. E., & Anderson, R. C. (1984) How many words are there in printed school English? *Reading Research Quarterly.* 19. pp. 304–330.

Nagy, W. E., Herman, P. A., & Anderson, R. C. (1985) Learning words from context. *Reading Research Quarterly.* 20. pp. 233–253.

National Literacy Trust (2018) *Adult literacy.* Available at: https://literacytrust.org.uk/parents-and-families/adult-literacy/

The Reading League (2016) *Reading league event Jan 2016 David Kilpatrick: Understanding reading development and difficulties.* Available at: www.youtube.com/watch?v=VBx3zBzrL5I&t=1094

Rosenshine, B. (2012) Principles of instruction: Research-based strategies that all teachers should know. *American Educator. Spring.* 2012. pp. 12–39.

Rosenshine, B., & Meister, C. (1992) The use of scaffolds for teaching higher-level cognitive strategies. *Educational Leadership.* April, 1992. pp. 26–33.

Sampson, G. (1921) *English for the English: A Chapter on National Education.* Cambridge, UK: University Press.

Stanovich, K. (1986) Matthew effects in reading: Some consequences of individual differences in the acquisition of literacy. *Reading Research Quarterly.* 22. pp. 360–407.

Stenhouse Publishers (2011) *Kelly Gallagher: Write Like This.* Available at: www.youtube.com/watch?v=OJFMhWtFVnA

Teaching Channel (2015) *I Do, We Do, You Do.* Getty Museum. Available at: www.youtube.com/watch?v=IOMF06TJAO4

Tomsett, J. (2015) This much I know about … what REALLY WORKS when preparing students for their examinations! In: *johntomsett.com.* 24th April, 2015. https://johntomsett.com/2015/04/24/this-much-i-know-about-what-really-works-when-preparing-students-for-their-examinations/

Willingham, D. T. (2009) *Why Don't Students like School? A Cognitive Scientist Answers Questions about How the Mind Works and What It Means for the Classroom.* San Francisco, CA: Jossey-Bass.

Willingham, D. T. (2017) *How to get your mind to read.* The New York Times. Online. 25th November, 2017. Available at: www.nytimes.com/2017/11/25/opinion/sunday/how-to-get-your-mind-to-read.html

Willingham, D. T., & Lovette, G. (2014) Can Reading Comprehension Be Taught? *Teachers College Record*: 26 September, 2014 Available at: www.tcrecord.org.proxy.its.virginia.edu ID Number: 17701.

Wood, D., Bruner, J., & Ross, G. (1976) The role of tutoring in problem solving. *Journal of Child Psychology and Psychiatry.* 17(1976). pp. 89–100.

Are we just doing data because we've been told to do data?

How data has increased the workload of teachers but how we can use it to improve teaching and learning

Like with so many things, data seems to have got lost in its own hype. We see it happen all the time: research shows us that feedback is valuable, but rather than seeing a boon in professional development about effective feedback, we instead see sales of red pens go through the roof as the most obvious form of feedback – marking – becomes all-important.

So it is with data. We were told that research showed that use of data was a really effective way to ensure better progress for students. As a fairly new teacher, this sounded plausible, and so I happily submitted my numbers each term to the spreadsheet, and waited for coloured graphs to come back to tell me who had achieved what.

The problem was, I already knew that: I was the one who had put the data in. So instead of the data informing my planning and teaching, it became just another thing to do. Instead of data being a tool to improve the quality of education, we instead ended up with the situation where education felt like a tool for providing the data. It felt like the numbers were just collected as a way of predicting outcomes at the end of a Key Stage, and rather than offering us any insight about how to improve things, it just pointed out that we weren't there yet.

I'm sure that carefully collected and analysed data can be a really powerful tool . . . but that isn't what happens in too many schools.

(Michael Tidd, deputy headteacher at a Nottinghamshire Primary School)

One of the most significant things that I have noticed increase over the years is data collection. Speaking to a number of experienced teachers, teachers who were in classrooms before the days of Excel spreadsheets, there has been a significant shift in the way we approach, collect and analyse data. Data for them would be a record sheet in their mark books that they would use to record how well their students were performing.

The rise of assessment and data collection has now become more prominent in the world of education. The necessity of comparing a country's education system with others around the world means that we need evidence to prove which systems are working. Within a country, we use data from schools to demonstrate the value that schooling has on student achievement. We compare schools with similar demographics. We look at the progress of various student groups. Parents, governing bodies, regulators and local authorities use data to measure which schools are doing well and which ones aren't. Unsurprisingly this fascination and dependency on data has filtered into schools, departments and classrooms. It has also increased the pressure on teachers and, in some cases, our students.

It is now common for teachers to be masters of spreadsheets. There is an expectation that we track, collate and monitor assessments in an effort to demonstrate that a) students are learning and making progress, and b) we are effective as teachers in the job we are doing. The necessity to prove our worth, to showcase that things are going well, to highlight trends is common place. Data has become one of the tools in which leaders in schools can pull us up and scrutinise what impact we are having. At its worst it has become a pressure on teachers. An unnecessary stress as we focus on accountability. But this pressure can lead us to collecting data on our students for the wrong reasons. It can become *proof* rather than what I personally see it as – a tool for teaching and learning.

I remember quite clearly my relationship with data in the early stages of my career. It was, if I am completely honest, an afterthought in most instances. The day-to-day teaching was what is was all about. As the Assessment, Recording and Reporting (ARR) calendar unfolded I would have deadlines to meet and data to input. Most of the time, naively, this input came only hours before the window closed. I would quickly scan my assessment sheets, look at previous data inputs, wrestle with my assumptions, worry over what a 'level 3.5' actually meant and then put in a score. It was the best I could do at the time. Looking back now, there's a worry that a large part of this data was merely a best guess. What was I actually recording? What was this data actually telling me? What was it actually assessing? More worrying is the following set of questions. What did I actually do with this data? What did collecting this data actually change in my classroom? What did it change in my teaching? Did it make any difference to the students I taught? If I'm honest, and this was my downfall with data and assessment, this numerical end-product had very little impact at all. It allowed the school to track. It met a required deadline. It gave students *something* to read when they received their reports. It gave line managers something to discuss – but that was it.

As time went on and results (especially GCSEs) became more and more important, something changed within me as well. I became fixated on *proving* my role as a teacher with data rather than using it to have any real impact on teaching and learning. I remember a number of department meetings in the cycle of data reviews where I would cringe at the assessment results of my classes. Times when students who should be reaching the higher echelons fell woefully short. Times when my class averages were below those of my colleagues. Times when I questioned whether I was a good teacher, whether my students were working hard enough, or whether I needed to rethink my beliefs about teaching. In this situation you have to ask yourself, are you actually using data effectively? There were also the times when results were good and an inflated ego followed. I would walk around proud in the knowledge that my grades were good and so must my teaching be. Instead of reflecting on why things had gone well, I would bathe in the glory.

Breaking a habit or culture is hard and trying to rethink an approach to data can be difficult. However, I think it is important that we find time to change the focus when it comes to data. Rather than it scrutinising us, maybe we should scrutinise it. If I asked you to think solely about how *you* use data and assessment, how might you answer these questions?

- Why do you collect data?
- What is it collecting information about?
- What does this tell you about student achievement?
- What does it *really* tell you about student achievement?
- What do you do with the data?
- Does the data help improve your teaching?
- *How?*
- How does it help improve student learning?
- How do the students use the data?
- What change does it have on their motivation and effort in your lesson?
- If I asked your students about their data and how well they were doing in your subject, would they be able to tell me accurately and in depth?
- Is the data you're collecting accurate?
- What do you do with data when you've collected and inputted it?
- Does it make any difference?
- Is there a better or more intelligent way to collect it?

If you are anything like me, your answers may not be clear cut. Sometimes we know we need to do a particular action but aren't quite sure why. Sometimes things are a little fuzzy or hazy. We know that we need to assess and ultimately collect data – that is pretty obvious. There's a whole separate debate about what type of data we collect but that is a management decision and something we can't influence without changing policies. We need to be able to analyse, at some level, what learning is taking place, and the use of formative/summative assessment data may contribute to a clearer picture. We need to be able to see what new things students have learnt that they didn't know before. We need to use data to be able to see if the way we are teaching is actually right for this class, this group of students or this individual. Data is information with great potential if used effectively. It's wrong to assume that data can tell us everything and the insistence from some corners to do so is unhelpful. But I do believe that if we approach data in a significantly different way it can really have an impact on what we do in lessons. This isn't about whole school data systems, data management or policies but a way to look at data in a more effective way for *you*. A way that might tell you some real things about what might be going on within your teaching and learning.

Ok, I've been asked to collect it, but what do I need to do with it?

For many a year I followed school policy and like all teachers I inputted data onto the school system when deadlines approached. Quite late on I realised that after the slog of this collection, I rarely did anything with it. I had this wealth of information in front of me but no plan of action. Of course, I would look at the usual things. Who is on track? Who are our C/D borderlines? Who might need a phone call home? These sorts of questions are very common but rarely led to anything significant that I didn't already know. Surely I was missing a trick.

In 2013, I visited our deputy head, Ian Gates, and in a very frank conversation where I probably said what he didn't want to hear, I explained that although I collected data, I didn't have a clue about how it actually helped me as a teacher. Ian offered one simple piece of advice. It was the beginning of my data awakening and provided me with my first principle.

---

1 Data should make us ask questions

Providing you have collected the right type of information from your assessments, the richness of the data should allow you to ask numerous questions that allow us to scratch beneath the surface. It should provide an insight into student understanding and help unpick the quality of learning that has taken place. But *providing you have collected the right type of information* is the key word of warning here.

For this data to be rich it needs to step away from the simple grade, percentage or mark that accompany most pieces of assessment. Although gathering these single figures can allow us to sort or rank order who has performed well, who has underachieved or who is coasting, it doesn't allow for deep interrogation. For instance, if two students both got 57/80 in an assessment, you might think that both have scored around 70 per cent and have therefore grasped a significant amount of the topic. That's a fair assumption. There is clearly "30 per cent" of things that didn't stick but this can be worked on when you meet the class post-test. However, what we must be consider, as highlighted by Nuthall (2007, p. 43), is:

- What did these two students get the 57 marks for?
- Even though both got 57, it may be for different things. Student A might have scored well in their ability to use scale factors, whereas student B might have struggled in this topic.

How do we know what exactly students have learnt, or not learnt, when the data is so broad? At best these single scores help to rank order or do a quick comparison against previous assessments/target grades. At worst they lead us to make assumptions that can be inherently wrong.

Some schools and teachers insist on more of a breakdown of results. Taking up a role at a new school, I found that they had gone a step further and had split an assessment, particularly exams, into three sections: multiple choice, short answer questions, and long answer questions. Although not ideal, at least it distinguished between question types. However, there are still the same questions. What does 7/18 on the short answer section tell us? What topics are weak areas for student A, student B, student C and so on? How do I know what areas I need to focus on in the post assessment lesson? The data is becoming slightly more workable, but there is still significant room for improvement.

In order for data to actually be of benefit it must be able to demonstrate what has actually happened. If we only look at a final grade we may come to the conclusion that a student needs to work harder or has done pretty well. If we have a bank of information then this can become more refined. A word of caution, though – *the data must be easy for teachers to input and simple in its manipulation*. If it takes us hours to input and even longer to look for trends, it probably isn't time well spent.

One method is discussed in *Driven by Data: A Practical Guide to Improve Instruction*, by Paul Bambrick-Santoyo (2010). Using a system, like Question Level Analysis (QLA), teachers gather information about *each* question that students have answered. They report the finite grades rather than grouping questions together. This gathering of information happens at regular assessments rather than at a final summative test when intervention is probably too late. Having data mapped out in detail like this allows the teacher to analyse the quality of answers to topics, questions and individual students and even make whole-class comparisons. Now, if I was reading this I would be thinking three things: 1) this sounds too complex for me, 2) this sounds like I need to buy a product which is probably too expensive, and 3) this seems like it will add to my workload. In the initial stage, as you set things up, it may take an investment in time. For me it took the creation of one spreadsheet template which I used over and over again.

This spreadsheet doesn't need to be all singing, all dancing, either. A simple spreadsheet lined up for the assessment with a breakdown of each question, their topic and the mark available is as complex as it needs be (see Figure 7.1). As you finish marking an assessment you simply input the marks for each question. If you're spreadsheet savvy you can even get it to traffic light how well questions were answered, provide an average for each question or even compare results. Your maths, science or IT departments should be able to help. Yes, there are tools that go further. Yes, there are buy in packages. But a simple breakdown on a spreadsheet is sufficient to delve into analysis and begin asking questions.

But wait! Input every finite grade?

I know. That sounds like a lot of work every time, but I assure you it isn't. With exam papers in hand, it simply requires you to flick through the pages and type in the numbers. A class of 30 takes no time at all once you get into the groove.

Question	1	2	3	4	5	6	7	8	9	10	11	12	13	14	15	16	17		Total	%	Grade	Target	3 Levels of progress	4 Levels of progress	5 Levels of progress
	Components of fitness	Somatotype	Diet	Healthy Active lifestyle	Principles of training	Strength	Open Skill	Age	Circulatory	Skeletal	Flexibility	Method of training	Media	Healthy Lifestyle	technology	Method of training	Respiratory								
Marks	1	1	1	1	1	1	1	4	5	5	1	3	4	2	4	3	8								
Name																									
Student A	1	1	1	1	0	1	0	3	2	2	1	2	3	1	3	2	0		24	51	B	B			
Student B	1	1	1	1	0	1	0	4	2	5	1	2	4	2	3	3	0		28	60	D	B			
Student C	1	1	1	1	0	1	2	2	2	5	1	1	4	1	0	1	1		25	53	D	B/C			
Student D	1	1	1	1	0	1	2	4	2	5	1	2	2	2	3	1	5		32	66	C	A'			
Student E	1	1	1	1	0	1	2	2	2	5	1	2	2	0	1	1	3		28	68	D	C			
Student F	1	1	1	1	1	1	2	4	2	3	1	3	4	2	4	2	7		40	85	A'	A'			
Student G	1	1	1	1	0	1	2	4	2	5	1	3	2	2	0	0	0		30	64	C	C			
Student H	1	1	1	1	0	1	2	4	2	5	1	3	4	0	4	2	4		32	68	C	B/C			
Student I	1	1	1	1	0	1	2	4	3	4	1	3	4	2	0	1	0		33	70	B	B			
Student J	1	1	1	1	0	1	0	2	2	5	1	2	2	2	4	2	4		27	57	B	A/B			
Student K	1	1	1	1	0	1	0	3	2	5	1	2	4	0	0	2	2		26	55	B	A/B			
Student L	1	1	1	1	0	1	1	4	2	5	1	2	2	2	4	1	3		32	68	C	B/C			
Student M	1	1	1	1	0	1	0	4	2	5	1	3	4	0	0	2	5		34	72	B	A'			
Student N	1	1	1	1	1	1	2	4	2	5	1	2	4	2	0	1	7		40	85	A'	A'			
Student O	1	1	1	1	0	1	0	4	2	5	1	1	1	1	1	1	0		22	47	B	A			
Student P	1	1	1	1	1	1	0	3	1	5	1	1	1	1	1	1	0		35	74	B	A'			
Student Q	1	1	1	1	0	1	2	4	2	5	1	2	4	2	3	2	4		34	72	B	B			
Student R	1	1	1	1	0	1	2	4	2	5	1	2	2	2	1	1	7					A'			
	1	1	1	1	0.1667	1	1.2778	3.5	2	4.6667	1	2.1667	3.1667	1.2778	2.0556	1.2778	3.2222								

Figure 7.1 Simple Data Spreadsheet

But that's still 30 minutes!

My comeback is this. We could just give an overall grade and hazard a guess at why students didn't perform well. We go a step further and group sections of a paper and input grades for those. Three sections in a typical exam (multiple choice, short answer, extended answer) and we only have to input three grades per child. Nuthall (2007, p. 43) points out a problem. He discusses the issue that if two students get the same grade/score on a test about life in Ancient Egypt, does that mean that both of these students understood the various sub topics associated with this area? Do they know whether girls went to school? Did they learn the same things as boys? His argument is they may know facts, but do they understand the underlying roles and social status of Ancient Egyptians.

He also takes it a step further and highlights that even though two students get the same grade, one may know more about one aspect, such as the lives of girls but not women in Egypt, yet the other student may know the exact opposite.

> But since they got the same numerical score, it is assumed that they must know the same things.

My argument is that by grouping grades we assume many things. We get a hunch. We sort of know. Even though it adds a few extra minutes to the process, inputting finite grades gives us more information. Borrowing an unrelated phrase from Ron Berger (2003, p. 95), grouped grades is like doing analysis with a meat cleaver, whereas finite grades allows analysis with a scalpel. I know which one gives me more information – information that could help me and my students address misconceptions. And surely that's what the collection of student data should do.

So just a simple spreadsheet will do?

There is a way to develop this spreadsheet further. Compare the spreadsheets in Figures 7.1 and 7.2. What differences do you notice? Both have things like question level breakdowns, marks on offer, averages per question, target grades, etc. Look closer though. The table in Figure 7.2 not only breaks down questions by topics, but also sub-topics. As pointed out, saying a student didn't do so well in the "technology" topic is helpful. But with a topic so vast, pinning it down to the fact it was the "technological development" element which they struggled in tells you with more clarity the areas that you need to recap. Many teachers using this approach even sub-categorise question type – whether it is a state, explain, describe or evaluate question. This is helpful when scrutinising exam technique and being precise about which types of question students struggle with.

With a rich source of teacher friendly information in front of you, what might you do with it? Take the set of data in Figure 7.2. Looking at it, what things might you be analysing? How would you analyse it? What are you looking for?

Figure 7.2 Detailed Data Spreadsheet

Detailed marks per question (rotated spreadsheet):

Name	SEN/PP	Q1 User groups concessions	Q2 Comp of fitness - Static strength	Q3 Gender flexibility	Q4 Functions of the blood	Q5 Principles of training - overload	Q6.1 Methods of training - Interval defi	Q6.2 Methods of training - Interval exa	Q7 Schools - Teachers influence	Q8 Amatuer - obtaining funding	Q9.1 Social groupings - family positive	Q9.2 Social groupings - family positive	Q10 Healthy lifestyle - Regular exercis	Q11 Components of fitness - agility	Q12.1 Biquette - definition	Q12.2 Biquette - Example	Q13 Leisure time-Reasons for increas	Q14.1 Sponsorship - types	Q14.2 Sponsorship - Unacceptable form	Q15 Diet - dehydration	Q16 Technology - Teachnological dev	Q17 Social groups - Influence on part
Question Marks		1	1	1	1	1	2	2	2	3	2	2	2	2	2	2	4	3	2	2	4	8
Student A	SEN	1	1	1	0	1	0	0	2	2	1	2	2	2	2	2	4	3	2	2	4	4
Student B		1	1	1	0	1	1	2	2	2	2	2	2	2	2	2	4	3	2	1	3	6
Student C	PP	1	1	1	1	1	2	2	2	2	2	2	2	2	2	2	4	3	3	2	4	7
Student D		1	1	1	1	1	2	2	2	3	2	2	2	2	2	2	3	3	3	2	4	6
Student E		1	1	1	1	1	2	2	2	2	2	2	2	2	2	2	4	3	2	2	4	6
Student F		1	1	1	1	1	2	2	2	3	2	2	2	2	2	2	4	3	2	2	4	8
Student G		1	1	1	1	1	1	2	2	3	2	1	2	2	2	2	4	3	2	2	4	8
Student H		1	1	1	1	1	1	2	2	2	1	1	1	1	1	2	3	3	2	2	3	3
Student I		1	1	1	1	1	2	2	2	3	2	2	2	2	2	2	4	3	2	2	4	6
Student J		1	1	1	1	1	0	2	2	2	2	2	2	2	1	2	3	3	2	2	4	6
Student K		1	1	0	0	1	0	0	2	2	2	2	1	2	1	1	4	3	1	1	3	3
Student L		1	1	1	1	1	2	2	2	2	2	2	2	2	1	2	4	3	2	2	4	6
Student M	SEN	1	1	1	0	1	0	2	2	2	2	2	2	2	1	2	4	3	2	2	4	5
Student N		1	1	1	1	1	2	2	2	2	2	2	2	2	1	2	4	3	2	2	4	6
Student O	PP	1	1	1	1	0	0	0	2	2	2	2	2	0	0	2	4	3	1	2	2	4
Student P		1	1	1	0	1	2	1	2	3	2	2	2	2	2	2	4	3	2	3	4	6
Student Q		1	1	1	1	1	1	2	2	2	2	2	2	2	0	2	4	3	2	3	4	6
Student R		1	0	1	0	1	1	1	2	2	2	2	2	2	2	2	3	3	2	1	3	3
Average		0.9	1.0	1.0	0.5	0.9	1.2	1.0	1.8	1.9	1.9	1.7	1.5	1.7	1.4	1.9	3.2	2.6	1.9	1.8	3.5	6.2

Summary totals and grades:

Name	Total	%	Grade	Target
Question Marks	49			
Student A	38	78	A	B/A
Student B	32	65	C	C
Student C	45	92	A'	B
Student D	42	86	A	A
Student E	39	80	A	A
Student F	47	96	A	A
Student G	46	94	A	A/A'
Student H	36	73	B	B
Student I	41	84	A	B
Student J	40	82	A	B
Student K	29	59	D	C/B
Student L	40	82	A	A
Student M	36	73	B	C
Student N	45	92	A	A
Student O	30	61	D	A
Student P	41	84	A	C/B
Student Q	40	82	A	A/A'
Student R	28	57	D	B/A
Average	38.6	78.8		C

A pretty solid foundation for this process would be to begin asking questions about successes, weakness, trends, comparisons and so on. The list of things you could look into is endless. A basic set of questions might be:

- Who has performed well?
- Who has not performed well?
- Who might have coasted?
- Are there any trends in particular student groups (Gender, SEN, Pupil Premium etc)?
- What topics were answered well?
- Answered well by everyone?
- What topics were not answered well and may need further intervention?
- What gaps are there in student achievement?
- Are my lessons pitched correctly that either support or challenge individuals?

If you have asked these questions, you might have spent 20 minutes looking at the sheet, got some fairly clear trends and then begun to plan follow up intervention. But how about working with data in the following, more analytical way. Bambrick-Santoyo (2010) suggests that for QLA to be effective, you should take note of the following guidance:

1. *Analysis must be conducted with test in hand*: This is an important point. As you analyse the data it is essential that you have the student's assessments with you. Data can tell you a lot but it can also paint a harsh picture. Things aren't always black and white. So by having your assessments to hand, once you identify an anomaly or something you may wish to question, you can quickly scan the papers to actually build up the full picture. Pete Pease, a director of learning at a school in Hampshire, agrees with this and says "*Data can sometimes just be seen as numbers. But what information can you get from this? Go back to the exam scripts, the work and the assessments*". Having them in hand also allows you to make personal notes on particular areas of strengths and weaknesses. This will be vital later on in the process and helps you build up a narrative of what has happened.

2. *Analysis must be deep*: With test in hand, the analysis you conduct must go below the surface. Pete Pease offers sound advice when he says "*The key thing to do is ask yourself, why did this student write the answer to this particular question? What was their reasoning? What is their thought process?*" By doing this we can quickly ascertain whether the error was due to a lack or content knowledge or lack of exam technique? Bambrick-Santoyo (2010) offers three ways to do this in a more effective way. *First* is to do the question and topic analysis side by side. At first glance, it may seem that the class struggled with topic of acids and alkalis. Your initial thought may be to reteach this whole topic again in your post assessment lesson. However, by quickly scanning through the student answers you actually notice that they simply have misinterpreted the reactivity series. This is easier to

rectify and less time consuming than reteaching the whole topic again. *Second*, search for separators. If a student or small group of students performed highly in a topic compared to the rest of the class, they could be given an extension/stretch task whilst you reteach the topic to the remaining students. It makes the follow up targeted, responsive and productive. *Third*, scan by student. Although a disappointing result may make you believe a student performed badly, maybe they did well at the start of the exam but poorly towards the end. Maybe it is more of a timing issue where they fail to allocate sufficient time for the whole paper. Not scanning each individual may make you miss this.

3. *Results from analysis must be turned around immediately*: "But where do we get the time to do this!", I hear you scream. Finding time to mark tests, analyse them and then do something with them takes time. This is why the way you mark (discussed in Chapter 4), how you collect data and how you analyse it **must** be quick and effective. The point this highlights is that if this whole process of marking a set of exams takes two or three weeks, depending on the subject we teach, we could have taught a further 10 to 15 lessons before we actually produce any follow up. Is this too long? Will the students clearly recollect the assessment they actually took and be able to remember reasons to attribute success/failure? An idea could be to have assessments windows that are synchronised across the whole school and time is allocated (whether through department time, staff meeting time, Twighlight INSET) to do it. If we want to have more of an impact, quick turnaround is essential. If time can't be allocated, the process itself must be rigorous but fast.

4. *Analysis must include effective analysis meetings and you need to prepare for them*: I'll talk about analysis meetings in more detail in a moment but in a nutshell, it is important that departments review assessment results collectively. However, preparing for these meetings is essential. Come to a meeting unprepared and it could take double, even triple the time. Preparing for it could help speed up your analysis as well. When I first tried to get to grips with QLA I would find myself looking at every minute detail. This took an age and contradicted everything I have just proposed, that data analysis should be rigorous but quick. However, I created a proforma (Figure 7.3) with some guidance from Katie Yezzi (principal of Troy Prep ES and co-author of *Practice Perfect*). You fill it out once for a class. The sheet accompanied me on the analysis process and prompted me to ask specific questions that would add value to any follow up. Its simplicity allows you to make notes as you mark the papers which is so important. Making comments as you go tells more of a story than numbers ever do. The pro-forma also helps focus on the analysis of the assessment data.

How can data actually improve teaching?

Have you ever been in that situation where your department does an assessment with a cohort or year group and when the results come in, yours are poorer than you had anticipated? It puts you into what a colleague of mine describes as the "pit of despair".

GCSE PE Data Analysis (DDI) DAF

Targeted students (how have these students performaed?):	Exam technique answered poorly (was it state questions, explain questions.....)
Who are the underachievers from this mock (2 grades or below):	
Performance of PP and SEN:	Any horizontal trends for particular students (started strongly on a test and then tailed off....?)
Praise (what has been answered well by students? Which questions in Particular? Which topics were answered well? Any particular groups? Any particular styles of questions?) *Please be prepared to share how you tought this*	Reteach (plan and practice):
Probe (what wasn't ansered well? Why?) Questions not answered well: Topics that may be a class weakness (including old topicsvs new topics):	Follow up (Has the gap been closed?)

Figure 7.3 DDI Sheet

You go through a mix of emotions and question the outcome. You wondered what went wrong, trying to locate whether it was your teaching or the efforts of the students that have led to this (what feels like) disastrous outcome.

The problem is that there could be many reasons for students' lack of achievement. One of these has to be the quality of the teaching. As much as students play a huge part in the process (and I will talk about their role later), the initial input comes from the teacher. It was the teacher instruction which led to misconceptions or misunderstanding. With this in mind it can be easy for us to retreat to our rooms and try and tackle the problem in isolation. When this has happened to me. I would feel too embarrassed to ask others for help because (stupidly) I didn't want to look weak. I would question my approach and then plan how to correct it. I would go back to the class and either read the riot act or re-teach the bits that students got wrong. Two questions arise from this:

1. Why is it not helpful to try and correct the problem on your own? Why do we sometimes let our pride hinder the process?

2. What is wrong with going back next lesson to reteach the errors and misconceptions?

What do you think? What issues are there with working this way? To help explore some of the problems that these questions raise I will once again draw upon the work of Pete Pease, who helped form my second principle of data.

2 Data *must* be a group activity and it *must* improve teaching

This is a principle that for some is common sense, but for others (me included) came as quite an eye-opener. I had primarily looked at data on my own, developed an idea about what needed doing and then gone back to lessons to reteach the topics that the class had performed poorly in. That seemed sensible. When I first sat down with Pete and he asked me the question that became pivotal, "*After an assessment, why might going back to your class and re-teaching the areas of misconception be a problem?*", I had absolutely no idea.

Pete's point was that if we work alone when analysing data and planning follow ups, more often than not we go back to lessons and re-teach the topic the same way we taught it before. We probably use the same analogy, the same examples, the same instruction, explanation and resources. His point was that doing it *that way* caused the misconception in the first place. In any other walk of life, if something I did had an undesirable result, I'd probably look for another way to do it better – usually after seeking advice or guidance. Pete made me realise the power of collaborative data follow-up. After collating and scrutinising the data on our own, attending a follow-up analysis meeting with colleagues is probably the most valuable thing you can do. As Pete eloquently puts it,

> *The value in assessment results is in the gathering around and tweaking lessons and teaching plans to make those lessons more effective. The act of working as a team with assessment results enables the expertise to spread and contributes to the essential open culture of improvement.*

The data analysis meeting Part of the process, as outlined earlier in the first principle, is preparing for a group analysis meeting. Using a pro-forma similar to Figure 7.3, you can unpick some of the strengths and weaknesses from your results before you meet with other teachers. You can also begin to pencil in an action plan on how you *might* follow this up in subsequent lessons. The analysis meetings can take many forms. One that I have been part of has involved the whole department, another a peer teacher.

Whole department data analysis meeting – Prior to the meeting, each teacher is given the whole assessment data for the year group or cohort. This openness helps break down the culture of data being a negative thing to measure a teacher by. Over time, it creates an environment where we can use data to support each other and help our development. By having everyone's data, we can see the bigger picture of how the department, and its students, have performed. For me it does two things. It allows me to see common trends which might have cropped up with our curriculum, and it also lets me spot expert teachers who I might learn from. Each teacher also brings their analysis sheet and assessments with them. The meeting is led by a member of staff (although the head of department may wish to take the initial lead) who facilitates, focuses on a few key areas and asks probing questions. Bambrick-Santoyo (2010) offers some guidance on the running of this meeting:

Let the data do the talking – Rather than tell teachers what to do, point to the data and ask them what it means.

Let the teacher do the talking – Teachers must own the assessment and analysis and they will do so if they find answers on their own.

Go back to specific test questions – Have copies of the assessment at the meeting.

Know the data yourself – By knowing the data school leaders can ensure meetings will be productive.

He also offers some phrases leaders can use to ground analysis meetings:

- Let's look at question ____. Why did the students get it wrong?
- What did the students need to be able to do to get that question right?
- What's so interesting is that they did really well on question ___, but struggled on question ___ on the same standard. Why do you think that is?
- So, what you're saying is ___ (paraphrase and improve good responses).

The process allows deep discussion about the reasons why students have or have not done so well. It unpicks the probable causes and brings them to the surface. From here you can focus in on specific areas. As Katie Yezzi once told me:

> In the meetings, we look at the one trend area, and then the question or two from that standard where there was a gap in understanding. We first look at an exemplar answer (we have them already, or you can have teachers come with them or do them on the spot). Then we look at the student work and we create a charted list of what they need to do to complete the exemplar and then what the specific gaps are in our students. Based on those gaps, as a group, we create objectives for future lessons.

And this is the key part. As Katie highlights, the teachers then work on future plans as a group. The collaborative nature of this allows something very powerful to happen. It allows teachers to learn from each other and develop their own practice.

I remember a story Pete told me when I first asked about the format. He explained that after the group had analysed the data together and shared their individual reflections from their own analysis, they began to work as a team to close gaps. Pete explained how he himself had a class that struggled with pie charts. Clearly, there was something in the way he had taught it that had led students to misunderstand the topic, which led to errors in the assessment. If he had worked alone he might not have been able to see what the issue was. However, during the whole department analysis meeting, the team focused in on the topic and a colleague, John Exley, shared with the team a simple way he taught the topic to students. Now, John taught the lower ability students, yet on this topic, his class outperformed everybody else's. Pete recollects that he had never thought of teaching the topic that way, yet it was so obvious. It transformed the way that they would all now teach it. It had improved teaching and learning. As Pete put it, it is the *"gathering around and tweaking lessons and teaching plans to make those lessons more effective"* that is the valuable element of this process. Data can do that.

Pete has been kind enough to offer some words of warning regarding this type of meeting, though. We should

> [b]e aware that if done badly, conversations can be superficial. "What did they do well in? What didn't they do well in? Let's teach those bits again" – What is this actually unpicking? You must have the exams/assessments to see what is actually going wrong.

The worst thing (as I have found out) is trying to implement department data meetings for the first time. To begin with, your colleagues may not see the benefit. Pete told me a number of stories of how it took some colleagues longer than others to get it. They would still go off and do things the way they always did and get the same results. But after a while, and by making the meetings more efficient, those colleagues would have that lightbulb moment and finally see the benefit. Reflecting on how the meeting is conducted and making tweaks is vital. He also provided some tips on how to get people on board. In essence, you need to make the benefits very obvious:

- Look for the bright spots first.
- What did a specific teacher do to get great grades/answers on a particular topic?
- Get them to share it.
- Did they teach it in a particular way?
- What resources did you use?
- How did you teach/model it?

Look for the positives from colleagues and focus on them. Get the discussion that stems from data to be about teaching and learning.

Peer data analysis meetings – In teaching, time is precious. Sometimes the delay between department meetings can be weeks or months, which makes the review of data too inconsistent. In science and maths departments at his school, Pete decided to make these meetings more regular and less reliant on the scheduling of department meetings by teaming up teachers with similar teaching groups. After assessments, these teachers would meet together and perform a review process similar to that of a whole department one. It may not bring together the wealth of experience that a larger meeting can, but it allows the review and interrogation process to be undertaken in a timely fashion. How these peer review teams are set up is entirely dependent on the focus of the department. It seems sensible to match teachers of similar ability sets together, but there are also benefits to matching experienced and novice teachers or making it random if your department doesn't set on ability. The core point remains the same – teachers are working together and discussing data and moving teaching and learning forward.

Probably the most important thing, and something I will talk about in my fourth principle, is how this helps students. Pete told me that for his students, "*The fear is 'If they don't get topic x, y and z, they say they don't get maths' when in fact it's not maths that's the problem, it's that they have struggled with some specific topics*". By undertaking detailed analysis, collaborating and planning effective follow up (re-teach), we can stop students making blanket statements and help tackle the real misconceptions.

But what about learning?

Nuthall (2007, p. 51) makes such an important point when it comes to knowing what a student has learnt. He talks about the how if we really want to know how well a topic or unit went, or how successful our activities were, we need to ascertain two things about each student:

> What did the student know and believe about each concept or idea before the unit began? What did each student know and believe about each concept or idea after the unit was finished?
>
> With these metrics we can work out what each student learned. Makes total sense. He also states that by doing this, we as educators can "work out what each activity contributed or failed to contribute to each student's knowledge and understanding".
>
> (Nuthall, 2007, p. 51)

One of the main reasons for collecting assessment data is to see what students have or have not learned. It's a way of finding out if things have actually been transferred from teacher to student. But as we know from Nuthall (2007, p. 35), students already know on average 50 per cent of what a teacher intends them to learn in a topic (even though this knowledge is not distributed evenly). The other problem, as pointed out by UCLA professor of psychology Robert Bjork, is that sometimes the things we are assessing are more performance rather than learning. So, what can we deduce from a student who gets 82 per cent on a test? If I hadn't provided you with the previous two research points you might say that the student has learnt quite a bit from your teaching. But what if that student already knew most of that topic anyway? What if they could have got 79 per cent on that test without you teaching them because they had been told a lot about it by their Uncle Simon who used to be a science teacher? What if they took the same test three months later and got 68 per cent? Does that mean that your teaching helped or not? This leads me to my third principle.

---

3 Data must help improve learning

The worry for me as a teacher, when teaching a topic, was that a student would say, "Oh we did this in Year 6". While teaching Year 7 Science in 2016 it happened more than once. I would instantly think, "What will this individual learn if they already know it?" Student self-assessments can actually be unreliable and sometimes they say they know something when in fact they don't, not to the level you want. However, it is worth knowing that students will invariably know some of what you are teaching as it can make the assessment data you have collected at the end of a unit misleading.

As a PE teacher at my first school, we made the conscious decision to perform a baseline assessment at the beginning of every new sport/activity we taught. We had to do this as differences in levels of physical literacy and fundamental skills between students were huge. If we didn't, I would be teaching skills and tactics to students who could already perform them to a high standard. Fine, my assessment grades would look good but how would these students have been challenged over the six to eight weeks I taught them? What new things would they have learned?

Transferring this to the classroom is a fairly simple process and can come in the form of "a diagnostic performance assessment (e.g. a short quiz or mini-assignment) to reveal students' prior knowledge of material" (Ambrose & Lovett, 2014, p. 9). You could call this a *pre-assessment*. There are a number of reasons from the realm of cognitive psychology/science why pre-assessment might be beneficial for learning, but here it just helps us measure how much has actually been learnt.

Although the process is quite simple, it may prompt a common argument: *Why waste time on pre-assessments when I have content to teach.* To counter this I would say, "But what if the content you teach is already known by a number of students – where is the challenge, who is making progress, and what will actually be learnt by these students?" Surely it's better to use the limited time you have to focus on what students don't yet know.

A pre-assessment can take a number of different forms. At its quickest, it could be a multiple-choice test that students sit at the start of every unit. This can be teacher, self or peer marked and would provide you with a measure of who knows what. As always with multiple-choice, you need to understand that guesses from students that lead to correct answers can skew the diagnosis. Having an option of "I don't know this" or even a confidence score (ranging from 1 – I don't know this to 10 – I am confident this is the answer) next to the question can help with this.

For more depth of pre-assessment you could design tests or exams that have short- or long-answer questions that encourage the student to provide more evidence of their understanding. As always with this type of assessment, the amount of marking that comes with it may cause you to dismiss it.

A final way could be that of a mini assignment which asks students to write an extended piece about the various topics being covered. Andy Tharby (2014) wrote about something similar he called "Benchmarks of brilliance", which students would create at the start of a year, term or unit. It allowed him to see what students were capable of and compare this against their final assessment. Although students can go into greater detail, the increased marking and difficulty of analysing the results may be deciding factors.

In my department we start every unit with a pre-test. It comes in the form of multiple choice questions taken from our exam board website and covers elements of the various topics we will be covering that term. It takes half a lesson to answer and a further 15 minutes to mark, but the results do show us to see who actually knows what. It allows us to pitch challenge adequately for various groups and, more importantly, see who *might* have learnt new information in this unit. Without them, how would I know if our assessment data at the end of the unit is accurate? How would I know if students actually learnt things or simply recapped topics? If things have improved, you can use this data to share teaching methods that might have aided the students get high scores. If scores have stayed the same or even decreased from pre to post assessment, then you can analyse your teaching methods with your colleagues and develop better methods for the future.

One final point relates to what assessment data is actually showing. Remembering Robert Bjork, does it show that learning has taken place or does it simply highlight performance? If a student scored well in an assessment in January but poorly on the same topic in a test in May, did learning happen? I once again urge you to consider this when looking at data.

Do students really care about data?

I had the pleasure of working briefly with Richard Cheetham MBE a while ago. Richard is a senior fellow in sports coaching at the University of Winchester, where he has worked since 2005. This followed three years teaching and coaching in New Zealand, and he has also worked with organisations such as the UCI World Cycling Elite Coach Education Programme and Fulham Football Club. I sought his help developing teaching methods in the PE curriculum. Lots of discussions about theory went back and forth and I asked numerous questions. At the end he made one simple statement. Not matter what we intend to do in classes with students, it's all about the culture. If students don't care or don't get on board, even the best teaching methods won't be as effective as they potentially could be. This leads me to my fourth principle.

---

4 Data must be transparent and involve students

Answer these questions – *Do you share assessment data with students? If so, how do you share it? Does it transform learning? Is it a key learning resource?*

Data can be a very effective tool for teachers, but involving students makes it even more powerful. I have had the privilege of visiting many classrooms and chatting to numerous students. I always ask the most stupid questions – "So how well are you doing?" "What are your grades like?" "What are the areas you need to work on?" Now these may not seem like stupid questions to you, but students are bombarded with numbers, percentages and grades and don't always understand what they mean. I think back to a history lesson I observed a few years back when I asked a student what grade they got in their last assessment and what it told them they needed to work on. They gave the best answer they could, partly out of politeness, but it was obvious that they didn't really know what their test results meant.

The other end of the spectrum is the bombardment of data at students. I've seen schools insist that every student knows their current grade, their predicted grade and target grade for every subject. *Every subject?* At this extreme the intention is to be informative, but many students forget, get stressed or don't care – not because they are unruly, but because there's too much information and they don't know what to do with it.

Striking the balance is key. We need systems in place that help students utilise data and make them aware of their progression, but it needs to be kept in perspective. It is an essential sort of feedback which students, if taught correctly, can use to make decisions and shape their learning behaviours. It builds upon the self-regulatory control that we hope students achieve. As Eckhart Tolle (2008, p. 62) once said, "Awareness is the greatest agent for change".

One of the best methods – and one I have adopted and adapted (see Figure 7.4) – came from Kristian Still, headteacher at the Focus Learning Trust. The idea was an Exam Feedback Tool that harnesses all the principles of QLA. The complex spreadsheet had the key elements: student assessment broken down into question by question analysis which details question topic and type. It also incorporated comparison tools for cohort, class or student analysis. A particular advantage of the spreadsheet was its ability to print off a student friendly data sheet that visually broke down every answer and scored them out of 100 per cent, allowed targets to be set and reflection to take place. The sheet is given to students during the post-test follow up lesson and brings them into the conversation. Too many times we tell students what they have done, what they need to do and what they must work on. With the data sheet in hand, they can see

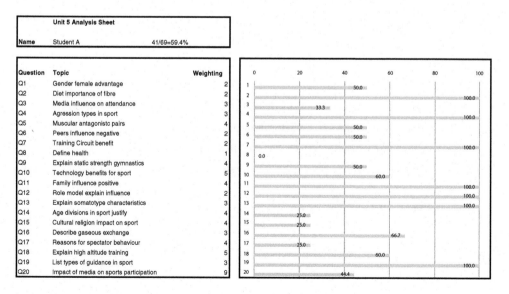

Figure 7.4 QLA Analysis Sheet

these areas themselves. They can identify successes they must reinforce. They can make decisions about subsequent learning and assessments. If we develop this as the norm, it allows students to use assessments to answer Hattie's (2007, p. 86) three key feedback questions: "Where am I going? How am I going? Where to next?"

If you watched its implementation in a lesson you would see it become the central resource for learning. Once the sheets are handed out, accompanied by the assessment paper, the teacher can re-teach common misconceptions as discussed in Principle 2. The focus then shifts to students, who have time to use the data sheet as a map for navigating their assessment. They can look at questions that the sheet has highlighted as strengths and reinforce good habits. They can look at questions that scored poorly and analyse why. With the percentage ranking they can also see how well a question was answered, whether it needs a lot of work or whether it needs only minor tweaks. Students can then (with support if needed) tackle the areas of weakness. The teacher might provide new instructions, allocate resources to allow individuals to work independently, or simply allow them to retry questions making use of the feedback.

Rachel Ingram, teacher of design and technology in Southampton, has adopted a similar approach, displaying student assessment results in the form of a graph on her walls. Students regularly check their performance, identify what areas need attention and take action. It shifts an element of responsibility to the student, which many thrive on. Again, it increases student involvement in the data process and makes it a source of feedback. It reinforces self-regulated learning.

Kristian uses a data sheet. Rachel uses a wall display. The key to both is that they turn quite complex data into something student friendly. They also take it a step further and make it the culture by insisting students regularly interact with it. When using data for any form of analysis, it might be worth asking these questions:

- Can the data be transformed into a student friendly version?
- Can it visually help students see areas of strength or weakness?
- How will you plan to share the data?
- How will students use the data?
- Will the data sheet provide rich feedback and allow students to act upon it?
- Will the data sheet reinforce self-regulation?
- How can you get students to engage with the sheet?
- What will they do once they have been given a sheet that helps move learning forward?
- How will you make it part of the classroom culture?

And finally

First, many assessments have traditionally been at the end of units. These units are usually organised into blocks. So the assessments generally assess what has been taught over the last few weeks/months. What about what was taught three months ago or at the start of Year 9? When will this be reassessed? It's important, as stated in Chapter 2, that assessments are cumulative. That way we not only get an idea of how students have performed over the last unit but are able us to see whether things have been learnt from some time before.

Second, a final thought comes from Nuthall (2007, p. 40), who says, "Achievement tests assess motivation before they assess learning". Nuthall talks about the influence of the test environment. Would your students perform better on a Monday period 3, a Wednesday after lunch on a hot summer's day, or in period 5 in the middle of winter? There are so many variables that potentially affect students' motivation to perform to the best of their ability. The data you collect may not be a fair reflection of what has been learnt. How annoying is it when the data says a group of students need to recap displacement reactions, only for them to tell you they know it but couldn't be bothered in the test. So how do we combat this? Culture, buy in and be transparent with students.

To recap

1. Data should make us ask questions.
2. Data *must* be a group activity and it *must* improve teaching.
3. Data *must* help improve learning.
4. Data *must* be transparent and involve students.

References

Ambrose, S. A., & Lovett, M. C. (2014) Prior knowledge is more important than content: Skills and beliefs also impact learning. In: Benassi, V. A., Overson, C. E., & Hakala, C. M. (Eds) *Applying Science of Learning in Education: Infusing Psychological Science into the Curriculum*. Retrieved from the Society for the Teaching of Psychology web site: http://teachpsych.org/ebooks/asle2014/index.php

Bambrick-Santoyo, P. (2010) *Driven by Data: A Practical Guide to Improve Instruction*. San Francisco, CA: Jossey-Bass.

Berger, R. (2003) *An Ethic of Excellence; Building a Culture of Craftsmanship with Students*. Portsmouth, NH: Heinemann.

Hattie, J., & Timperley, H. (2007) The power of feedback. *Review of Educational Research*. 77(1). pp. 81–112.

Nuthall, G. (2007) *The Hidden Lives of Learners*. Wellington: NZCER Press.

Tharby, A. (2014) A benchmark of brilliance. In: *Reflecting English: In Search of Classroom Answers*. 5th February, 2014. Available at: https://reflectingenglish.wordpress.com/2014/02/05/a-benchmark-of-brilliance/

Tolle, E. (2008) *A New Earth: Awakening to Your Life's Purpose*. Farmington Hills, MI: Gale Cengage.

Getting a little better at getting a little better

Chris Moyse

Teachers are drowning in advice; a plethora of initiatives and ever moving goalposts that make the job an ever-increasing challenge. Many of these external directives seem disconnected from the daily role of the teacher. Not this book.

What Dave Fawcett has managed so successfully is to curate the very best in teaching expertise. Thoroughly researched, he presents a compelling case to go back to basics and focus on the things that make the biggest difference to children's learning. Actionable, accessible and concrete guidance to establish effective routines to better manage classrooms; building the foundations for great teaching.

Great teaching is not just a process, though; it's an art. Mastery of this art takes time and requires the successful application of a range of core skills. This book presents you with a range of tools to develop that mastery. Basic yet highly effective tools that allow its user to unlock the vast potential of the children they teach.

For those starting out in teaching, this book is a goldmine. For those more experienced, the in-depth and pragmatic approach that is its hallmark will be reaffirming and challenging in equal measure. Much of this book is common sense but that doesn't mean it's common practice.

So how can we use this book to get a little better?

Legendary basketball coach John Wooden constantly emphasised the importance of becoming better rather than winning – getting better rather than being good. He urged his players to try their hardest to improve on that day, to make that practice a masterpiece. He suggested that we can apply ourselves each day to becoming a little better and by doing so we become a lot better.

Mastery is not about perfection. It's about a process, a journey. A person who masters their art stays on that path day after day, year after year. This person is willing to try, and fail, and try again. To make the quickest progress though you don't take big steps. Just small steps. Great and lasting success is achieved through small consistent steps towards challenging yet realistic goals. Slow and steady is also the best way to overcome your resistance to change. As John Wooden (1997, p. 143) says in his book, *Wooden*, "Don't look for the big, quick improvement. Seek the small improvement one day at a time. That's the only way it happens – and when it happens, it lasts".

So don't think big, think small. Take one idea at a time from this book and set yourself a realistic improvement goal based on that one idea. Something that may be difficult yet possible. Goals that cause you, often unconsciously, to increase your focus, effort and commitment to that goal persist longer and make better use of these effective strategies. Focus on making progress rather than proving yourself as then we deal with difficulties more easily. We then see setbacks as informative, rather than signs of personal failure. Getting a little better is the goal.

The only real path to success is through the practising and establishing of unexciting, often mundane yet often challenging daily disciplines which over time lead to big changes. Don't look for a magic bullet. The solution already exists. It exists within the pages of this book. Is it magic? No! It's just the power of daily routines compounded over time. And as you read through these well researched pages, you will be presented with the components of teacher expertise, guiding us all to what works rather than what looks good.

So absorb the knowledge and narrow your concentration to one thing at a time. Go small. When you want the absolute best chance to succeed at anything, your approach should always be the same. Go small. Going small is ignoring all the things you could do and doing what you should do. Not all things matter equally, and whilst this book offers you a wealth of evidence-informed strategies, it is important to focus down on the thing you need to do rather than you want to do; the one thing that your children will benefit the most from you doing a little better. Extraordinary results are determined by how narrow you can make your focus. When you think big, success becomes time-consuming and overly complicated. As a result a teacher can feel overwhelmed and overloaded. Success starts to feel out of reach and so we settle for less. We often get lost trying to do too much, ultimately achieve very little and over time this can lead to a lowering of expectations. As a busy teacher you only have a finite amount of time and energy, so don't spread yourself thin. When you go small you will inevitably be looking at just one thing to do and that's where the magic does start. The key is continually developing over time as success builds sequentially; one thing at a time. As Daniel Coyle (2012, p. 77) says in his book *The Little Book of Talent*, "think like a gardener, work like a carpenter". Be patient and develop great habits over time – work on horticultural time but do what needs to be done as accurately as possible. The devil's in the detail.

Experts and achievers operate differently. They have an eye for the essential and an eye for the detail. They reflect on what matters to drive their daily work. They always work from a clear sense of priority. Success is about doing the right thing rather than doing everything right, so select carefully. Choose the right thing. That is, the strategy or technique that you hope will make the biggest difference to the children and practise this one thing until it becomes part of your daily routine. Relentlessly pursue this goal, seeking regular feedback on your progress from a colleague you trust. Finding and keep adding +1s to your teaching repertoire – small gains and wins that lead to a compound effect of big changes. Many of these +1s detailed in the book are easy to do, yet equally easy not to bother to do. Turn these small daily disciplines into massive success by sweating the detail and these small wins will create great momentum – essential on the path to mastery.

The most successful people make getting to the heart of things the heart of their approach. Choose from the wealth of evidence-informed strategies in this book but set limitations. Doing this helps to choose the essential. By choosing the essential, we create impact with less effort. This book provides you with the basics, some of which may seem trivial and ordinary. But they aren't. They are fundamental to your progress as a teacher. This book will help you eliminate the non-essential and focus on what works. Focus is your most important tool in becoming more effective and the most important factor in determining whether you'll achieve a goal or stick to creating a new habit. Maintain your focus on one goal and habit at a time. Multitasking is less efficient as your focus and attention is split. Starting small will narrow your focus and keep your energy and enthusiasm going.

Remember this Russian proverb:

"If you chase two rabbits, you will not catch either one".

So challenge yourself and set a *goal* as a result of reading *Relearning to Teach*. To do this effectively, consider these guiding questions:

What specifically do you want to accomplish? How would things be better for you and your children when that happens?

How will you know when you have achieved this goal?

A month from now what changes would you like to have in place?

What will you notice when you have achieved this goal?

What do you already do that is helping you achieve this goal?

What ideas from Dave's book could help too?

What will you focus on?

When will you achieve this goal by?

Now write down your goal in this way:

By ... (Short-term date)

I am ... (What will be different in what you are doing? Record this in the present tense with the implication that the goal has already been achieved.)

So that ... (What is the impact of this goal and focus?)

When you have achieved this goal, what next? What will be your next +1? The answers lie within yourself and this meticulously researched book.

Now get on with the business of getting a little better at being a little better.

References

Coyle, D. (2012) *The Little Book of Talent*. New York: Random House Books.
Wooden, J. (1997) *Wooden: A Lifetime of Observations and Reflections on and off the Court*. New York: McGraw-Hill Education.

Index